The Kovels'
Illustrated Price Guide
to
DEPRESSION GLASS
and
AMERICAN DINNERWARE

Second Edition

Ralph and Terry Kovel
Illustrations by Don Hall

CROWN PUBLISHERS, INC. NEW YORK

BOOKS BY RALPH AND TERRY KOVEL

American Country Furniture 1780–1875
Dictionary of Marks—Pottery and Porcelain
A Directory of American Silver, Pewter and Silver Plate
The Kovels' Antiques & Collectibles Price List
The Kovels' Book of Antique Labels
The Kovels' Collector's Guide to American Art Pottery
The Kovels' Collectors' Source Book
The Kovels' Bottle Price List
The Kovels' Illustrated Price Guide to Royal Doulton
Kovels' Know Your Antiques, Revised
Kovels' Know Your Collectibles
Kovels' Organizer for Collectors
The Kovels' Price Guide for Collector Plates, Figurines, Paperweights, and
    Other Limited Editions

Published by Crown Publishers, Inc., 225 Park Avenue South, New York, New York 10003,
    and represented in Canada by the Canadian MANDA Group
Manufactured in the United States of America

Library of Congress Cataloging-in-Publication Data

Kovel, Ralph M.
The Kovels' Illustrated price guide to depression
glass and American dinnerware

1. Depression glass—Catalogs.   2. Ceramic tableware—
United States—History—20th century Catalogs.
I. Kovel, Terry H.   II. Title.   III. Title: Illustrated
price guide to depression glass and American dinnerware.
NK5439.D44K68   1983   738.2'0973'0750973   83-2084
ISBN 0-517-54974-3
10 9 8 7 6 5 4 3

Contents

Acknowledgments

B & B Collectibles, Terre Haute, Indiana; J. Barry, Aurora, Illinois; Lee Barry, Dallas, South Dakota; Tom & Phyllis Bess; Elizabeth Boyce, Terre Haute, Indiana; Buckeys Antiques, Buckeystown, Maryland; Jerry Burke, Meshoppen, Pennsylvania; Collector's Pantry, Clay, New York; Depression Glass Daze, Otisville, Michigan; Doug's Antiques, Shamrock, Texas; Henry & Joyce Engel, Clyde, Ohio; Fenn's Antiques, Mansfield, Missouri; Fenner's Antiques, Brooklyn, New York; Lillian Fuenta, Brooklyn, New York; The Glaze, Springfield, Missouri; The Hall Teapot Man; Don & Pat Hoffman; Barbara Howell, Oakdale, Pennsylvania; Sharon & Bob Huxford, Covington, Indiana; Ann Kerr, Sidney, Ohio; Nora Koch, Otisville, Michigan; Luther Kolstad Antiques, Gaylord, Minnesota; Laub's Loft, Neponset, Illinois; Martha Little, Caledonia, Ohio; National Depression Glass Association, Shawnee Mission, Kansas; Maxine Nelson, Huntington Beach, California; Olmar Collectibles, Kearney, Nebraska; Sue & Ian Paul, Champaign, Illinois; Robinson Sales, Branford, Connecticut; Second Time Around, Milford, Michigan; Gary & Bonnie Tefft; 'Tiques & Stuff, Rosendall, New York; Western Reserve Depression Glass Club, Cleveland, Ohio; Catherine Yronwode, Columbia, Missouri.

Special thanks to Jo Cunningham and all the people at the American Pottery, Earthenware, and China Show and to the many authors whose books helped us with our research. The artwork, editing, and layout by Crown Publishers, especially Pam Thomas and Jake Goldberg, the photographs by Don Hall, and the sketches by Jeffrey Clark, all added to the information and appeal of this book. Another round of thank-yous to them and to the many on our staff who typed, collated, proofed, and did the other jobs that help us look like experts.

Depression Glass

Introduction

Pastel-colored glassware in matching sets became popular about 1925. The Fostoria Glass Company of Fostoria, Ohio, made the first of these glass sets, which included dinner plates, coffee cups, and other pieces to be used at a dinner table. The glassware was expensive and its popularity led to similar pieces being made by other companies that were able to produce a less expensive glass.

Inexpensive glass was made by a method called tank molding: silica sand, soda ash, and limestone were heated, and the molten glass mixture was passed through pipes to the automated pressing mold. Patterns were acid etched or tooled into the mold so the finished glassware had some design. Because the pressing process made a glass that often had flaws or bubbles, patterns used as decoration were often lacy in appearance to help hide the flaws.

During the late 1960s interest in the inexpensive pastel glass led to several books and the term "Depression glass" came into general use, even though the glassware was made before, during, and after the Depression. The name has gradually come to include other glassware made from 1925 through the 1970s. Our price list includes the lacy types, the pseudo-Sandwich glass patterns, the hobnail variations, the solid colored wares of ruby, cobalt, or green and the many opaque glass patterns.

Depression-glass designs can be divided into groups. The etched designs—e.g., "Adam" or "Cherry Blossom"—were made first, from about 1925 to 1935. Pastel colors were used.

Raised designs, often with fruit and flower patterns—e.g., "Open Rose" and "Sharon"—were made in the mid-1930s. Strong colors like cobalt blue or royal ruby, opaque glass, pastels, and clear glass were popular.

Geometric wares—e.g., "Hobnail" and "Ribbon"—were made during the late 1920s and again in the late 1930s and early 1940s. Simple outlines and bold colors predominated. Art Deco-influenced geometric designs include "Imperial Octagon" and "United States Octagon."

Enameled or silk-screen patterns were developed during the 1940s. White enameled designs were added to the glass. Cobalt blue, royal ruby, and clear glass were the most popular colors that were decorated this way. Shirley Temple glasswares and "Sailboats" are two such enameled patterns.

A few patterns, "Floral & Diamond Band" for example, were made to resemble the cut glass of the nineteenth century, particularly the "Lacy Sandwich" pattern made by the Sandwich, Massachusetts, glassworks. About ten such pseudo-Sandwich patterns were made, and most of them were referred to as "Sandwich" in the manufacturers' catalogs.

Depression glass utility wares were also made. The dishes were made for use in the kitchen and not on the table—e.g., ice-box dishes, lemon reamers, canister sets.

Opaque glass was popular in the 1930s. Each of the colors was given a special name by the company that produced it—e.g., "Monax" or "Ivrene." (See Glossary for color names and descriptions.)

The opaque green glass was known by a variety of names. Jade green is the generic name used by many companies. Jade-ite was the green color used by Anchor Hocking. Jadite was a color of glass and a pattern of green kitchenware made by Jeannette Glass Company. To avoid unnecessary confusion, we have chosen to always spell the word *jadite* in this book. Delphite, an opaque blue glass, is sometimes spelled delfite in the ads; but we have chosen to always use the *delphite* spelling.

This book is not an in-depth study of Depression glass. The beginner who needs more information about patterns, manufacturers, and color groups or how and where to buy should see the Bibliography and club lists we have included.

Hundreds of patterns, many not listed in the more expensive books, are included here. But if you wish to specialize in one pattern of Depression glass, there may be a book available with many color pictures. There may also be a book available with special information about the factory making your pattern. The best way to learn about Depression glass is to attend the regional and national shows devoted to glass. Your local newspaper or the collectors' publications listed in this book will print the dates and locations.

Be sure to read the Glossary of terms on page 251. It includes special names and sizes used by Depression glass collectors that may be unfamiliar. There is a list of reproductions on page 108 and a list of known glass patterns and manufacturers on page 112.

This book is a price report. Prices are actual offerings in the marketplace. They are not averages. The high and low prices represent different sales. Prices reported are not those from garage or house sales or flea markets. They are only from dealers who understand the Depression glass market and who sell at shops, at shows, or through national advertising.

Collector Clubs and Publications

DEPRESSION GLASS DAZE
Box 57
Otisville, MI 48463

THE GLASS COLLECTOR
P.O. Box 27037
Columbus, OH 43227

GLASS REVIEW
P.O. Box 542
Marietta, OH 45750

NATIONAL DEPRESSION GLASS ASSOCIATION
NEWS & VIEWS
8337 Santa Fe Lane
Shawnee Mission, KS 66212

THE NATIONAL JOURNAL
P.O.Box 3121
Wescosville, PA 18106

THE PADEN CITY PARTY LINE
13325 Danvers Way
Westminster, CA 92683

Bibliography

Florence, Gene. *The Collector's Encyclopedia of Depression Glass,* Fifth Edition. Paducah, Kentucky: Collector Books, 1982.

————. *Pocket Guide to Depression Glass,* Revised Third Edition. Paducah, Kentucky: Collector Books, 1983.

Fountain, Mel. *Swankyswigs, with Price Guide.* Privately printed, 1979 (201 Alvena, Wichita, KS 67203).

Klamkin, Marian. *The Collector's Guide to Depression Glass.* New York: Hawthorn Books, 1973.

Kovel, Ralph and Terry. *Kovels' Know Your Collectibles.* New York: Crown Publishers, Inc., 1981.

McGrain, Pat. *1981 Price Survey.* Privately printed, 1980 (Box 219, Frederick, MD 21701).

Stout, Sandra McPhee. *Depression Glass in Color.* Des Moines, Iowa: Wallace-Homestead Book Co., 1970.

————. *Depression Glass Number Two.* Des Moines, Iowa: Wallace-Homestead Book Co., 1971.

————. *Depression Glass Price Guide.* Des Moines, Iowa: Wallace-Homestead Book Co., 1975.

————. *Depression Glass III.* Des Moines, Iowa: Wallace-Homestead Book Co., 1976.

Warner, Ian. *Swankyswigs, A Pattern Guide and Check List.* Privately printed, 1982 (Depression Glass Daze, Box 57, Otisville, MI 48463).

Weatherman, Hazel Marie. *Colored Glassware of the Depression Era.* Privately printed, 1970 (P.O. Box 4444, Springfield, MO 65804).

————. *Colored Glassware of the Depression Era 2.* Privately printed, 1974 (P.O. Box 4444, Springfield, MO 65804).

————. *The Decorated Tumbler.* Privately printed, 1978 (P.O. Box 4444, Springfield, MO 65804).

————. *Price Guide to the Decorated Tumbler.* Privately printed, 1979 (P.O. Box 4444, Springfield, MO 65804).

Weiss, Jeffrey. *Cornerstone Collector's Guide to Glass.* New York: Simon & Schuster, 1981.

Color Names

AMBER	Topaz, golden glow
BLUE GREEN	Ultramarine
CLEAR	Crystal
CREAM OPAQUE	Cremax, clambroth
DEEP BLUE	Ritz blue, colbalt, dark blue, deep blue
GREEN	Springtime green, emerald, imperial green, forest green
IVORY	Ivrene, chinex
MEDIUM BLUE	Madonna
OPAQUE BLACK	Black
OPAQUE BLUE	Delphite
OPAQUE GREEN	Jadite
OPAQUE WHITE	Milk white, monax
PINK	Rose Marie, rose, rose pink, rose tint, rose glow, nu-rose, wild rose, flamingo, cheri-glo
PURPLE	Burgundy, amythyst
RED	Royal ruby, ruby red, carmen

Accordion Pleats, see Round Robin

Adam

Adam, sometimes called Chain Daisy or Fan & Feather, is a glass pattern made from 1932 to 1934 by the Jeannette Glass Company, Jeannette, Pennsylvania. Sets can be found in crystal, green or pink. A few pieces are known in yellow, but this does not seem to have been a standard production color. It has been reproduced in green or pink.

CRYSTAL
Pitcher, Round Base 14.00

GREEN
Ashtray	12.00 To 13.00
Bowl, Covered, 9 In. ...	30.00 To 60.00
Bowl, Oval, 10 In.	10.00 To 19.50
Bowl, 4 3/4 In.	6.00 To 10.00
Bowl, 5 3/4 In.	8.50 To 16.00
Bowl, 7 3/4 In.	14.50
Butter, Covered	210.00
Cake Plate	14.00 To 16.50
Candleholder, Pair	30.00
Candy Container, Covered	55.00
Coaster	5.00 To 12.00
Creamer	9.00 To 12.00
Cup & Saucer	14.50 To 20.00
Pitcher, 32 Oz., Round Base	85.00
Pitcher, 32 Oz., 8 In.	27.50
Plate, Grill, 9 In.	8.00 To 12.50
Plate, 7 3/4 In.	5.00 To 7.00
Plate, 9 In.	10.00 To 14.50
Platter, 11 3/4 In.	8.00 To 14.00
Salt & Pepper	67.50
Saucer	1.00 To 3.50
Sherbet	15.00 To 18.00
Sugar & Creamer	20.00 To 44.00
Sugar, Covered	27.50 To 31.00
Tumbler, 4 1/2 In.	15.00 To 20.00
Tumbler, 5 1/2 In.	25.00 To 29.00
Vase, 7 1/2 In.	25.00 To 40.00

PINK
Ashtray	15.00 To 24.50
Bowl, Covered, 9 In. ...	26.00 To 43.00
Bowl, 4 3/4 In.	9.00 To 12.00
Bowl, 5 3/4 In.	8.50 To 10.00
Bowl, 7 3/4 In.	12.00 To 14.00
Butter, Covered	65.00 To 95.00
Cake Plate	9.00 To 25.00
Candleholder, Pair	42.00 To 49.75
Candy Container, Covered	40.00 To 55.00
Coaster	10.50 To 18.50
Creamer	9.00 To 12.50
Cup & Saucer	19.00 To 22.50
Pitcher, Round Base	35.00
Pitcher, 8 In.	16.00 To 22.50
Plate, Grill, 9 In.	9.00 To 14.00
Plate, Sherbet, 6 In.	3.50
Plate, 7 3/4 In.	5.50 To 8.00
Plate, 9 In.	11.00 To 19.00
Platter, 11 3/4 In.	8.00 To 15.00
Relish	7.00 To 12.00
Salt & Pepper	38.00 To 45.00
Saucer	1.75 To 3.00
Sherbet	9.00 To 16.75
Sugar	10.00
Sugar & Creamer, Covered	27.50 To 38.50
Sugar, Covered	11.50 To 28.00
Tumbler, Footed, 4 1/2 In.	11.00 To 17.50
Tumbler, 5 1/2 In.	35.00 To 40.00
Vase	119.50 To 125.00

Akro Agate

Picture a marble cake with the irregular mixture of colors running through the batter. This is what Akro Agate is like, a marbleized mixture of colored glass. The Akro Agate Company, Clarksburg, West Virginia, made marbles at first. The marbleized dinnerware and children's sets were made in many colors from 1932 to 1951.

BLUE
Ashtray, Leaf-Shaped, Marbleized . . 4.00
Vase, Marbleized, 4 1/4 In. 4.00

GREEN
Cup & Saucer, Child's 12.00

Plate, Child's 6.00
Saucer, Child's 4.00
Teapot, Child's, Covered 15.00
Vase, Marbleized, 4 1/4 In. 4.00

IVORY
Cornucopia, 6 1/4 In. 2.00

PINK
Cup & Saucer, Child's 17.00

PUMPKIN
Planter, Oval, 8 In. 38.00

Alice

An 8 1/2 inch plate, cup and saucer were apparently the only pieces made in the Alice pattern. This 1940s pattern was made by the Anchor Hocking Glass Company, Lancaster, Ohio, in jadite or opaque white with a pink or blue border.

JADITE
Cup & Saucer 2.00

WHITE
Bowl, 5 In. 1.00
Cup & Saucer 1.50
Plate, Rolled Edge, 6 In. .... .75
Plate, Rolled Edge, 7 1/4 In. 1.00
Plate, Rolled Edge, 9 In. 1.50
Saucer, Child's, Gold Rim .... .50
Saucer, Swirl .... .50

Alpine Caprice, see also Caprice

Caprice and Alpine Caprice were made from the same molds. Alpine Caprice has a satin finish, Caprice is transparent. Alpine Caprice, made by the Cambridge Glass Company, Cambridge, Ohio, about 1936, was made in blue, crystal or pink satin finished glass.

BLUE
Cigarette Box, Covered 45.00

Dish, Jelly, 2-Handled 30.00
Plate, Footed, 8 In. 32.50
Plate, 6 1/2 In. 14.50
Tray 35.00

CAPRICE
Blue, Bowl, Footed Console 40.00

American

American is a pattern made to resemble the pressed glass of an earlier time. It was introduced by Fostoria Glass, Moundsville, West Virginia, in 1915. The pattern was made only in crystal, never in colored glass. It is similar to Cube pattern, but after looking carefully, you will soon learn to tell the two patterns apart.

CRYSTAL

Ashtray, Square	6.50	Jar, Jam, Covered	25.00
Candleholder, Pair	30.00	Relish, 2 Part, 12 In.	18.00
Celery, 10 In.	14.00	Saltshaker	6.50
Cup & Saucer	6.50	Sherbet, 4 1/2 In.	8.00
Custard, Flared, 6 Oz.	6.00	Tray, Round, 13 In.	25.00
Goblet, 7 In.	10.00	Tray, Utility, Handled, 9 In.	20.00

American Beauty, see English Hobnail

American Pioneer

Panels of hobnail-like protrusions and plain panels were used in the design of American Pioneer. It was made by Liberty Works, Egg Harbor, New Jersey, from 1931 to 1934. Crystal, green and pink dishes are easily found, amber is rare.

AMBER
Plate, Handled, 11 1/2 In. 16.00

CRYSTAL
Cup 4.00
Cup & Saucer 4.75
Sugar & Creamer, 3 1/2 In. 10.00
Sugar, 3 1/2 In. 4.50
Vase, 8 1/4 In. 25.00

GREEN
Cake Plate 10.00
Cup & Saucer .... 8.00 To 9.00
Plate, Handled, 11 1/2 In. 11.00
Plate, 8 In. .... 4.00 To 4.50
Sugar & Creamer, 2 3/4 In. 13.00 To 15.00
Tray, Handled 12.50

PINK
Bowl, Handled, 9 In. 9.00
Creamer 5.00
Cup & Saucer .... 4.75 To 6.00
Plate, Handled, 11 1/2 In. 8.00
Plate, 8 In. .... 3.00 To 4.50
Sugar & Creamer, 2 3/4 In. 10.00
Vase, Ruffled, 7 In. 45.00
Vase, 8 1/4 In. 25.00

American Sweetheart

In 1930 Macbeth-Evans Glass Company introduced American Sweetheart. At first it was made in pink, but soon other colors were added. The pattern continued in production until 1936. Blue, pink, red, cremax and monax pieces were made. Sometimes a gold, platinum, green, pink, red or smoky black trim was used on monax pieces. There is a center design on most plates, but some monax plates are found with plain centers. One of the rarest items in this pattern is the monax sugar bowl lid. The bowls are easy to find but the lids seem to have broken.

BLUE
Plate, 9 In. 79.50
Saucer 37.50

CREMAX
Bowl, 6 In. 5.00
Bowl, 9 In. 20.00

CRYSTAL
Cup & Saucer 10.00

MONAX
Bowl, Oval, 11 In. . . . . . 37.00 To 45.00
Bowl, 6 In. . . . . 7.00 To 12.50
Bowl, 9 In. . . . . 30.00 To 49.75
Creamer . . . . 5.00 To 10.00
Cup . . . . 7.00 To 8.00
Cup & Saucer 12.00
Plate, Chop, 11 In. . . . . . 10.00 To 12.00
Plate, Server, 12 In. 12.50
Plate, Server, 15 In. . . 130.00 To 200.00
Plate, 6 In. 3.50
Plate, 8 In. . . . . 4.50 To 6.00
Plate, 9 In. . . . . 4.00 To 8.00
Plate, 9 3/4 In. . . . . 11.00 To 15.00
Platter, Oval, 13 In. . . . . 28.00 To 40.00
Salt & Pepper . . . . 190.00 To 225.00
Saucer . . . . 1.00 To 3.50
Sherbet . . . . 6.00 To 13.50
Soup, Cream . . . . 36.50 To 42.50
Soup, Flat . . . . 32.00 To 39.00
Sugar . . . . 4.00 To 8.00
Sugar & Creamer . . . . . . 11.00 To 13.00
Sugar, Covered 150.00
Tidbit, 2 Tier . . . . 40.00 To 55.00

PINK
Bowl, Oval, 11 In. . . . . . 22.50 To 25.00
Bowl, 3 3/4 In. 17.50
Bowl, 6 In. . . . . 5.50 To 9.50
Bowl, 9 In. . . . . 15.00 To 18.00
Creamer . . . . 5.00 To 8.50
Cup . . . . 8.00 To 11.00
Cup & Saucer . . . . 9.00 To 14.00
Pitcher, 7 1/2 In. . . . . 250.00 To 475.00
Pitcher, 8 In. . . . . 125.00 To 300.00
Plate, Server, 12 In. . . . . 8.00 To 13.50
Plate, 6 In. 2.50
Plate, 8 In. . . . . 5.50 To 6.00
Plate, 9 In. . . . . 4.75 To 7.50
Plate, 9 3/4 In. . . . . 11.00 To 15.00
Platter, Oval, 13 In. . . . . 12.00 To 19.75
Salt & Pepper . . . . 65.00 To 225.00
Saucer 2.00

Sherbet	3.75 To 12.50
Soup, Cream	25.00 To 30.00
Soup, Flat	17.50 To 23.00
Sugar	5.00 To 8.00
Sugar & Creamer	11.00 To 17.50
Tidbit, 2 Tier	125.00
Tumbler, 3 1/2 In.	29.00 To 39.75
Tumbler, 4 In.	15.00 To 19.00

RED

Cup	80.00

Cup & Saucer	68.50 To 135.00
Plate, Server, 12 In. ..	145.00 To 250.00
Plate, 8 In.	65.00 To 75.00
Saucer	40.00
Sugar & Creamer	195.00

SHERBET

Metal Holder	3.00 To 4.00

SMOKE

Sugar & Creamer	175.00

Anniversary

Although pink Anniversary pattern was made from 1947 to 1949, it is still considered Depression glass by collectors. Crystal pieces are shown in a 1949 catalog. Later amethyst and milk glass pieces were made. From 1970 to 1972 crystal and an iridescent Carnival-glass-like amber color were used. The pattern was the product of the Jeannette Glass Company, Jeannette, Pennsylvania.

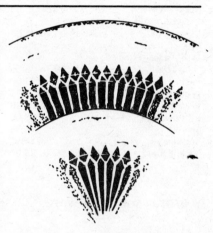

CRYSTAL

Bowl, 4 7/8 In.	2.00 To 2.50
Bowl, 5 3/4 In.	2.25
Bowl, 6 3/4 In.	3.50
Butter, Covered	10.00 To 22.00
Cake Plate	3.00 To 5.00
Candy Container	3.00
Cookie Jar, Covered	15.00
Creamer	3.00
Cup	2.00 To 3.00
Cup & Saucer	2.00 To 3.50
Cup, Punch	.75 To 1.50
Plate, 9 In.	4.00
Sandwich Server	5.00
Saucer	1.00
Sherbet	2.00
Soup, Flat	2.00 To 5.00
Sugar	2.25
Sugar & Creamer	5.00
Sugar, Covered	4.50 To 5.75
Tidbit, 2 Tier	14.00

IRIDESCENT

Bowl, Footed	10.00
Candleholder, Flat	6.00

Candy Container, Footed	3.00
Creamer	2.50
Cup	1.50
Cup & Saucer	2.75 To 5.00
Plate, 6 In.	1.25 To 5.00
Saucer	1.00
Soup, Flat	7.00
Tidbit, 3 Tier	12.00

PINK

Butter, Covered	35.00 To 38.00
Candy Container, Covered	33.00
Goblet, Wine	9.00 To 12.50
Sherbet, Footed	4.00
Vase, Wall	12.00

Apple Blossom, see Dogwood

Apple Blossom Border, see Blossoms & Band

Aunt Polly

U.S. Glass Company, a firm with factories in Indiana, Ohio, Pennsylvania and West Virginia, made Aunt Polly glass. The pattern can be found in blue, green or iridescent. Pink pieces have been reported. The pattern was made in the late 1920s.

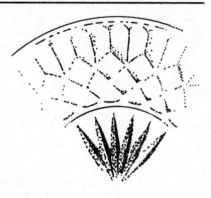

BLUE
Bowl, Oval 32.00
Bowl, 4 3/8 In. .... 5.00 To 6.50
Bowl, 4 3/4 In. 11.00
Butter, Covered ...... 90.00 To 125.00
Candy Container, Footed, Handled
    .... 15.00 To 25.00
Creamer 20.00
Dish, Pickle, Handled,
    4 3/8 In. .... 12.00 To 26.00
Pitcher .... 100.00 To 125.00
Plate, 6 In. .... 4.00 To 5.25
Plate, 8 In. .... 7.00 To 9.00
Saltshaker 68.00
Sherbet 6.50
Tumbler 14.50
Vase, Footed, 6 1/2 In. . 20.00 To 25.00

GREEN
Butter, Covered 230.00

IRIDESCENT
Butter .... 49.75 To 75.00

Aurora, see Petalware

Avocado

Although the center fruit looks more like a pear, the pattern has been named Avocado. It was made originally from 1923 to 1933 by the Indiana Glass Company, Dunkirk, Indiana, in crystal, green or pink. In 1973 a reproduction line of pitchers and tumblers appeared in amethyst, blue, frosted pink, green and pink. In 1982 amber colored creamer and sugar, cup and saucer, plate and serving dishes were made. The pattern is sometimes called Sweet Pear or No. 601.

CRYSTAL
Bowl, 7 1/2 In. .... 6.00 To 8.00

GREEN
Bowl, Oval, 2-Handled, 8 In.
    .... 16.00 To 22.00
Bowl, 3-Legged, 6 In. ... 20.00 To 27.00

Bowl, 7 1/2 In. 35.00
Creamer .... 19.00 To 29.00

Cup	25.00 To 27.50	Bowl, 9 1/2 In.	65.00
Plate, 8 1/4 In.	13.00 To 15.00	Cup	25.00
Sherbet	37.50 To 44.75	Plate, 6 1/4 In.	8.50
Sugar	20.00 To 27.00	Plate, 8 1/4 In.	10.00
Sugar & Creamer	50.00 To 60.00	Relish, Footed, 6 In.	26.00

PINK
Bowl, Oval, 2-Handled, 8 In. 15.00

B Pattern, see Dogwood

Ballerina, see Cameo

Banded Cherry, see Cherry Blossom

Banded Fine Rib, see Coronation

Banded Petalware, see Petalware

Banded Rainbow, see Ring

Banded Ribbon, see New Century

Banded Rings, see Ring

Basket, see No. 615

Block Optic

Beaded Block

Imperial Glass Company, Bellaire, Ohio, made Beaded Block from 1927 into the 1930s. It was made in amber, crystal, green, ice blue, pink or red. Frosted or iridescent pieces were also made, giving the pattern the name Frosted Block by some collectors. Some iridescent pink pieces made recently have been found marked with the IG trademark used from 1951 to 1977.

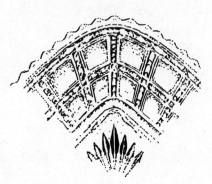

BLUE
Bowl, 9 1/4 In. 15.00
Soup, Cream . . . . 18.00 To 18.50
Vase 45.00

CRYSTAL
Bowl, 2-Handled, 4 1/2 In. 5.00
Celery, 8 1/2 In. 13.00
Creamer 9.00
Sugar 7.50

GREEN
Plate, Square, 7 3/4 In. 8.00
Plate, 8 3/4 In. 9.00
Rose Bowl 17.75
Sugar 15.00

OPALESCENT
Soup, Cream 12.00

PINK
Bowl, 2-Handled, 4 1/2 In. 12.00
Creamer 9.00
Plate, Square, 7 3/4 In. 4.50
Sugar 9.00
Vase, 6 In. . . . . 6.00 To 10.00

VASELINE
Plate, Square, 7 3/4 In. . . 2.00 To 10.00
Soup, Cream 18.50
Vase 24.75

Bee Hive, see Queen Anne

Berwick, see Boopie

Beverage with Sailboats, see White Ship

Big Rib, see Manhattan

Block, see Block Optic

Block Optic

Block Optic, sometimes called Block, was made from 1929 to 1933 by the Hocking Glass Company, Lancaster, Ohio. Slight variations in the design of some pieces like creamers and sugars show that the pattern was redesigned at times. Crystal, green or pink pieces are common. Yellow examples are harder to find. Some pieces were made with black stems, or a black flat foot.

CRYSTAL
Butter 10.00
Candy Container, Covered 12.50 To 18.00
Cup 2.00
Goblet, 4 1/2 In. .... 3.50 To 7.50
Goblet, 5 3/4 In. .... 2.25 To 8.00
Pitcher, Rope Top, 8 1/2 In. 12.00 To 20.00
Pitcher, 8 In. .... 19.00 To 20.00
Plate, 6 In. .... 1.00 To 7.00
Plate, 8 In. 1.50
Plate, 9 In. .... 3.00 To 6.00
Saucer 2.00
Sherbet, Footed, 4 3/4 In. 8.00
Sugar 5.00
Tumbler, 4 In. 3.00
Tumbler, 5 In. 2.00
Whiskey, 2 1/2 In. 3.50

GREEN
Bowl, Mayonnaise, 4 In. 15.00
Bowl, 4 1/4 In. .... 3.00 To 6.00
Bowl, 5 1/4 In. .... 4.50 To 6.50
Bowl, 7 In. .... 3.50 To 6.50
Bowl, 8 1/2 In. .... 9.00 To 11.50
Butter Tub .... 23.00 To 28.00
Candy Container, 6 1/4 In. 12.50 To 18.00
Coaster 3.50
Creamer, Cone-Shaped ... 4.00 To 8.00
Cup .... 1.25 To 4.00
Cup & Saucer .... 5.00 To 7.00
Goblet, 4 1/2 In. .... 6.50 To 25.00
Mug .... 20.00 To 29.00
Nappy, 5 1/2 In. 5.00
Night Set, Bottle & Tumbler 26.00 To 40.00
Pitcher, Bulbous, 8 In. .. 24.00 To 33.00
Pitcher, 8 1/2 In. .... 18.00 To 37.00
Plate, Grill, 9 In. 12.00
Plate, 6 In. .... 1.00 To 2.50
Plate, 8 In. .... 2.00 To 4.00
Plate, 9 In. .... 8.50 To 12.00
Plate, 10 1/4 In. 6.00

Salt & Pepper, Flat 38.00
Salt & Pepper, Footed .. 15.00 To 20.00
Sandwich Server, 10 1/4 In. 28.00 To 55.00
Saucer .... 2.50 To 4.50
Sherbet, Round, 3 1/4 In. . 2.75 To 4.50
Sherbet, 4 3/4 In. ...... 8.50 To 12.50
Sugar & Creamer, Cone-Shaped
.... 13.50 To 15.00
Sugar, Cone-Shaped ...... 4.50 To 5.50
Sugar, Flat 6.00
Sugar, Footed, 4 1/4 In. 7.00
Tumbler, Flat, 4 In. 8.75
Tumbler, Footed, 5 In. ... 8.75 To 12.00
Tumbler, Footed, 6 In. ... 9.00 To 14.75
Tumbler, Footed, 7 In. 13.00
Tumbler, 3 1/2 In. ...... 7.50 To 10.00
Tumbler, 5 1/4 In. ...... 8.50 To 12.00
Whiskey, 2 1/2 In. 15.00

PINK
Butter 12.00
Butter Tub 18.00
Candy Container, Covered, 6 1/4 In. 30.00
Creamer, 4 In. 6.00
Cup .... 2.25 To 4.75
Goblet, 4 1/2 In. 14.50
Goblet, 5 3/4 In. .... 9.00 To 12.50
Pitcher, 8 In. .... 30.00 To 34.00
Pitcher, 8 1/2 In. ...... 20.00 To 32.50
Plate, 6 In. .... 1.50 To 3.50
Plate, 8 In. .... 2.00 To 4.00
Plate, 10 1/4 In. 9.50
Saltshaker, Footed 17.00
Sandwich Server .... 27.50 To 37.00
Saucer, 6 1/8 In. .... 3.50 To 4.50
Sherbet, 3 1/4 In. .... 2.75 To 4.00
Sherbet, 4 3/4 In. 5.00
Sugar & Creamer, Cone-Shaped
.... 10.00 To 15.00

Sugar, Cone-Shaped ...... 7.00 To 7.50
Tumbler, Flat, 4 In. ...... 5.00 To 8.00
Tumbler, Flat, 5 In. ..... 8.50 To 10.00
Tumbler, Footed, 5 In. ... 8.50 To 11.00
Tumbler, 3 1/2 In. 9.00
Whiskey, 2 1/2 In. 14.00

YELLOW
Creamer .... 5.00 To 8.50
Cup .... 4.00 To 6.00

Cup & Saucer .... 7.00 To 8.00
Goblet, 7 1/4 In. ...... 18.00 To 23.00
Plate, 6 In. .... .75 To 2.50
Plate, 8 In. .... 3.50 To 4.50
Salt & Pepper .... 60.00 To 69.50
Sherbet, 3 1/4 In. .... 4.00 To 7.50
Sherbet, 4 3/4 .... 10.00 To 11.00
Sugar .... 6.00 To 8.50
Sugar & Creamer, Round 18.00
Tumbler, Footed, 5 In. .. 12.00 To 15.00

Blossoms & Band

Jenkins Glass Company, Kokomo, Indiana, made Blossoms & Band glass in 1927. The pattern, sometimes called Apple Blossom Border, was made in crystal, green, pink or iridescent marigold, the Carnival glass color.

CRYSTAL
Bowl, 12 In. 20.00

MARIGOLD
Sugar 15.00

PINK
Bowl, Ruffled, 12 In. 8.00

Boopie

With a name like Boopie, it must have some other attraction. This Anchor Hocking pattern was made in the late 1940s and 1950s. Only glasses of various sizes are known, including the 3 1/2 ounce, 4 ounce, 6 ounce and 9 ounce. The pattern came in crystal, forest green or royal ruby.

CRYSTAL
Tumbler, Footed, 4 1/2 In.   1.25 To 4.50
Tumbler, Footed, 5 1/2 In.   1.25 To 5.00
Tumbler, Footed, 7 In. 6.50
Tumbler, 3 1/2 In. 2.50

GREEN
Parfait 5.00
Sherbet .... 3.50 To 4.00

Tumbler, Footed, 4 1/2 In. 4.50
Tumbler, Footed, 5 1/2 In. 6.00
Tumbler, Footed, 7 In. 6.50

RED
Tumbler, Footed, 5 1/2 In. 5.00

Bouquet & Lattice, see Normandie

Bowknot

The Bowknot pattern remains a mystery. The manufacturer is still unidentified. The swags and bows of the pattern were mold-etched. There does not seem to be a full dinner set of this pattern. Only the 7 inch plate, cup, sherbet, two sizes of bowls and two types of 10 ounce tumblers have been found. Green pieces are found easily and one writer reports the pattern was also made in crystal.

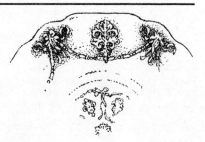

GREEN

Bowl, 5 1/2 In.	8.00	Plate, 7 In.	5.00 To 6.50
Cup	4.50 To 7.00	Sherbet	6.50

Bridal Bouquet, see No. 615

Bubble

Names of Depression glass patterns can be depressingly confusing. Bubble is also known as Bullseye, the original name given by Anchor Hocking Glass Company, or as Provincial, a 1960s name. Bubble was made in many colors, originally in crystal, pale blue or pink. Dark green was issued in 1954. Later, milk white and ruby red were made.

BLUE

Bowl, 4 1/2 In.	2.50 To 6.00
Bowl, 5 1/4 In.	3.50 To 6.50
Bowl, 8 3/8 In.	5.00 To 8.00
Creamer	5.00 To 19.00
Cup	3.00
Cup & Saucer	2.75 To 5.50
Plate, Grill, 9 3/8 In.	4.75 To 10.00
Plate, 6 3/4 In.	1.25 To 2.50
Plate, 9 3/8 In.	3.00 To 5.00
Platter, Oval, 12 In.	1.75 To 8.00
Saucer	1.00 To 2.50
Soup, Dish	4.00 To 9.50
Sugar	6.00 To 12.00
Sugar & Creamer	3.75 To 25.00

CRYSTAL

Bowl, 4 1/2 In.	.50 To 2.00

Bowl, 5 1/2 In. .... 1.00 To 2.00
Bowl, 8 3/8 In. .... 2.50 To 4.00
Candleholder, Pair ...... 7.50 To 12.00
Creamer .... 2.00 To 3.00
Cup .... 1.25 To 2.50
Cup & Saucer .... 2.00 To 2.50
Plate, 6 3/4 In. 1.00
Plate, 9 3/8 In. .... 1.00 To 2.00
Saucer .... .50
Soup, Dish .... 1.50 To 2.75
Sugar .... 2.00 To 2.50
Sugar & Creamer 6.50
Tumbler, Footed, 7 In. 10.00
Tumbler, 4 In. 2.00
Tumbler, 5 In. 2.00

GREEN
Bowl, 4 In. 4.00
Bowl, 4 1/2 In. 4.75
Bowl, 5 1/4 In. .... 2.50 To 5.00
Creamer .... 4.00 To 8.00
Cup 3.00

Cup & Saucer 4.50
Parfait 2.00
Plate, 9 3/8 In. .... 5.00 To 8.00
Saucer .... 1.50 To 2.50
Sugar .... 1.25 To 6.00
Sugar & Creamer .... 8.50 To 9.75

PINK
Bowl, 8 3/4 In. .... 4.00 To 6.00

RED
Bowl, 4 In. 4.50
Bowl, 4 1/2 In. 2.00
Creamer 2.50
Cup 3.50
Cup & Saucer .... 5.00 To 7.50
Pitcher .... 37.50 To 45.00
Plate, 9 3/8 In. 5.00
Tumbler, Juice, 4 In. ..... 1.00 To 6.50
Tumbler, 5 In. .... 4.00 To 9.00
Tumbler, 6 In. .... 5.00 To 10.00
Tumbler, 7 In. .... 9.00 To 12.00

Bullseye, see Bubble

Burple

Burple is not a mistype but a real name used
by the factory. Anchor Hocking Glass Company, Lancaster, Ohio, made a forest green
or ruby red dessert set in this pattern in the
1940s. There are also two sizes of bowls.

FOREST GREEN
Bowl, 8 1/2 In. 5.00
Tumbler, Footed, Swirl, 5 7/8 In. .. 4.50
Tumbler, Footed, Swirl, 6 3/4 In. .. 5.00

GREEN
Bowl, 4 In. 3.50
Sherbet, Footed, 4 In. 3.00

Butterflies & Roses, see Flower Garden with Butterflies

Buttons & Bows, see Holiday

By Cracky

A strange cracked ice look to the glass must have inspired the name By Cracky for this pattern. It was made in the late 1920s by L. E. Smith Glass Company, Mt. Pleasant, Pennsylvania. A luncheon set with sherbets, an 8 inch octagon plate, candleholder and flower frog were made. The luncheon set dish had several compartments. Amber, canary yellow, crystal and green pieces were made. The pieces have an overall pattern.

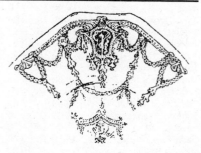

AMBER
Plate, Octagonal, 8 In.	2.00
Tray, Snack, 3 Part	2.50

CRYSTAL
Decanter, No Stopper	4.00
Plate, Octagonal, 6 In.	1.00
Plate, Octagonal, 8 In.	1.50
Plate, Round, 7 In.	1.50
Plate, Round, 8 In.	1.50
Sherbet, Crimped	1.50
Sherbet, Round	1.50
Tumbler, 3 5/8 In.	2.00

GREEN
Plate, Octagonal, 6 In.	1.00

Cabbage Rose, see Sharon

Cabbage Rose with Single Arch, see Rosemary

Cameo

Cameo is understandably called Ballerina or Dancing Girl because the most identifiable feature of the etched pattern is the silhouette of the dancer. This pattern must have sold well when made by Hocking Glass Company from 1930 to 1934 because many different pieces were made, from dinner sets and servers, to cookie jars and lamps. The pattern was made in crystal with a platinum rim, green, pink or yellow. In 1981 reproductions were made of both pink and green Cameo salt and pepper shakers.

CRYSTAL
Compote, 5 In.	17.50
Cup	2.50 To 3.75
Plate, Grill, 10 1/2 In.	7.00
Plate, Sherbet, 6 In.	1.50 To 2.00
Plate, 7 In.	2.50 To 3.00
Sugar & Creamer	25.00

GREEN
Bowl, Console, 3-Legged, 11 In.	35.00 To 48.00
Bowl, Oval, 10 In.	10.00 To 16.00
Bowl, 5 1/2 In.	13.00 To 18.00
Bowl, 7 1/4 In.	22.00 To 34.00
Bowl, 8 1/4 In.	18.75 To 25.00

Butter .... 105.00 To 150.00
Butter Tub .... 65.00 To 90.00
Cake Plate, Footed ...... 6.00 To 18.00
Candleholder, Pair .... 59.00 To 100.00
Compote, 5 In. .... 15.00 To 20.00
Cookie Jar, Covered .... 15.00 To 38.00
Creamer, 3 1/4 In. ..... 10.50 To 18.00
Cup .... 9.00 To 11.00
Cup & Saucer .... 11.00 To 12.50
Decanter & Stopper .... 35.00 To 79.50
Goblet, 3 1/2 In. ...... 22.75 To 27.50
Goblet, 4 In. .... 42.75 To 45.00
Goblet, 6 In. .... 28.50 To 37.50
Ladle, Mayonnaise 11.00
Pitcher, 5 3/4 In. .... 125.00 To 145.00
Pitcher, 56 Oz., 8 1/2 In. 26.00 To 38.00
Pitcher, 6 In. .... 29.00 To 47.00
Plate, Grill, Handled, 10 1/2 In. ... 6.50
Plate, Grill, 10 1/2 In. ... 5.00 To 12.00
Plate, Handled, 11 1/2 In. 8.00 To 16.00
Plate, Sherbet, 6 In. ...... 2.00 To 4.50
Plate, Square, 8 1/2 In. . 10.00 To 25.00
Plate, 8 In. .... 1.75 To 7.00
Plate, 9 1/2 In. .... 8.50 To 15.00
Platter, 12 In. .... 9.25 To 14.00
Relish .... 8.00 To 15.00
Salt & Pepper .... 30.00 To 60.00
Sherbet, 3 1/8 In. ...... 8.00 To 9.50
Sherbet, 4 7/8 In. ..... 17.00 To 25.00
Soup, Cream .... 35.00 To 44.00
Soup, Dish .... 22.00 To 28.00
Sugar 8.00
Sugar & Creamer, 4 1/4 In. 10.50 To 28.00
Sugar, 3 1/4 In. .... 6.00 To 10.00
Sugar, 4 1/4 In. .... 10.00 To 14.00
Tray, Domino .... 55.00 To 60.00
Tumbler, Flat, 4 In. .... 14.00 To 16.50
Tumbler, Flat, 4 3/4 In. . 16.00 To 20.00
Tumbler, Flat, 5 1/4 In. . 16.00 To 24.50
Tumbler, Footed, 3 1/4 In. 30.00 To 55.00
Tumbler, Footed, 5 In. .. 16.50 To 18.50
Tumbler, Footed, 5 3/4 In. 24.00 To 26.00
Tumbler, 3 3/4 In. ..... 14.00 To 17.00
Tumbler, 5 In. .... 14.00 To 20.00
Vase, 5 3/4 In. .... 75.00 To 84.50
Vase, 8 In. .... 14.50 To 22.00
Vinegar Bottle .... 15.00 To 20.00

PINK
Plate, 10 In. .... 29.75 To 34.75

Cameo

YELLOW
Bowl, Oval, 10 In. ..... 23.00 To 38.00
Bowl, 5 1/2 In. ...... 12.50 To 19.75
Candy Container, Covered 48.50
Creamer .... 12.00 To 18.00
Cup .... 3.00 To 7.00
Cup & Saucer .... 5.00 To 10.00
Pitcher, Plain, 8 1/2 In. 49.75
Plate, Grill, Closed Handle,
  10 1/2 In. ...... 3.00 To 10.00
Plate, Sherbet, 6 In. ...... 2.00 To 3.50
Plate, 8 In. .... 3.50 To 8.00
Plate, 9 1/2 In. .... 5.00 To 9.00
Platter, 12 In. .... 22.50 To 24.50
Saltshaker 22.00

Saucer . . . . 1.75 To 3.50	Sugar, 3 1/4 In. . . . . 8.50 To 11.00
Sherbet, 3 1/8 In. 20.00	Tumbler, Footed, 4 3/4 In. 12.50 To 14.00
Sherbet, 4 7/8 In. . . . . . 22.00 To 32.50	Tumbler, Footed, 5 In. . . 10.00 To 18.00
Sugar & Creamer . . . . . . 18.50 To 22.00	Tumbler, 5 In. . . . . 9.50 To 15.00

Candlewick

Candlewick was made by Imperial Glass Company, Bellaire, Ohio, from 1937 to the 1980s. Many similar patterns have been made by other companies. The beaded edge is the only design. Although the glass was first made in crystal it has also been produced in black, nut brown, sunshine yellow, ultra blue or verde (green). Some pieces of crystal are decorated with gold.

BLUE
Vase, Handled, 8 1/2 In. 15.00

CRYSTAL
Ashtray 4.00
Basket, Handled, 5 X 6 1/2 In. . . . 33.00
Bowl, 10 1/2 In. 14.00
Bowl, 2-Handled, 6 In. 7.00
Candleholder, 2 Part, Pair 30.00
Coaster, 4 3/4 In. . . . . 4.00 To 6.00
Cup & Saucer 6.00

Plate, 2-Handled, 12 In. 12.00
Plate, 8 In. 6.00
Relish, 2 Part, 6 1/2 In. . . 11.00 To 12.00
Relish, 6 Part, 10 1/2 In. 18.00
Salt & Pepper, Footed 33.00
Sandwich Server 17.00

Cape Cod

Cape Cod was a pattern made by the Imperial Glass Company, Bellaire, Ohio, from 1932. It is usually found in crystal, but was also made in amber, blue or ruby.

CRYSTAL
Bowl, 6 In. 4.00
Compote 12.00
Goblet, Ball Stem, 6 5/8 In. 4.00
Goblet, 6 1/4 In. . . . . 2.00 To 7.00
Plate, 6 3/4 In. . . . . 2.50 To 3.50
Plate, 8 In. . . . . 4.50 To 4.75
Relish, 2 Part, Handled 17.50
Salt & Pepper, 3 1/2 In 17.00
Sherbet, Ball Stem, 5 In. . . 3.00 To 4.75
Tumbler, Footed, 5 1/8 In. 3.00
Tumbler, 7 In. 7.00

RUBY
Bowl, Rimmed, 6 In. 8.00
Plate, 8 In. 8.00
Sherbet . . . . 9.00 To 12.00

Caprice, see also Alpine Caprice

Caprice was advertised in 1936 as the most popular crystal pattern in America. Over 200 pieces were made in the line. Frosted pieces were called Alpine Caprice, the name given by the maker, Cambridge Glass Company, Cambridge, Ohio. The sets were made in amber, amethyst, blue, crystal or pink.

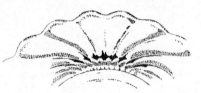

BLUE

Bowl, Crimped, Footed, 12 In. ... 35.00
Bowl, Crimped, Handled, 4 In. ... 12.50
Bowl, Footed, Handled, 7 In.
.... 15.00 To 20.00
Bowl, Footed, 10 1/2 In. 39.00
Candy Container, Covered,
Footed. 53.00
Coaster, 3 1/2 In. 25.00
Creamer 12.00
Cruet 18.50
Cup & Saucer 32.00
Dish, Jelly, Handled, 5 1/2 In. 12.00 To 17.50
Pitcher, Ball, 80 Oz. . 200.00 To 240.00
Plate, Footed, 14 1/2 In. 36.00
Plate, 6 In. 8.50
Plate, 6 1/2 In. .... ·12.00
Plate, 8 1/2 In. 16.00
Relish, 3 Part, 8 1/2 In. 35.00
Salt & Pepper .... 30.00 To 35.00
Sherbet 27.50
Sugar 12.00
Sugar & Creamer, Medium 32.00
Tray, Oval 28.50
Tray, Sugar & Creamer, Small 40.00
Vase 25.00

CRYSTAL

Bowl, Footed, 10 3/4 In. 30.00
Bowl, Footed, 13 In. ... 20.00 To 28.00

Bowl, Oval, Handled, 11 In. 32.00
Bowl, Square, Footed, 10 In. 32.00
Bowl, 4 1/2 In. 10.00
Bowl, 10 1/2 In. ...... 23.00 To 30.00
Candleholder, Pair, 7 In. 20.00 To 28.00
Cigarette Box, Covered, 3 1/2 In. 20.00
Coaster 3.00
Compote, Footed, 7 In. 6.75
Compote, Footed, 8 In. 14.00
Compote, 5 1/2 In. 25.00
Creamer .... 6.00 To 7.50
Cruet & Stopper 32.00
Cup & Saucer .... 13.50 To 15.00
Dish, 7 In. 8.00
Goblet, Champagne 10.00
Jar, Mustard, Covered 25.00
Plate, 6 1/2 In. 7.50
Plate, 7 3/4 In. .... 6.50 To 9.00
Plate, 8 1/2 In. .... 7.75 To 12.00
Plate, 14 In. .... 22.00 To 23.00
Relish, 2 Part, 5 1/2 In. 13.00
Relish, 3 Part, 7 1/2 In. 18.00
Relish, 3 Part, 8 1/2 In. . 12.00 To 20.00
Salt & Pepper .... 9.50 To 12.00
Saucer 5.00
Sugar & Creamer ...... 14.00 To 17.50
Sugar, 3 In. 7.50
Tumbler, Footed, 7 In. 15.00

Centaur

The Egyptian Sphinx included in the border gave this pattern its original name of Sphinx. Collectors now call it Centaur. It was made by the Lancaster Glass Company, Lancaster, Ohio, in the 1930s. Both green and yellow glass was made.

GREEN

Ashtray, Footed 4.00
Bowl, Footed, Scalloped, 3 In. 4.00

Chain Daisy, see Adam

Chantilly

As late as the 1960s the Jeannette Glass Company, Jeanette, Pennsylvania, made a pattern called Chantilly which is collected by Depression glass buffs. It was made in crystal or pink.

CRYSTAL
Candy Container, Covered, 3 Part   75.00
Goblet, Sherry 58.00
Pitcher, Martini 200.00
Saltshaker, Handled 22.00

Cherry, see Cherry Blossom

Cherry-Berry, see also Strawberry

Two similar patterns, Cherry-Berry and Strawberry, can be confusing. If the fruit pictured is a cherry, then the pattern is called Cherry-Berry. If the strawberry is used, then the pattern has that name. The dishes were made by the U.S. Glass Company in the early 1930s in amber, crystal, green or pink.

GREEN
Bowl, 7 1/2 In. 11.00
Sherbet 6.50

PINK
Sherbet 6.50

Cherry Blossom

Cherry Blossom is one of the most popular Depression glass patterns. It has been called Banded Cherry, Cherry, or Paneled Cherry Blossom by some collectors. The pattern was made by the Jeannette Glass Company, Jeannette, Pennsylvania, from 1930 to 1939. Full dinner sets and serving pieces were made in a wide range of colors. Pieces were made in crystal, delphite, green, jadite, pink or red. Because the pattern is popular and because some pieces, especially the butter dish, sell for high dollars, reproductions were made from 1973. These were made in blue, delphite, green or pink.

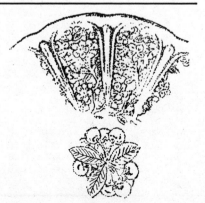

BLUE

Plate, Child's	7.50
Tray, Handled	9.50

CRYSTAL

Bowl, Console	45.00
Bowl, Oval, 9 In.	18.00
Bowl, 5 3/4 In.	16.00
Bowl, 8 In.	15.00
Bowl, 8 1/2 In.	15.75
Butter	70.00
Pitcher, Allover Design, 6 1/2 In.	29.00
Plate, 7 In.	11.50 To 14.75
Plate, 9 In.	12.00
Saucer	3.50
Sherbet	10.00
Sugar & Creamer, Covered	28.00
Sugar, Covered	15.00 To 17.50
Tray, Handled, 10 1/2 In.	13.50 To 17.50
Tumbler, Design On Top, 4 1/4 In.	8.00 To 12.00
Tumbler, Design On Top, 5 In.	30.00

DELPHITE

Bowl, Handled, 9 In.	18.00
Bowl, Round, 8 1/2 In.	40.00
Bowl, 4 3/4 In.	7.50 To 12.75
Candleholder, Pair	24.75
Child's Set, 14 Piece	125.00 To 175.00
Creamer	14.00
Cup & Saucer	16.00
Pitcher, Footed, 8 In.	80.00
Pitcher, 6 3/4 In.	79.00
Pitcher, 8 In.	75.00
Plate, 6 In.	7.00 To 8.50
Plate, 8 In.	14.00
Plate, 9 In.	11.00 To 16.00
Saucer	2.50 To 6.50
Saucer, Child's	4.00
Sherbet	14.00 To 15.00
Sugar	12.00
Sugar & Creamer	32.00 To 35.00
Tray, Handled, 10 1/2 In.	12.00 To 17.50
Tumbler, Allover Design, 3 3/4 In.	16.00
Tumbler, Footed, 4 1/2 In.	16.00 To 20.00
Water Set, 6 Tumblers	195.00

GREEN

Bowl, Console, 3-Legged, 10 1/2 In.	34.00 To 40.00
Bowl, Oval, 9 In.	16.00 To 19.50
Bowl, 4 3/4 In.	7.00 To 12.50
Bowl, 5 3/4 In.	14.00 To 30.00
Bowl, 8 1/2 In.	14.00 To 21.00
Butter, Covered	55.00 To 95.00
Cake Plate, 10 1/4 In.	15.00 To 18.75
Coaster	6.00 To 10.00
Creamer	10.00 To 15.00
Cup	13.50 To 15.00
Cup & Saucer	15.00 To 22.50
Mug	85.00 To 129.50
Pitcher, Allover Design, 6 3/4 In.	35.00 To 42.00
Pitcher, Flat, 8 In.	25.00 To 39.00
Plate, Grill, 9 In.	13.00 To 18.00
Plate, 6 In.	3.00 To 5.00
Plate, 7 In.	11.00 To 16.00
Plate, 9 In.	10.00 To 16.00
Platter, Divided, 13 In.	32.00 To 39.00
Platter, Oval, 11 In.	20.00 To 22.50
Platter, 13 In.	29.00
Saucer	3.50 To 4.50
Sherbet	9.00 To 14.00
Soup, Dish	30.00 To 45.00
Sugar & Creamer, Covered	26.00 To 34.00
Sugar, Covered	17.50 To 26.00
Tray, Handled, 10 1/2 In.	12.00 To 16.00
Tumbler, Design On Top, Flat, 4 1/4 In.	12.00 To 18.00
Tumbler, Flat, 3 1/2 In.	11.00 To 16.00
Tumbler, Footed, 3 3/4 In.	11.00 To 15.00
Tumbler, Footed, 4 1/2 In.	25.00 To 32.50
Water Set, Design On Top, 6 Tumblers, 4 In.	130.00

PINK

Bowl, Console, 10 1/2 In.	32.00 To 48.00
Bowl, Handled, 9 In.	9.00 To 24.75
Bowl, Oval, 9 In.	15.00 To 22.50
Bowl, 4 3/4 In.	6.00 To 12.50
Bowl, 5 3/4 In.	20.00 To 25.00
Bowl, 8 1/2 In.	14.50 To 22.00
Butter, Covered	35.00 To 65.00
Cake Plate	14.00 To 17.50
Child's Set	150.00
Coaster	7.00 To 13.75
Creamer	8.00 To 16.00
Creamer, Child's	22.00
Cup	10.00 To 13.00
Cup & Saucer	14.50 To 18.00
Cup & Saucer, Child's	25.00 To 28.75
Mug, 7 Oz.	135.00
Pitcher, Flat, Allover Design	30.00 To 35.00
Pitcher, Footed, Design On Top, 8 In.	32.50
Plate, Child's, 6 In.	5.00 To 7.00
Plate, Sherbet, 6 In.	3.50 To 4.50
Plate, 7 In.	11.00 To 14.75
Plate, 9 In.	10.00 To 14.50

Platter, Divided, 13 In. . 28.00 To 40.00
Platter, 11 In. . . . . 8.00 To 19.75
Saucer . . . . 2.50 To 4.00
Saucer, Child's . . . . 3.00 To 4.00
Sherbet . . . . 3.00 To 12.50
Soup, Dish . . . . 30.00 To 42.50
Sugar . . . . 4.75 To 10.00
Sugar & Creamer, Child's 40.00
Sugar & Creamer, Covered 25.00 To 35.00
Sugar, Child's 25.00
Sugar, Covered . . . . 12.00 To 20.00
Tray, Handled, 10 1/2 In. 10.00 To 18.00
Tumbler, Design On Top, 4 1/4 In.
. . . . 10.00 To 12.00
Tumbler, Design On Top, 5 In.
. . . . 28.00 To 35.00
Tumbler, Flat, 3 1/2 In. . 11.00 To 14.50
Tumbler, Footed, Allover Design, 3 3/4 In.
. . . . 11.00
Tumbler, Round Foot, 3 3/4 In.
. . . . 10.00 To 14.00

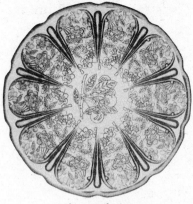

Cherry Blossom

Tumbler, Scalloped Foot, Allover Pattern,
  4 1/2 In. 22.00

Chinex Classic, see also Cremax

Chinex Classic and Cremax are very similar
patterns made by Macbeth-Evans Division of
Corning Glass Works from about 1938 to
1942. Chinex and Cremax are both words
with two meanings. Each is the name of a
pattern and the name of a color used for
other patterns. Chinex is ivory color, Cremax
is a bit whiter. Chinex Classic, the dinnerware pattern, has a piecrust edge, and just
inside the edge is an elongated feathered
scroll. It may or may not have a decal-
decorated center and a colored edging. The
Cremax pattern has just the piecrust edge.
The decals used on Chinex Classic are either
floral designs or brown-toned scenics.

Creamer 4.75
Cup & Saucer . . . . 2.50 To 5.75
Cup, Red Band 2.00
Plate, Sherbet, 6 1/4 In. . . 1.50 To 2.50
Plate, 9 3/4 In. . . . . 4.00 To 4.50
Saucer 1.00
Soup, Dish 18.00
Sugar & Creamer, Footed 14.00

IVORY
Bowl, 5 3/4 In. 2.50
Cake Plate, 11 1/2 In. . . . 6.50 To 10.00

IVORY WITH DECAL
Butter 19.75
Plate, 9 3/4 In. . . . . 3.50 to 5.00

Christmas Candy

Christmas Candy, sometimes called Christmas Candy Ribbon, was made by the Indiana Glass Company, Dunkirk, Indiana, in
1937. The pattern, apparently only made
in luncheon sets, was made in crystal, a light
green called seafoam green, a bright blue
called teal blue and a dark emerald green.

CRYSTAL
Cup & Saucer 4.00
Plate, 8 In. 3.00
Plate, 11 In. 6.00
Saucer 1.50
Sugar & Creamer . . . . 8.50 To 10.00

Christmas Candy Ribbon, see Christmas Candy

Circle

Circles ring the Circle pattern made by Hocking Glass Company, Lancaster, Ohio, in the 1930s. It is often found in green, but is less available in crystal or pink.

CRYSTAL
Pitcher, 8 In. 14.00
Tumbler, 3 3/4 In. 3.00

GREEN
Bowl, 5 1/2 In. 5.00
Cup .... 2.00 To 3.00
Cup & Saucer .... 3.50 To 6.00
Goblet, 5 3/4 In. .... 5.50 To 7.50
Pitcher, 8 In. 28.00
Plate, 6 In. .... 1.75 To 2.00
Plate, 8 In. 5.00
Saucer .... 1.00 To 1.25
Sherbet .... 4.00 To 5.50

PINK
Cup 2.50
Sherbet 4.00
Tumbler, 3 3/4 In. 3.50

Circular Ribs, see Circle

Classic, see Chinex Classic

Cloverleaf

Three-leaf clovers form part of the border of Cloverleaf pattern made by Hazel Atlas Glass Company from 1930 to 1936. It was made in black, crystal, green, pink or topaz.

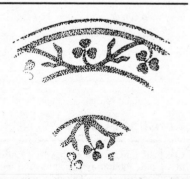

BLACK
Creamer .... 7.00 To 10.00
Cup 8.00
Cup & Saucer .... 4.00 To 12.50
Plate, 8 In. .... 9.00 To 12.00
Salt & Pepper .... 55.00 To 77.75
Saucer 4.00
Sherbet 18.00
Sugar .... 7.00 To 10.00
Sugar & Creamer ...... 13.00 To 22.00

CRYSTAL
Saucer 2.00
Sugar & Creamer 16.50

GREEN
Bowl, 4 In. .... 12.00 To 14.00
Bowl, 5 In. .... 9.00 To 15.00
Bowl, 7 In. .... 25.00 To 26.00

Bowl, 8 In. .... 60.00 To 62.00
Candy Container, Covered 25.00 To 52.00
Creamer .... 5.00 To 7.50
Cup .... 4.00 To 6.00
Cup & Saucer .... 4.00 To 9.00
Plate, Grill, 10 1/4 In. 15.00
Plate, 6 In. .... 2.50 To 5.50
Plate, 8 In. .... 3.50 To 8.50
Relish 18.00
Salt & Pepper .... 15.00 To 28.00
Saucer .... 1.00 To 2.50
Sherbet .... 1.25 To 5.50
Sugar .... 5.00 To 7.50
Sugar & Creamer 12.00
Tumbler, Flat, 4 In. .... 16.00 To 22.00
Tumbler, Footed, 5 3/4 In. 15.00 To 18.00

PINK
Bowl, 4 In. 12.00
Bowl, 5 In. 17.50

Cup 6.00
Cup & Saucer .... 5.00 To 7.50
Plate, 8 In. .... 3.50 To 5.25
Saucer .... .75 To 2.00
Sherbet .... 3.75 To 5.50
Tumbler, Flat, 4 In. 22.50

TOPAZ
Bowl, 5 In. 12.00
Candy Container, Covered 12.00
Creamer 9.50
Cup & Saucer 15.00
Plate, 6 In. 4.50
Plate, 8 In. 7.00
Saltshaker .... 39.00 To 45.00
Sherbet .... 6.50 To 8.00
Sugar .... 6.00 To 8.00
Sugar & Creamer 16.50
Tumbler, Footed, 5 3/4 In. 18.00

Colonial

Sometimes this pattern is called Knife & Fork, although Colonial is the more common name. It was made by Hocking Glass Company, Lancaster, Ohio, from 1934 to 1936. Colors include crystal, green, opaque white or pink.

CRYSTAL
Bowl, 9 In. 10.00
Butter, Covered .... 25.00 To 32.50
Cream & Sugar, Open 23.00
Creamer .... 5.50 To 8.50
Cup 4.50
Cup & Saucer .... 7.00 To 8.00
Goblet, 4 In. .... 6.00 To 7.00
Goblet, 4 1/2 In. 9.75
Goblet, 5 1/4 In. 8.00
Goblet, 5 3/4 In. 8.00
Pitcher, Ice Lip, 7 3/4 In. 18.00 To 23.00
Plate, Grill, 10 In. .... 7.00 To 10.50
Plate, 8 1/2 In. .... 2.50 To 3.50
Plate, 10 In. .... 9.50 To 13.00
Platter, 12 In. 7.50
Saltshaker 22.00
Saucer 1.00
Sherbet, 3 3/8 In. 3.00
Soup, Dish 7.00
Sugar .... 4.00 To 5.00
Sugar & Creamer 15.00
Sugar & Creamer, Covered 21.50 To 25.00

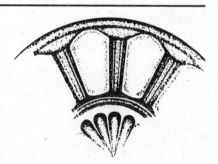

Sugar, Covered 15.00
Tumbler, Flat, 3 In. 3.00
Tumbler, Footed, 4 In. .... 4.00 To 7.50
Whiskey .... 5.00 To 6.00

GREEN
Bowl, 4 1/2 In. .... 7.00 To 12.00
Bowl, 9 In. .... 11.00 To 20.00
Butter, Covered .... 45.00 To 55.00
Celery .... 80.00 To 125.00
Creamer .... 10.00 To 14.00
Cup .... 7.50 To 9.50
Cup & Saucer .... 9.50 To 15.00
Goblet, 3 3/4 In. ...... 18.00 To 19.00
Goblet, 4 In. .... 13.00 To 20.00
Goblet, 5 1/4 In. ...... 15.00 To 20.00
Goblet, 5 3/4 In. ...... 20.00 To 24.00

Plate, Grill, 10 In. . . . . 6.50 To 29.00
Plate, Sherbet, 6 In. . . . . . . 1.00 To 3.50
Plate, Sherbet, 8 1/2 In. . . 5.50 To 8.00
Plate, 10 In. 38.00
Platter, 12 In. . . . . 11.00 To 18.00
Salt & Pepper 120.00
Soup, Cream 31.00
Soup, Dish 35.00
Sugar & Creamer . . . . . . 20.00 To 28.00
Sugar, Covered . . . . 14.00 To 22.75
Tumbler, Footed, 3 1/2 In. 12.50 To 22.00
Tumbler, Footed, 4 In. 15.50
Whiskey . . . . 6.50 To 9.00

PINK
Bowl, Oval, 10 In. . . . . . 10.00 To 14.00
Bowl, 4 1/2 In. 9.50
Bowl, 5 1/2 In. 19.50
Bowl, 9 In. 14.00
Celery 65.00
Cup . . . . 3.00 To 5.50

Pitcher, Ice Lip, 7 In. . . . 28.00 To 30.00
Pitcher, Ice Lip, 7 3/4 In. 33.00 To 52.00
Plate, Grill, 10 In. 15.00
Plate, 8 1/2 In. . . . . 3.50 To 5.00
Plate, 10 In. 18.00
Platter, 12 In. 11.00
Salt & Pepper 95.00
Saltshaker . . . . 42.50 To 50.00
Sherbet . . . . 3.50 To 7.00
Sugar 7.00
Tumbler, Footed, 3 1/4 In. 8.50
Tumbler, 3 In. . . . . 9.00 To 10.00
Tumbler, 4 In. . . . . 6.50 To 10.00
Tumbler, 5 In. 19.00
Whiskey . . . . 6.00 To 7.00

WHITE
Cup 12.00
Cup & Saucer 14.00
Plate, 10 In. 12.00

Colonial Block

A small set of dishes, mostly serving pieces, was made in Colonial Block pattern by Hazel Atlas Glass Company, a firm with factories in Ohio, Pennsylvania and West Virginia. The dishes were made in the 1930s in green or pink and in white in the 1950s.

GREEN
Candy Container, Covered 20.00 To 22.00
Sherbet 2.50

Sugar & Creamer 13.00
Sugar, Open 9.00

PINK
Bowl, 7 In. 8.50
Sugar 6.25

Colonial Fluted

Federal Glass Company made Colonial Fluted pattern from 1928 to 1933. It was made in crystal or green.

GREEN
Bowl, 4 In. 2.75
Bowl, 6 In. 2.50
Bowl, 7 1/2 In. . . . . 7.00 To 10.00
Creamer 10.00
Cup & Saucer . . . . 4.00 To 5.00
Plate, 8 In. . . . . 2.00 To 2.50
Saucer 1.25

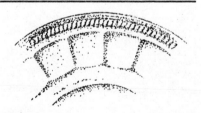

Sherbet 3.75
Sugar & Creamer . . . . 7.00 To 12.00
Sugar, Covered . . . . 8.00 To 9.00

Colony

Colony is a pattern that has also been called Elongated Honeycomb or Hexagon Triple Band because of the features in the molding. It was made by Hazel Atlas Glass Company in the 1930s in crystal, green or pink.

CRYSTAL

Bowl, 8 1/2 In.	25.00
Candleholder, Short, Pair	20.00
Candy Container, 3-Legged	10.00
Cocktail Shaker	9.00 To 10.00
Compote, Covered	20.00 To 25.00
Creamer	5.00
Cup	7.50
Cup & Saucer	8.50 To 12.00
Mayonnaise Set, 3 Piece	27.50
Plate, 8 In.	5.00 To 6.00
Plate, 10 In.	12.00
Salt & Pepper	27.50
Sandwich Server	25.00
Sherbet, Footed	6.00
Sugar	7.00
Sugar & Creamer	25.00
Tumbler, Flat, Juice, 3 In.	7.00

Columbia

Columbia pattern can be found in crystal but is rare in pink. It was made by Federal Glass Company, Columbus, Ohio, from 1936 to 1942.

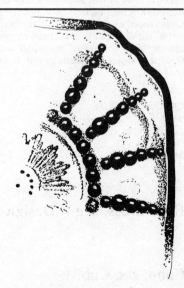

CRYSTAL

Bowl, Ruffled, 10 1/2 In.	5.00 To 10.00
Bowl, 5 In.	5.00 To 5.50
Bowl, 8 1/2 In.	6.50 To 8.00
Butter, Covered	9.00 To 17.50
Celery, 5 1/2 In.	15.00
Coaster, 4 In.	1.00
Cup	3.00 To 3.50
Cup & Saucer	4.00 To 7.50
Plate, Chop, 11 3/4 In.	3.00 To 7.00
Plate, 6 In.	.75 To 2.50
Plate, 9 1/2 In.	2.00 To 5.00
Saucer	1.00 To 1.75
Soup, Dish	5.50 To 9.00

PINK

Plate, 9 1/2 In.	9.50 To 10.50

Coronation

Coronation was made by Anchor Hocking Glass Company, Lancaster, Ohio, from 1936 to 1940. Most pieces are crystal or pink, but there are also ruby red sets. The pattern is sometimes called Banded Fine Rib or Saxon. Some of the pieces are confused with those in Lace Edge pattern.

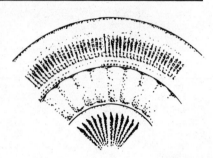

PINK
Bowl, 4 1/4 In.	1.00 To 3.00
Bowl, 8 In.	6.50 To 7.00
Cup	2.50 To 3.00
Cup & Saucer	5.50
Plate, Sherbet, 6 In.	1.25 To 2.50
Saucer	1.50
Sherbet	2.25 To 4.50
Tumbler, 5 In.	8.00

RUBY RED
Bowl, 4 1/4 In.	3.50 To 5.00
Bowl, 8 In.	7.75 To 10.00

Cremax, see also Chinex Classic

Cremax and Chinex Classic are confusing patterns. There is an added piece of molded design next to the fluted rim trim on Chinex Classic. Also the name Cremax and Chinex refer to colors as well as patterns. Cremax, made by Macbeth-Evans Division of Corning Glass Works, was popular in the late 1930s to the early 1940s. It is a cream-colored opaque glass sometimes decorated with floral or brown-tinted decals or with a colored rim.

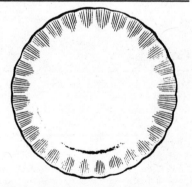

CREAM-COLORED
Bowl, 9 In.	10.00
Cup & Saucer	7.00
Plate, 11 1/2 In.	6.50 To 7.50
Saucer	3.00

CREAM-COLORED WITH DECAL
Cup & Saucer	4.50
Plate, 6 1/4 In.	3.50

Criss Cross, see X Design

Cube, see Cubist

Cubist

Cubist or Cube, molded with the expected rectangular and diamond pattern, was made by Jeannette Glass Company from 1929 to 1933. It was made in crystal, green, pink or ultramarine. It has been made recently in amber or avocado.

AMBER
Creamer	3.00
Sugar & Creamer	12.00
Tumbler, Footed, 4 In.	8.00
Tumbler, Footed, 4 1/4 In.	8.00

CRYSTAL
Bowl, 4 1/2 In.	1.00
Bowl, 5-Legged	18.00
Bowl, 6 1/2 In.	3.00 To 4.00
Creamer, 2 In.	4.00
Jar, Powder, Covered	12.00
Plate, Sherbet, 6 In.	.50 To 1.00
Sugar & Creamer, 2 In. ...	1.75 To 5.00
Sugar, 2 In.	1.00 To 4.00
Tray, Handled, 7 1/2 In. ..	2.50 To 3.00

GREEN
Bowl, 4 1/2 In.	2.50 To 5.50
Bowl, 6 1/2 In.	7.00 To 10.00
Butter, Covered	30.00 To 50.00
Candy Container, Covered	14.50 To 25.00
Coaster	2.50 To 6.00
Creamer, 3 In.	4.00 To 6.00
Cup	4.00 To 6.00
Cup & Saucer	6.00 To 8.50
Jar, Powder, Covered ...	12.00 To 17.00
Pitcher, 8 3/4 In.	125.00
Plate, 6 In.	1.00 To 2.00
Plate, 8 In.	1.50 To 5.50
Salt & Pepper	16.50 To 22.50
Saucer	1.50
Sherbet	3.00 To 7.00
Sugar & Creamer, Covered	16.00 To 20.00
Sugar, Covered	7.00 To 14.75
Sugar, 3 In.	3.25 To 5.50
Tumbler, 4 In.	27.50

PINK
Bowl, Deep, 4 1/2 In.	2.75 To 5.00
Bowl, 4 1/2 In.	2.25 To 4.50
Bowl, 6 1/2 In.	4.75 To 7.50
Butter, Covered	35.00 To 45.00
Candy Container	18.50 To 20.00
Coaster	3.00 To 5.00
Creamer, 2 In.	1.50
Creamer, 3 In.	3.25 To 4.50
Cup	3.00 To 4.50
Cup & Saucer	5.75
Jar, Powder, Covered	9.00 To 15.00
Pitcher, 8 3/4 In.	115.00
Plate, Sherbet, 6 In.	.75 To 2.50
Plate, 8 In.	2.50 To 4.50
Salt & Pepper	16.00 To 17.50
Saucer	1.50 To 1.75
Sherbet	4.00
Sugar & Creamer, 2 In. ...	3.25 To 5.50
Sugar & Creamer, 3 In. ..	8.50 To 12.00
Sugar, 2 In.	1.50 To 1.75
Sugar, 3 In.	3.00 To 5.00
Tumbler, 4 In.	20.00

Daisy, see No. 620

Daisy Petals, see Petalware

Dancing Girl, see Cameo

Dewdrop

Although Dewdrop was made in 1954 and 1955, it is collected by some Depression glass buyers. It was made by Jeannette Glass Company, Jeannette, Pennsylvania, in crystal.

CRYSTAL
Creamer 4.00
Punch Bowl & 6 Cups 15.00
Snack Plate 5.00

Diamond, see Windsor

Diamond Pattern, see Miss America

Diamond Point, see Petalware

Diamond Quilted

Imperial Glass Company, Bellaire, Ohio, made Diamond Quilted in the late 1920s and early 1930s. The pattern is sometimes called Flat Diamond. It was made in amber, black, blue, crystal, green, pink or red.

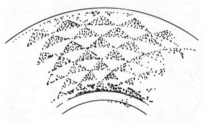

BLACK
Plate, 8 In. 6.50
Sugar 8.00

BLUE
Cup 9.00
Plate, 8 In. .... 6.00 To 9.50
Sugar .... 5.00 To 8.00

CRYSTAL
Cup & Saucer 5.00
Sugar 4.50

GREEN
Bowl, Handled, 5-1/2 In. 6.00
Candleholder, Round, Footed 8.00
Console Set, Rolled Edge 30.00
Creamer 5.00
Cup 4.00
Plate, 6 In. 2.00
Plate, 8 In. .... 3.00 To 3.50
Saucer 1.50

Sherbet .... 3.00 To 4.00
Soup, Cream 6.50
Sugar 6.75
Sugar & Creamer ...... 12.00 To 15.00

PINK
Bowl, Crimped, 7 In. ..... 4.00 To 6.00
Bowl, Handled, 5 1/2 In. 6.00
Candleholder, Pair ..... 10.00 To 14.50
Candy Container, Covered 16.00
Cup & Saucer .... 5.00 To 5.50
Goblet, 6 In. 6.00
Plate, Sherbet, 6 In. 2.00
Plate, 8 In. .... 3.50 To 4.50
Sherbet .... 1.25 To 4.00
Soup, Cream 6.50
Sugar .... 4.00 To 5.50
Sugar & Creamer .... 9.00 To 15.00

Diana

Diana is one of the many Depression glass patterns with swirls in the glass, which often causes confusion. Federal Glass Company, Columbus, Ohio, made this pattern, sometimes called Swirled Sharp Rib, from 1937 to 1941. It was made in amber, crystal, green or pink.

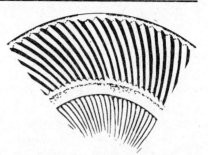

AMBER
Bowl, Console, 11 In. .... 5.00 To 9.50
Bowl, 5 In. .... 2.00 To 4.00
Bowl, 9 In. .... 6.00 To 6.50
Candy Container, Covered 35.00
Creamer 4.50
Cup 4.00
Cup & Saucer .... 2.25 To 5.50
Plate, 6 In. 1.50
Plate, 9 1/2 In. .... 4.00 To 5.00
Plate, 11 3/4 In. .... 3.50 To 6.50
Platter, 12 In. 6.00
Salt & Pepper .... 40.00 To 60.00
Saucer .... 1.50 To 2.00
Soup, Cream .... 5.00 To 10.00
Soup, Dish 7.50
Sugar .... 2.00 To 4.50
Sugar & Creamer ...... 10.00 To 12.00
Tumbler, 4 1/8 In. 7.00

CRYSTAL
Bowl, Console, 11 In. 3.50
Bowl, Scalloped Edge, 12 In. 5.00 To 10.50
Bowl, 5 In. 2.00
Bowl, 9 In. 6.00
Candy Container, Covered 8.00 To 14.00
Cup & Saucer, Demitasse . 2.50 To 5.00

Cup, Demitasse 2.00
Plate, 6 In. .... .50 To 1.25
Plate, 9 1/2 In. .... 2.75 To 4.00
Platter, 12 In. 4.00
Sandwich Server, 11 3/4 In. 5.50
Saucer .... .50 To 2.00
Saucer, Demitasse, Silver Rim 1.00 To 1.25
Soup, Cream 5.00
Tumbler, 4 1/8 In. 6.00

PINK
Bowl, Console, 11 In. 10.00
Bowl, Salad, 9 In. .... 6.00 To 8.00
Bowl, 5 In. .... 3.00 To 5.00
Candy Container, Covered 15.00
Coaster 3.25
Cup 6.00
Plate, 6 In. .... 1.25 To 2.00
Plate, 9 1/2 In. .... 5.75 To 8.00
Platter, 11 3/4 In. 5.00
Salt & Pepper .... 25.00 To 39.50
Saucer .... 1.00 To 3.00

Dogwood

Dogwood is decorated with a strange flower that has been given many names. Collectors have called this pattern Apple Blossom, B pattern, Magnolia or Wild Rose. It was made from 1930 to 1934 by Macbeth-Evans Glass Company. It is found in cremax, crystal, green, monax, pink or yellow.

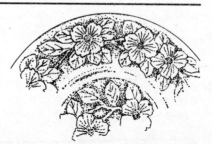

CREMAX
Bowl, 8 1/2 In. 20.00
Cup & Saucer .... 32.50 To 37.50

CRYSTAL
Plate, 8 In. 2.50
Sherbet 8.00
Sugar 5.00

GREEN
Cup .... 10.00 To 20.00
Cup & Saucer .... 16.00 To 24.75
Plate, 6 In. .... 3.00 To 3.50
Sugar 29.75

MONAX
Plate, Server, 12 In. .... 24.00 To 27.50

PINK
Bowl, 5 1/2 In. .... 10.00 To 13.50
Bowl, 8 1/2 In. .... 25.00 To 40.00
Bowl, 10 1/4 In. 135.00
Cake Plate, 13 In. ..... 60.00 To 75.00
Creamer, Thin .... 8.00 To 10.00
Creamer, 3 1/4 In. 10.00
Cup .... 5.00 To 9.00
Cup & Saucer .... 8.50 To 12.50
Pitcher, American Sweetheart Style,
    8 In. 625.00
Pitcher, 8 In. .... 98.00 To 112.50
Plate, Grill, 10 1/2 In. ... 7.50 To 13.00
Plate, Server, 12 In. .... 15.00 To 22.00
Plate, 6 In. .... 2.50 To 6.00
Plate, 8 In. .... 2.50 To 4.00
Plate, 9 1/4 In. .... 10.00 To 19.00
Platter, Oval, 12 In. 250.00

Dogwood

Relish 20.00
Saucer .... 1.50 To 3.50
Sherbet .... 14.50 To 18.75
Sugar & Creamer, Thick . 11.00 To 20.00
Sugar & Creamer, Thin . 10.75 To 24.75
Sugar, Thick, 3 1/4 In. 6.00
Sugar, Thin, 2 1/2 In. 7.00
Tidbit, 2 Tier 75.00
Tumbler, Decorated, 4 In. 20.00 To 22.50
Tumbler, Decorated, 4 3/4 In.
    .... 20.00 To 28.00
Tumbler, Decorated, 5 In. 28.00 To 29.50
Tumbler, Etched, 4 3/4 In. 10.00 To 15.00

Doric

Doric was made by Jeannette Glass Company, Jeannette, Pennsylvania, from 1935 to 1938. The molded pattern has also inspired another name for the pattern, Snowflake. It was made in crystal, delphite, green, pink or yellow. A few white pieces may have been made.

DELPHITE
Candy Container,
    3 Part, 6 In. .... 3.25 To 6.00
Sherbet .... 4.00 To 4.50

GREEN
Bowl, 4 1/2 In. .... 5.00 To 6.00
Bowl, 5 1/2 In. 22.50
Bowl, 8 1/4 In. .... 9.00 To 11.00
Butter, Covered .... 45.00 To 65.00
Cake Plate .... 13.00 To 17.50

Candy Container, Covered, Footed
    .... 22.00 To 34.00
Candy Container, 3 Part 4.00
Coaster 11.00
Creamer .... 7.00 To 10.00
Cup 5.50
Plate, Grill, 9 In. 8.00
Plate, Sherbet, 6 In. 3.00

Plate, 7 In. .... 10.00 To 12.00
Plate, 9 In. 8.00
Platter, 12 In. .... 10.00 To 17.50
Relish, 4 X 2 In. .... 8.00 To 14.00
Relish, 4 X 4 In. .... 5.50 To 8.00
Salt & Pepper .... 20.00 To 37.00
Saucer .... 1.50 To 2.50
Sherbet .... 7.50 To 9.00
Sugar 9.00
Sugar & Creamer, Covered 35.00
Sugar, Covered 16.00
Tray, Handled, 10 In. 8.00
Tumbler, 4 In. 25.00
Tumbler, 4 1/2 In. ..... 45.00 To 55.00

PINK

Bowl, 4 1/2 In. .... 2.50 To 6.50
Bowl, 8 1/4 In. 10.00
Cake Plate 12.00
Candy Container, Covered 27.50
Candy Container, 3 Part 4.00

Coaster 8.50
Creamer .... 6.00 To 10.00
Cup .... 4.25 To 5.50
Cup & Saucer .... 5.50 To 9.25
Plate, Grill, 9 In. .... 8.00 To 9.00
Plate, Sherbet, 6 In. ...... 2.00 To 3.00
Plate, 9 In. .... 2.00 To 9.00
Platter, 12 In. .... 9.00 To 15.00
Relish, Aluminum Tray, 4 X 8 In. . 28.00
Relish, 4 X 4 In. .... 4.50 To 5.50
Relish, 4 X 8 In. .... 5.00 To 12.00
Salt & Pepper .... 24.00 To 30.00
Saucer .... 2.00 To 2.25
Sherbet .... 6.00 To 10.00
Sugar & Creamer, Covered 20.00 To 22.50
Sugar, Covered .... 6.00 To 7.50
Tray, Handled, 10 In. 10.50
Tray, 8 X 8 In. .... 9.00 To 15.00
Tumbler, 4 In. .... 19.00 To 22.50
Tumbler, 4 1/2 In. ..... 19.00 To 22.50

Doric & Pansy

The snowflake-like design of Doric alternates
with squares holding pansies, so of course
the pattern is named Doric & Pansy. It too
was made by Jeannette Glass Company but
only in 1937 and 1938. It was made in crystal, pink and ultramarine.

CRYSTAL
Cup & Saucer 7.00

GREEN
Bowl, 4 1/2 In. 4.75
Candy Container, Clover Shape ... 5.00
Coaster 9.00
Creamer 8.00
Plate, 6 In. 3.00
Saltshaker 27.50
Sugar, Open 160.00

PINK
Bowl, 4 1/2 In. .... 3.50 To 5.00
Child's Set, 14 Piece 200.00
Coaster 5.50
Cup & Saucer .... 5.00 To 6.50
Plate, Sherbet, 6 In. 4.50
Plate, 9 In. 6.00
Salt & Pepper 30.00
Saucer .... 1.00 To 3.00
Sugar, Child's 35.00
Sugar, Covered 8.00

Tumbler, 4 1/2 In. 13.00

ULTRAMARINE
Bowl, Handled, 9 In. ... 22.00 To 33.00
Bowl, 4 1/2 In. 12.00
Creamer, Child's 16.00
Cup & Saucer .... 14.50 To 17.50
Cup & Saucer, Child's 37.50
Plate, Child's 6.50
Plate, 7 In. 24.00
Plate, 9 In. 25.00
Saucer .... 2.50 To 3.50
Saucer, Child's .... 3.50 To 4.00
Sugar 90.00
Sugar & Creamer 325.00
Sugar, Child's 29.00
Tray, Handled, 10 In. .. 20.00 To 26.00
Tumbler, 4 1/2 In. ..... 30.00 To 39.50

Doric with Pansy, see Doric & Pansy

Double Shield, see Mt. Pleasant

Double Swirl, see Swirl

Drape & Tassel, see Princess

Dutch, see Windmill

Dutch Rose, see Rosemary

Early American, see Princess Feather

Early American Hobnail, see Hobnail

Early American Rock Crystal, see Rock Crystal

Elongated Honeycomb, see Colony

English Hobnail, see also Miss America

Westmoreland Glass Company, Grapeville, Pennsylvania, made English Hobnail pattern from the 1920s through the 1970s. It was made in amber, blue, cobalt, crystal, green, pink or turquoise. Red English Hobnail has been made in the 1980s, a darker amber in the 1960s.

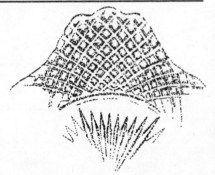

AMBER

Candy Container, Cone-Shaped ..	40.00
Lamp, 9 1/4 In.	75.00 To 98.00
Salt & Pepper	40.00

BLUE

Bottle, Cologne, Stopper	33.00
Bowl, Powder, 5 In.	35.00

CRYSTAL

Bowl, Oval, 12 In.	21.00
Bowl, 4 1/2 In.	2.00
Bowl, 6 In.	8.00 To 15.00
Candleholder, Double Stemmed, Pair	32.00
Candy Container, Covered	15.00
Celery	10.00
Cup	4.00
Goblet, Round Base, 6 1/4 In.	1.50
Goblet, Square Base, 6 1/4 In.	9.00
Goblet, 5 In.	12.50

Goblet, 5 1/2 In. 9.50
Jar, Jam, Chrome Cover & Underplate 6.00
Lamp, 6 1/2 In. 30.00
Plate, Sherbet, 6 1/2 In. 3.00
Plate, 8 In. 4.00
Salt & Pepper 65.00
Sherbet . . . . 6.00 To 15.00
Sugar & Creamer . . . . . . 8.00 To 15.00
Tumbler, Footed, 6 1/4 In.   5.00 To 9.00

GREEN
Ashtray, Round, 4 1/2 In. 15.00
Bottle, Cologne, Stopper 25.00
Bowl, 4 1/2 In. 7.50
Box, Cigarette, Covered . 25.00 To 35.00
Candleholder, 3 1/2 In. 15.00
Candy Container, Cone-Shaped,
   Covered . . . . 14.50 To 45.00
Candy, Covered, Footed 36.00
Jar, Jam, Covered 27.50
Lamp, 6 1/4 In. 65.00

Lamp, 9 1/4 In. . . . . 85.00 To 90.00
Plate, 8 In. . . . . 5.50 To 11.00
Plate, 10 In. 12.00
Salt & Pepper 95.00
Salt Dip, Footed, 2 In. . . . 9.50 To 12.50
Sugar & Creamer, Footed 25.00
Tumbler, 4 In. 15.00

PINK
Ashtray, Round, 4 1/2 In. 29.50
Bottle, Cologne, Stopper   25.00 To 30.00
Candleholder, 8 1/2 In., Pair 55.00
Candy Container, Cone-Shaped . . 40.00
Goblet, 6 1/4 In. . . . . . . 20.00 To 22.00
Jar, Jam 10.00
Lamp, Electric, 6 1/4 In.   50.00 To 65.00
Plate, Round, 8 In. . . . . 8.00 To 9.00

TURQUOISE
Bottle, Cologne, Stopper 39.75
Lamp, 9 1/4 In. 99.50

Fairfax

Fairfax was made by Fostoria Glass Company, Fostoria, Ohio, from 1927 to 1944. It is a very plain pattern. The same shapes were used to make other patterns with etched design. The glass was made in amber, black, blue, green, orchid, pink, ruby or topaz.

BLUE
Butter, Covered 125.00
Goblet, 8 1/4 In. 22.50

TOPAZ
Bowl, 6 In. 7.50
Cup & Saucer 8.00
Plate, 6 In. 3.00
Plate, 7 In. 4.50
Plate, 9 In. 7.00
Relish, 8 1/2 In. 12.00
Sugar 7.00

Fan & Feather, see Adam

Fine Rib, see Homespun

Fire-King, see also Philbe

Fire-King or Fire-King Oven Glass is the name of a kitchenware made by Anchor Hocking Company, Lancaster, Ohio, in 1942 through the 1950s. A matching dinnerware set is called Philbe, It was made in crystal and pale blue.

BLUE
Baker, Individual 1.50
Bowl, Measuring 12.00
Bowl, Mixing, Rolled Edge, 7 In. . . . 6.00
Bowl, Mixing, 8 1/2 In. . . . 7.50 To 8.00
Bowl, Mixing, 10 1/8 In. . . 9.00 To 12.00

Casserole, Covered, 5 In. . 4.50 To 5.00
Casserole, Covered, 8 In. 9.00
Casserole, Covered, 9 In. 8.00
Casserole, Knob Lid, 5 1/2 In. . . . 12.00
Casserole, Knob Lid, 7 In. 12.00
Casserole, Knob Lid, 8 3/4 In. . . . 15.00
Casserole, Pie Plate Cover, 8 1/4 In. 20.00
Custard, 4 In. . . . . 1.50 To 2.00
Custard, 8 In. . . . . 1.50 To 2.00
Hot Plate, Handled 12.50
Jar, Refrigerator, Covered, 5 In.
    . . . . 2.00 To 5.00
Loaf Pan, Covered, 5 X 9 In. 4.00 To 12.00

Measuring Cup, 1 Lip . . . . . 6.00 To 9.00
Mixing, 3 Piece 30.00
Nurser, 4 Oz. 10.00
Nurser, 8 Oz. 14.00
Percolator Top . . . . 2.00 To 3.00
Pie Plate, Juice Saver, 10 3/8 In. . 20.00
Pie Plate, 8 3/8 In. . . . . . . 2.00 To 4.50
Pie Plate, 9 In. . . . . 5.00 To 5.25

CRYSTAL
Casserole, Covered, 1 1/2 Qt. . . . 17.00
Hot Plate 4.00

Fire-King Dinnerware, see Philbe

Flat Diamond, see Diamond Quilted

Floragold

The iridescent marigold color of Carnival glass was copied in this 1950s pattern made by Jeannette Glass Company, Jeannette, Pennsylvania. The pattern is called Floragold or Louisa, the name of the original Carnival glass pattern that was copied. Pieces were made in the iridescent and in ice blue, crystal, shell pink and reddish yellow.

CRYSTAL
Ashtray 2.50
Bowl, Ruffled, 5 1/2 In. 3.50
Bowl, Ruffled, 8 1/2 In. 7.00
Bowl, Ruffled, 9 1/2 In. 5.00
Bowl, Ruffled, 12 In. 6.50
Butter, Covered, Oblong 14.00
Butter, Round 12.00
Candy Container, Oval, 5 1/4 In. . . 4.00
Creamer . . . . 3.25 To 5.00
Tray, 13 1/2 In. 11.00

IRIDESCENT
Ashtray . . . . 2.50 To 5.50
Bowl, Ruffled, 5 1/2 In. 3.00
Bowl, Ruffled, 8 1/2 In. . . 5.00 To 7.00
Bowl, Ruffled, 9 1/2 In. 4.50
Bowl, Ruffled, 10 1/2 In. 6.00
Bowl, Square, 4 1/2 In. . . . 3.00 To 4.50
Bowl, Square, 8 1/2 In. . . 6.50 To 12.00
Bowl, 9 1/2 In. 22.50
Butter, Covered, Oval . . . 8.00 To 12.50
Butter, Covered, Round . 30.00 To 33.00
Candleholder, Double, Pair 30.00

Candy Container, Footed . . 3.50 To 4.50
Cheese & Cracker 45.00
Creamer . . . . 3.50 To 5.00
Cup . . . . 3.00 To 4.00
Cup & Saucer . . . . 7.00 To 9.00
Pitcher . . . . 18.00 To 20.00
Plate, 13 1/2 In. . . . . . . 11.50 To 13.50
Platter, 11 3/4 In. 12.50
Saucer 5.00
Sherbet . . . . 6.00 To 7.50
Sugar . . . . 3.50 To 6.00
Sugar & Creamer, Covered 13.50
Sugar, Covered 10.00
Tumbler, Footed, 5 In. . . . 8.50 To 11.00

PINK
Ashtray 3.75
Bowl, Ruffled, 5 1/2 In. 2.75
Bowl, Ruffled, 8 1/2 In. 3.00
Bowl, Ruffled, 12 In. 5.00
Bowl, 9 1/2 In. 20.00
Cup 3.00
Tumbler, 5 In. 9.50

Floral

Poinsettia blossoms are the decorations on Floral pattern made by Jeannette Glass Company from 1931 to 1935. The pattern was made in amber, crystal, delphite, green, jadite, pink, red or yellow.

CRYSTAL

Ashtray	12.00
Plate, 9 In.	5.00
Sherbet	7.50 To 16.50
Tumbler, 4 In.	19.50

GREEN

Bowl, Covered, 8 In.	17.00 To 24.00
Bowl, Oval, 9 In.	8.00 To 11.50
Bowl, 4 In.	10.00 To 15.00
Bowl, 7 1/2 In.	8.00 To 14.00
Butter	69.50 To 82.50
Candleholder, Pair	50.00 To 90.00
Candy Container, Covered	24.00 To 32.50
Coaster	5.00 To 8.50
Creamer	6.00 To 15.00
Cup	6.50 To 10.00
Cup & Saucer	11.00 To 15.00
Pitcher, Cone-Shaped, 8 In.	17.50 To 30.00
Pitcher, 10 1/4 In.	205.00 To 225.00
Plate, 6 In.	2.00 To 4.00
Plate, 8 In.	6.00 To 9.00
Plate, 9 In.	10.00 To 14.50
Platter, 10 3/4 In.	8.00 To 12.00
Relish	7.00 To 12.00
Salt & Pepper	28.00 To 37.50
Saucer	5.50
Sherbet	7.00 To 12.00
Sugar	4.00 To 9.00
Sugar & Creamer, Covered	24.50 To 28.00
Sugar & Creamer, Open	15.00 To 17.50
Sugar, Covered	9.50 To 20.00
Tray, 6 In.	8.00 To 14.50
Tumbler, Footed, 4 In.	10.00 To 15.00
Tumbler, Footed, 4 3/4 In.	10.00 To 14.00
Tumbler, Footed, 5 1/4 In.	24.75 To 32.50

PINK

Bowl, Oval, 9 In.	8.00 To 10.00
Bowl, Vegetable, Covered, 8 In.	12.00 To 25.00
Bowl, 4 In.	7.00 To 12.00
Bowl, 7 1/2 In.	8.00 To 14.00
Butter, Covered	55.00 To 72.00
Candleholder, Pair	40.00 To 50.00
Candy Container, Covered	14.00 To 26.00

Coaster	5.00 To 8.00
Creamer	5.50 To 12.00
Cup	5.00 To 7.00
Cup & Saucer	10.00 To 12.00
Pitcher, Cone-Shaped, 8 In.	16.00 To 24.00
Pitcher, 10 1/4 In.	165.00 To 175.00
Plate, 6 In.	2.00 To 3.50
Plate, 8 In.	5.00 To 6.50
Plate, 9 In.	8.00 To 10.50
Platter, 10 3/4 In.	7.00 To 15.00
Relish	5.00 To 10.00
Salt & Pepper, 4 In.	25.00
Salt & Pepper, 6 In.	25.00 To 30.00
Saucer	3.00 To 5.50
Sherbet	6.75 To 11.00
Sugar	5.25 To 8.00
Sugar & Creamer, Covered	18.00 To 22.50
Sugar, Covered	7.50 To 18.00
Tray, 6 In.	9.00 To 15.00
Tumbler, Footed, 4 In.	9.50 To 13.00
Tumbler, Footed, 5 1/4 In.	21.00
Tumbler, 4 3/4 In.	9.00 To 12.00
Water Set, 7 Piece	85.00

Floral & Diamond Band

Floral & Diamond Band was made by the U.S. Glass Company in the 1920s. It features a large center flower and pressed diamond bands of edging. The pattern was made in black, green or pink. Some pieces are iridescent marigold color and are considered Carnival glass called Mayflower by the collectors.

GREEN

Bowl, 8 In.	10.00
Butter	75.00
Compote	12.00 To 13.00

Creamer, 4 3/4 In.	10.00 To 12.00
Pitcher	85.00
Sherbet	1.00 To 4.00
Sugar, Covered	25.00

PINK

Bowl, 4 1/2 In.	6.00
Bowl, 8 In.	14.00
Butter, Covered	65.00 To 80.00
Pitcher	27.50 To 85.00
Sugar & Creamer, Covered	34.50
Tumbler, 4 In.	8.25 To 10.50
Tumbler, 5 In.	13.00 To 18.00

Floral Rim, see Vitrock

Florentine No. 1

Florentine No. 1, also called Poppy No. 1, is neither Florentine in appearance nor decorated with recognizable poppies. The plates are hexagonal, differentiating them from Florentine No. 2. The pattern was made by the Hazel Atlas Glass Company from 1932 to 1935 in cobalt blue, crystal, green, pink or yellow.

CRYSTAL

Creamer	4.00
Cup	4.00 To 4.50
Cup & Saucer	3.50 To 6.50
Plate, 6 In.	2.00
Plate, 8 In.	4.00
Plate, 10 In.	1.75 To 7.50
Platter	8.50
Platter, 11 1/2 In.	8.50
Salt & Pepper	16.00 To 24.00
Sherbet	2.50 To 6.00
Sugar	3.50 To 6.00
Sugar & Creamer	10.00 To 12.50
Tumbler, Footed, 3 3/4 In.	7.00

GREEN

Bowl, 5 In.	8.00 To 9.50
Bowl, 8 1/2 In.	16.00
Creamer	5.00 To 15.50
Cup & Saucer	8.00 To 14.00
Pitcher, Footed, 6 1/2 In.	28.00 To 38.00
Plate, 8 1/2 In.	2.50 To 6.25
Plate, 10 In.	7.00 To 10.00
Plate, Grill, 10 In.	7.00 To 10.00
Platter, 11 1/2 In.	5.00 To 19.75

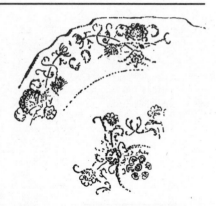

Saucer	2.00
Sherbet	5.50 To 8.50
Sugar	5.00 To 7.00
Sugar & Creamer	19.00 To 25.00
Sugar, Covered	12.00 To 25.00
Sugar, Ruffled	24.75
Tumbler, Footed, 3 3/4 In.	7.00 To 12.00
Tumbler, Footed, 4 3/4 In.	12.50
Tumbler, Footed, 5 1/4 In.	18.00

PINK

Bowl, Vegetable, Covered	38.00 To 39.75
Bowl, 5 In.	7.50 To 8.00
Bowl, 8 1/2 In.	18.75 To 25.00
Butter, Covered	150.00 To 165.00
Creamer	9.00 To 12.00
Creamer, Ruffled	18.00

Cup .... 5.00 To 6.00
Cup & Saucer .... 7.50 To 12.75
Pitcher, Footed, 6 1/2 In. 32.00 To 55.00
Plate, Sherbet, 6 In. ...... 3.50 To 4.75
Plate, 8 1/2 In. .... 5.00 To 8.50
Platter, 11 1/2 In. 9.00
Saltshaker .... 19.00 To 19.75
Saucer 3.00
Sherbet .... 3.50 To 8.50
Sugar .... 4.75 To 12.00
Sugar & Creamer, Ruffled 32.00 To 37.50
Sugar, Covered .... 14.00 To 19.50
Sugar, Ruffled .... 15.00 To 17.50

YELLOW
Ashtray, 5 1/2 In. 35.00
Bowl, 8 1/2 In. .... 19.50 To 33.00
Creamer .... 7.25 To 9.50
Cup 7.00
Pitcher, Footed, 6 1/2 In. 35.00 To 43.00
Pitcher, 7 1/2 In. 35.00
Plate, Grill, 10 In. .... 7.50 To 9.50
Plate, 10 In. 11.50
Salt & Pepper 35.00
Sherbet .... 6.50 To 7.50
Sugar 8.00
Tumbler, 3 3/4 In. ..... 12.00 To 15.00

Florentine No. 2

Florentine No. 2, sometimes called Poppy No. 2 or Oriental Poppy, was also made by Hazel Atlas Company from 1932 to 1935. It has round plates instead of the hexagonal pieces of Florentine No. 1. It was made in amber, cobalt, crystal, green, ice blue or pink.

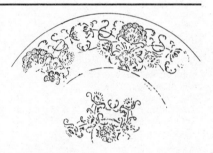

AMBER
Candy Container 35.00
Creamer 5.50
Gravy Boat 30.00
Plate, Sherbet, 6 In. 3.00
Saucer 2.50
Sherbet 15.00
Tumbler, Footed, 5 In. 24.00

CRYSTAL
Candleholder 12.00
Compote 8.00
Creamer .... 4.00 To 5.50
Cup .... 3.00 To 5.00
Cup & Saucer .... 4.75 To 6.00
Pitcher, Flat, 7 1/2 In. 37.00
Pitcher, Footed, Cone-Shaped, 7 1/2 In.
.... 12.00
Plate, Grill, 10 1/4 In. .... 5.00 To 6.00
Plate, Sherbet, 6 In. 2.00
Plate, 6 1/4 In. 2.00
Plate, 8 1/2 In. .... 2.50 To 4.50
Platter, 11 In. 10.00
Salt & Pepper 25.00
Saucer .... 1.00 To 1.50
Sherbet 6.00
Soup, Cream .... 1.00 To 7.50
Sugar 4.00
Sugar & Creamer .... 8.00 To 12.00

Tumbler, Footed, 4 In. 7.50
Tumbler, Water, 4 In. .... 5.00 To 8.00
Tumbler, 5 In. 12.50

GREEN
Ashtray, 5 1/2 In. ..... 14.50 To 25.00
Bowl, Vegetable, Covered 25.00
Bowl, 4 1/2 In. .... 6.00 To 10.00
Bowl, 8 In. .... 12.00 To 15.00
Butter, Covered .... 50.00 To 70.00
Candleholder, Pair ... 45.00 To 59.75
Candy Container, Covered 65.00
Celery, 10 In. 11.00
Coaster, 3 1/4 In. ...... 7.50 To 12.00
Compote, Ruffled 40.00
Creamer .... 6.00 To 7.50
Cup .... 2.00 To 6.50
Cup & Saucer .... 6.00 To 9.50
Pitcher, Cone-Shaped, 6 1/4 In. .. 25.00
Pitcher, Cone-Shaped, 7 1/2 In. .. 35.00
Pitcher, Flat, 7 1/2 In. 45.00
Pitcher, 8 In. 58.00
Plate, Grill, 10 1/4 In. .... 6.00 To 8.00
Plate, Sherbet, 6 In. ...... 2.00 To 5.00
Plate, 8 1/2 In. .... 3.00 To 5.50

Plate, 10 In. . . . . 7.75 To 10.00
Platter, 11 In. . . . . 9.00 To 10.00
Relish 11.50
Salt & Pepper . . . . 28.00 To 35.00
Saucer . . . . 1.50 To 3.25
Sherbet . . . . 4.00 To 6.00
Soup, Cream . . . . 5.75 To 9.50
Sugar . . . . 5.00 To 7.50
Sugar & Creamer . . . . 5.00 To 10.00
Sugar & Creamer, Covered 28.75
Tumbler, Footed, 3 1/4 In. 7.00 To 11.00
Tumbler, Footed, 4 In. . . . . 7.00 To 9.00
Tumbler, Footed, 5 In. . . 18.00 To 20.00
Tumbler, 3 1/2 In. . . . . . . 8.00 To 9.00
Tumbler, 4 In. . . . . 7.00 To 13.75
Tumbler, 5 In. 14.00

ICE BLUE
Compote, Ruffled 40.00

PINK
Bowl, 4 1/2 In. . . . . 5.00 To 7.75
Candy Container, Covered 70.00 To 85.00
Compote, Ruffled . . . . . . 12.00 To 15.00
Plate, 10 In. 8.00
Relish 12.50
Soup, Cream . . . . 6.00 To 12.00
Tumbler, Footed, 4 1/2 In. 10.00
Tumbler, 5 In. 25.00

YELLOW
Ashtray, 3 3/4 In. . . . . . 17.00 To 18.75
Ashtray, 5 1/2 In. 25.00
Bowl, Vegetable, Oval, Covered,
  9 In. . . . . 25.00 To 40.00
Bowl, 4 1/2 In. . . . . . . 11.00 To 14.00
Bowl, 6 In. . . . . 24.00 To 35.00
Bowl, 8 In. . . . . 16.00 To 27.50
Butter, Covered . . . . . . 80.00 To 125.00
Candleholder, Pair . . . . . 35.00 To 50.00
Candy Container, Covered 125.00
Creamer . . . . 5.50 To 12.50
Cup . . . . 6.00 To 7.00

Florentine No.2

Cup & Saucer . . . . 8.00 To 10.00
Gravy Boat . . . . 30.00 To 35.00
Gravy Boat, Underplate . 50.00 To 75.00
Pitcher, Cone-Shaped, 7 1/2 In.
  . . . . 17.00 To 24.00
Pitcher, 7 1/2 In. 127.50
Plate, Grill, 10 1/4 In. . . . 6.00 To 12.00
Plate, Sherbet, 6 In. . . . . . . 2.00 To 3.00
Plate, 8 1/2 In. . . . . 3.75 To 7.00
Plate, 10 In. . . . . 8.50 To 12.00
Platter, Gravy, 11 1/2 In. 29.50
Platter, Oval, 11 In. . . . . . 9.00 To 12.00
Relish . . . . 13.00 To 22.50
Salt & Pepper . . . . 32.00 To 35.00
Saucer . . . . 1.50 To 3.00
Sherbet, Footed . . . . 6.50 To 8.50
Soup, Cream . . . . 10.00 To 15.00
Sugar . . . . 6.00 To 7.00
Sugar & Creamer . . . . . . 13.00 To 15.00
Sugar & Creamer, Covered 24.00 To 30.00
Sugar, Covered . . . . 12.50 To 22.00
Tray, Condiment . . . . 49.50 To 75.00
Tumbler, Footed, 3 1/4 In. 5.00 To 8.50
Tumbler, Footed, 4 In. . . . 6.00 To 12.00
Tumbler, Footed, 5 In. . . 18.00 To 25.00
Tumbler, Juice, 3 1/2 In. . 9.00 To 10.00
Tumbler, Water, 4 In. . . . 9.50 To 16.00

Flower, see Princess Feather

Flower & Leaf Band, see Indiana Custard

Flower Basket, see No. 615

Flower Garden with Butterflies

There really is a butterfly hiding in the flowers on this U.S. Glass Company pattern called Flower Garden with Butterflies, Butterflies and Roses, Flower Garden or Wildrose with Apple Blossom. It was made in the late 1920s in a variety of colors including amber, black, blue, canary, crystal, green, pink or yellow.

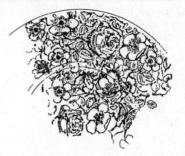

GREEN
Cup & Saucer 25.00
Plate, 8 In. 20.00

PINK
Candleholder, 4 In., Pair 95.00
Cup 70.00
Cup & Saucer 100.00
Tray, Rectangular 36.00

Flower Rim, see Vitrock

Forest Green

There is no need to picture Forest Green in a black-and-white drawing because it is the color that identifies the pattern. Anchor Hocking Glass Company, Lancaster, Ohio, made this very plain pattern from 1950 to 1957. Other patterns were also made in this same deep green color, but these are known by the pattern name.

GREEN
Ashtray .... 2.00 To 3.00
Bowl, 4 3/4 In. 3.00
Bowl, 7 1/2 In. 5.00
Butter Tub, Round 6.50
Creamer, Square 3.50
Cup & Saucer 3.25
Dish, Boat-Shaped, 8 X 6 X 3 In. .. 5.00
Goblet, Ball Stem, 5 1/4 In. 2.00
Goblet, Crystal Base, 5 3/8 In. 2.50
Pitcher, Ice Lip, 6 3/4 In. 10.00
Plate, 6 1/2 In. 1.50
Plate, 8 In. 2.50
Platter, Rectangular ...... 8.00 To 8.50
Punch Bowl, 12 Cups 24.00
Salt & Pepper 6.00
Saucer .... 1.00 To 2.50
Serve-A-Snack, Oblong 2.00
Soup, Dish, 6 In. 3.50
Sugar & Creamer .... 5.25 To 9.00
Tray, Beaded, Handled, Scalloped, 5 X 7 In.
.... 2.50
Tumbler, Curved, 3 3/8 In. 1.25
Tumbler, Curved, 4 1/4 In. 1.50
Tumbler, Curved, 5 In. 1.75
Tumbler, Straight, Heavy Bottom, 5 1/2 In.
.... 2.50
Tumbler, Straight, 4 1/4 In. 1.50
Tumbler, Straight, 4 3/4 In. 1.50
Vase, Bud, Crimped, 6 3/8 In. 2.50
Vase, Coolidge .... 2.00 To 2.50
Vase, Corset-Shaped, 9 In. 3.25
Vase, Crimped, 3 1/4 In. 1.25
Vase, Flared, 10 In. 4.50
Vase, Flared, 5 In. 2.25
Vase, Footed, Swirled, 9 1/2 In. ... 3.50
Vase, Harding .... 2.00 To 2.50
Vase, Ivy, 3 3/4 In. 1.50
Vase, Rectangular, 4 1/4 X 5 1/2 X 3 1/2 In.
.... 2.00
Vase, Rectangular, 6 1/4 X 5 1/2 X 3 1/2 In.
.... 2.50
Vase, Straight, 9 1/2 In. 3.00

Fortune

Anchor Hocking made Fortune pattern in 1937 and 1938. The simple design was made in crystal or pink.

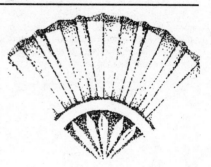

PINK
Bowl, Handled, 4 1/2 In. .. .75 To 3.50
Bowl, 4 In. .... 2.00 To 2.50
Bowl, 4 1/2 In. .... 2.00 To 3.00
Candy Container, Covered 10.00 To 14.75
Cup .... 1.00 To 3.00
Saucer 2.00
Tumbler, 3 1/2 In. .... 1.00 To 4.00
Tumbler, 4 In. .... 4.00 To 4.75

Fostoria, see American

Frosted Block, see Beaded Block

Fruits

Pears, grapes, apples and other fruits are displayed in small bunches on the pieces of Fruits pattern. Hazel Atlas and several other companies made this pattern about 1931 to 1933. Pieces are known in crystal, green, pink and iridized finish.

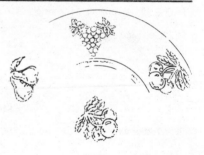

CRYSTAL
Tumbler, 4 In. 8.50

GREEN
Bowl, 5 In. 8.00
Bowl, 8 In. .... 30.00 To 35.00
Cup .... 3.00 To 5.00
Cup & Saucer .... 1.75 To 6.50
Pitcher 86.00
Plate, 8 In. .... 3.00 To 6.50
Saucer .... 1.00 To 3.50
Sherbet .... 5.00 To 9.00
Tumbler, 4 In. 12.00

PINK
Cup .... 4.00 To 4.50
Sherbet .... 3.50 To 4.00

Georgian

Georgian, also known as Lovebirds, was made by the Federal Glass Company, Columbus, Ohio, from 1931 to 1936. The pattern shows alternating sections with birds in one, a basket of flowers in the next. It was made in crystal or green. Notice that it is mold-etched and in no way resembles the Fenton glass pattern called Georgian.

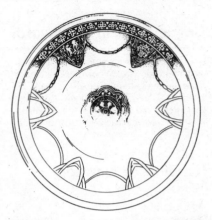

CRYSTAL

Bowl, 4 1/2 In.	4.50
Bowl, 6 1/2 In.	52.00
Cup & Saucer	8.00
Plate, 9 1/4 In.	12.00
Platter, 11 1/2 In.	49.00
Sugar & Creamer, 3 In.	10.00
Sugar, 4 In.	4.00
Tumbler, 5 1/4 In.	50.00

GREEN

Bowl, Deep, 6 1/2 In. . .	40.00 To 42.00
Bowl, Vegetable, Oval, 9 In.	32.50 To 49.50
Bowl, 4 1/2 In.	4.00 To 6.00
Bowl, 5 3/4 In.	9.50 To 15.00
Bowl, 7 1/2 In.	35.00
Butter, Covered	30.00 To 60.00
Creamer, 3 In.	5.75 To 8.00
Creamer, 4 In.	8.00 To 8.50
Cup	3.25 To 4.50
Cup & Saucer	3.25 To 12.75
Hot Plate	27.00
Plate, Sherbet, 6 In.	2.00 To 3.50
Plate, 8 In.	4.00 To 6.00
Plate, 9 1/4 In.	11.00 To 18.50
Platter, 11 1/2 In.	32.00 To 40.00
Saucer	1.75 To 3.00
Sherbet	7.00 To 10.00
Sugar & Creamer, Covered, 3 In.	24.50 To 47.50
Sugar & Creamer, 4 In. .	16.00 To 18.00
Sugar, Covered, 3 In. ...	17.00 To 18.00
Sugar, 4 In.	5.00 To 7.00

Georgian Fenton

Fenton Glass Company made this Georgian pattern tableware from about 1930. It came in many colors, some pale but many in the popular dark shades. Look for amber, black, crystal, green, pink, cobalt blue, ruby or topaz.

AMBER

Goblet, 5 1/2 In.	3.00
Plate, 5 3/4 In.	2.00
Tumbler, 4 In.	3.00

COBALT BLUE

Tumbler, 3 1/4 In.	3.00

PINK

Bowl, 4 1/2 In.	5.00
Cup & Saucer	8.00
Plate, Sherbet, 6 In.	2.50
Plate, 8 1/2 In.	3.00

RUBY

Sherbet, Flared, 2 3/8 In.	4.00
Sherbet, Stemmed, 4 1/8 In.	5.00

Gladiola, see Royal Lace

Grape, see also Woolworth

Grape design is sometimes confused with the pattern known as Woolworth. Both have grapes in the pattern. Grape was made by Standard Glass Manufacturing Company Lancaster, Ohio, in the 1930s. Full dinnerware sets were made in green, rose or topaz.

Green
Plate, 8 In. 4.00

PINK
Plate, 8 In. 3.00

Hairpin, see Newport

Hammered Band

The octagonal plate and serving pieces of this set of dishes are edged with a border that gave the name Hammered Band to the design. It was made by the L. E. Smith Glass Company, Mt. Pleasant, Pennsylvania, in the early 1930s. The pattern was made in black, green or pink. The pattern is sometimes called Melba or Pebbled Band.

BLACK
Plate, 9 In. 3.00
Sugar 3.50
Tumbler, Footed, 4 1/4 In. 4.50

PINK
Plate, 6 In. 1.50
Saucer 1.00

Hanging Basket, see No. 615

Harp

The pattern name Harp describes the small lyre-shaped instruments that are included on the borders of these pieces of glass. This Jeannette Glass Company pattern was made from 1954 to 1957. Pieces are found in crystal, crystal with gold trim, light blue and pink.

CRYSTAL
Ashtray, Gold Trim .... 2.00 To 4.00

Cake Plate, 9 In. .... 8.00 To 14.00
Cup & Saucer .... 4.50 To 10.50
Plate, Gold Trim, 7 In. .... 3.00 To 6.25
Plate, 6 In. 2.00
Tray, Handled, 12 3/4 X 10 In. .. 12.00
Vase .... 3.00 To 8.00

Heritage

Federal Glass Company, Columbus, Ohio, made Heritage in the 1930s through the 1960s. Evidently the serving pieces were made in blue, light green or pink, but the plates and dinnerware pieces were made only in crystal.

CRYSTAL
Bowl, 5 In. .... 2.50 To 4.50
Bowl, 8 1/2 In. .... 8.00 To 16.75
Bowl, 10 1/2 In. .... 8.00 To 10.00
Cup .... 1.50 To 3.75
Cup & Saucer .... 4.00 To 6.00
Plate, 8 In. .... 2.50 To 3.50
Plate, 9 1/4 In. .... 5.50 To 7.00
Plate, 12 In. 6.50
Saucer .... .50 To 1.50
Sugar .... 5.50 To 9.00

Hex Optic, see Hexagon Optic

Hexagon Optic

Hexagon Optic, also called Honeycomb or Hex Optic, really does have an accurate, descriptive name. Pink or green sets of kitchenware were made in this pattern by Jeannette Glass Company, Jeannette, Pennsylvania, from 1928 to 1932. In the years near 1960 some iridized sets and some blue-green pieces were made.

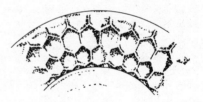

GREEN
Pitcher, 5 In. 10.00
Plate, Sherbet, 6 In. 1.25
Plate, 8 In. 3.75
Salt & Pepper .... 12.00 To 22.00
Sugar 4.00
Tumbler, 2 1/2 In. 4.00
Tumbler, 3 3/4 In. .... 3.50 To 4.00
Tumbler, 5 1/4 In. 4.00

PINK
Bowl, 4 1/4 In. .... .75

Bowl, 7 1/2 In. 8.75
Butter, Covered 29.00
Cup, Closed Handle 3.50
Ice Bucket 7.50
Mixing Bowl, 7 1/4 In. 7.00
Plate, 8 In. .... 2.50 To 4.50
Salt & Pepper .... 12.00 To 22.00
Tumbler, Footed, 7 In. .... 4.50 To 9.50
Tumbler, 5 3/4 In. .... 3.50 To 5.00

Hexagon Triple Band, see Colony

Hinge, see Patrician

Hobnail, see also Moonstone

Hobnail is the name of this pattern, although many similar patterns have been made with the hobbed decorations. Hocking Glass Company, Lancaster, Ohio, made this pattern from 1934 to 1936. It was made in crystal or pink. Some pieces were made with red rims or black feet.

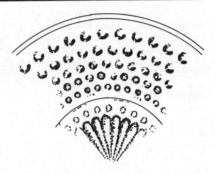

CRYSTAL
Candleholder, 4 In., Pair	18.00
Cup & Saucer	4.50
Goblet, Water, 7 1/2 In. ..	4.00 To 6.00
Pitcher, 7 In.	12.00
Plate, 8 1/2 In.	2.50
Salt & Pepper	75.00
Sherbet	2.00 To 2.50
Tumbler, Footed, 5 In.	4.50
Tumbler, 6 In.	4.00
Whiskey, Footed	3.00 To 4.00

PINK
Cup	1.25 To 3.00

Cup & Saucer	3.25 To 8.50
Pitcher, 7 In.	25.00
Plate, Sherbet, 6 In.	1.25 To 1.50
Plate, 8 1/2 In.	2.00 To 3.75
Saucer	1.50
Sherbet	2.50 To 4.50
Tumbler, 3 1/2 In.	3.50

Holiday

Holiday is one of the later Depression glass patterns. It was made from 1947 through 1949 by Jeannette Glass Company. The pattern is found in dinnerware sets of crystal, iridescent or pink. A few pieces of opaque shell pink were made. The pattern is sometimes also called Buttons & Bows or Russian.

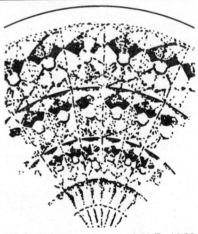

CRYSTAL
Bowl, 5 1/8 In.	6.00
Candleholder, Pair	55.00
Creamer	3.50 To 4.50
Pitcher, 6 3/4 In.	24.50
Tumbler, Footed, 4 In.	4.00
Tumbler, 4 In.	11.00

IRIDESCENT
Pitcher, Milk, 4 3/4 In. .	21.00 To 25.00
Plate, 10 1/2 In.	5.00
Tumbler, Footed, 4 In. ...	9.50 To 12.50

PINK
Bowl, Console, 10 3/4 In.	52.50 To 65.00
Bowl, Vegetable, Oval, 9 1/2 In.	
....	9.50 To 16.00
Bowl, 5 1/8 In.	4.50 To 6.00

Bowl, 8 1/2 In.	11.00 To 16.00
Butter, Covered	28.00 To 35.00
Butter, Ruffled	7.50
Cake Plate	40.00 To 59.50
Candleholder, Pair	44.00 To 70.00
Creamer	2.00 To 5.50
Cup	3.75 To 5.00

Cup & Saucer 6.50
Pitcher, Milk, 4 3/4 In.

.... 30.00 To 60.00
Pitcher, 6 3/4 In. ...... 19.00 To 27.00
Plate, Chop, 13 3/4 In.

.... 54.00 To 65.00
Plate, 10 1/2 In. .... 6.00 To 12.00
Plate, 6 In. .... 2.00 To 8.50
Plate, 9 In. .... 6.50 To 9.50
Platter, Oval, 11 3/8 In. .. 7.00 To 9.50

Saucer .... 1.25 To 3.00
Sherbet .... 3.50 To 7.50
Soup, Dish .... 20.00 To 35.00
Sugar 4.00
Sugar & Creamer, Covered 17.50 To 19.50
Sugar, Covered .... 10.00 To 12.00
Tumbler, Footed, 4 In. .. 10.00 To 28.00
Tumbler, Footed, 6 In. .. 47.50 To 60.00
Tumbler, 4 In. .... 10.00 To 12.50

Homespun

Homespun, often called Fine Rib, is a cause of confusion. Several writers have presented different views about whether this is really one pattern or two. We prefer to call all of these pieces Homespun because that is the way most collectors use the name. Jeannette Glass Company made crystal, light blue or pink pieces in this pattern in 1939 and 1940. Hazel Atlas made other pieces in crystal or cobalt blue.

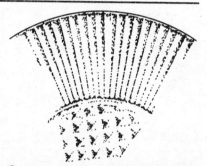

CRYSTAL
Butter, Covered .... 24.75 To 55.00
Jar, Mustard, Covered 10.00
Plate, Child's .... 2.50 To 6.00
Saucer, Child's 4.50
Tumbler, Footed, 6 1/2 In. 10.00
Tumbler, 4 In. 3.00
Tumbler, 5 1/4 In. 3.50

PINK
Bowl, Handled, 4 1/2 In.

.... 3.50 To 4.50
Bowl, 5 In. 10.00
Bowl, 8 1/4 In. 10.00
Butter, Covered .... 45.00 To 47.00
Coaster 5.00
Creamer 6.00

Cup .... 3.25 To 5.00
Cup & Saucer 6.50
Plate, Child's 7.50
Plate, 6 In. .... 1.25 To 2.50
Plate, 9 1/4 In. .... 5.00 To 8.50
Platter, Oval, 13 In. ..... 7.00 To 12.00
Saucer 2.00
Saucer, Child's 3.50
Sherbet .... 3.50 To 6.00
Soup, Cream 5.00
Sugar .... 5.00 To 5.50
Sugar & Creamer ...... 10.00 To 12.50
Tumbler, Footed, 4 In. .... 4.50 To 6.00
Tumbler, 4 In. .... 7.00 To 8.50
Tumbler, 5 1/2 In. ..... 11.50 To 12.50

Homestead

In the early 1930s the L. E. Smith Company, Mt. Pleasant, Pennsylvania, made Homestead pattern in amber, black, green or pink.

AMBER
Snack Tray, 3 Part 1.50

PINK
Sugar 2.50

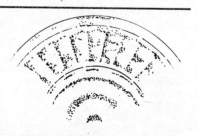

Honeycomb, see Hexagon Optic
Horizontal Fine Rib, see Manhattan
Horizontal Ribbed, see Manhattan
Horizontal Rounded Big Rib, see Manhattan
Horizontal Sharp Big Rib, see Manhattan
Horseshoe, see No. 612

Imperial Optic Rib

Imperial Optic Rib was made by Imperial Glass Company, Bellaire, Ohio, about 1927. Pieces were made in amberina, blue, crystal, green or were iridized.

Bowl, 7 3/4 In.	3.50
Plate, 8 In.	7.50
Sherbet	1.75
Sherbet Liner, 6 1/4 In.	1.00

AMBERINA

Bowl, Handled, 4 3/4 In.	1.50

BLUE

Plate, 8 In.	7.50

Imperial Plain Octagon

Imperial Plain Octagon was called Molly in the original ads from 1927. It was made of crystal, green or pink glass.

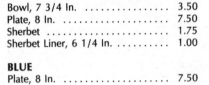

GREEN

Bowl, Deep, Floral Cut, 7 1/2 In.	7.00
Bowl, Handled, 8 3/4 In.	8.00
Plate, Handled, 6 3/4 In.	3.00
Plate, Handled, 10 1/2 In.	6.00 To 7.00
Saucer	1.00

PINK

Bowl, Handled, Floral Cut, 8 3/4 In.	8.50

Indiana Custard

The design makes the old name Flower & Leaf Band clear but the collectors prefer to call this pattern Indiana Custard. It is an opaque glassware of custard color or ivory made by the Indiana Glass Company. The sets were made from the 1930s to the 1950s. Some pieces have bands that are decorated with pastel colors. The same pattern was made of milk glass in 1957. It was called Orange Blossom.

IVORY

Bowl, Vegetable, Oval, 9 1/2 In.	11.00 To 19.50
Bowl, 4 7/8 In.	3.00 To 6.50
Bowl, 5 3/4 In.	9.00 To 16.00
Bowl, 8 3/4 In.	24.25
Butter, Covered	40.00 To 50.00
Creamer	8.00 To 9.75
Cup & Saucer	25.00 To 29.75
Plate, 5 3/4 In.	4.00
Plate, 8 7/8 In.	9.00
Plate, 9 3/4 In.	9.75 To 15.00
Platter, 11 1/2 In.	20.00 To 25.00
Saucer	3.75
Sugar	7.50 To 8.00
Sugar & Creamer, Covered	23.00 To 25.00
Sugar, Covered	13.00 To 20.00

Iris

The design of Iris is unusually bold for Depression glass. Molded representation of stalks of irises fill the center of a ribbed plate. Other pieces in the pattern show fewer irises but the flower is predominate. Edges of pieces may be ruffled or beaded. It was made by Jeannette Glass Company, Jeannette, Pennsylvania, from 1928 to 1932 and then again in the 1950s and 1970s. Early pieces were made in crystal, iridescent or pink, later pieces in blue-green or reddish yellow. The pattern is also called Iris & Herringbone.

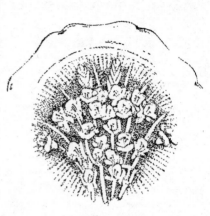

CRYSTAL
Bowl, Ruffled, 4 1/2 In. 3.00
Bowl, Ruffled, 5 In. ...... 3.00 To 4.50
Bowl, Ruffled, 8 In. ...... 6.00 To 9.00
Bowl, Ruffled, 9 1/2 In. .. 7.00 To 8.00
Bowl, Ruffled, 11 In. 9.00
Butter, Covered .... 20.00 To 25.00
Candleholder, Pair ..... 14.00 To 17.50
Candy Container, Covered 40.00 To 70.00
Coaster .... 32.50 To 35.00
Creamer .... 1.75 To 12.00
Cup .... 8.00 To 8.50
Cup & Saucer 12.50
Cup, Demitasse 16.00
Goblet, 4 In. .... 9.00 To 10.00
Goblet, 4 Oz., 5 3/4 In.
.... 12.00 To 12.50
Goblet, 4 1/2 In. .... 7.00 To 10.50
Goblet, 8 Oz., 5 3/4 In.
.... 11.00 To 12.50
Pitcher, 9 1/2 In. ...... 12.00 To 25.00
Plate, 8 In. 15.00
Plate, 9 In. .... 12.00 To 17.00
Plate, 11 3/4 In. .... 9.00 To 11.50
Saucer .... 2.75 To 4.25
Sherbet, 2 1/2 In. ...... 8.00 To 10.00
Sherbet, 4 In. .... 6.50 To 10.00
Sugar 3.00
Sugar & Creamer, Covered 13.00 To 20.00
Sugar, Covered .... 7.50 To 10.00
Tumbler, Flat, 4 In. 55.00
Tumbler, Footed, 6 In. ... 8.00 To 11.50
Tumbler, Footed, 7 In. ... 8.50 To 12.50
Vase, Footed, 9 In. ...... 8.00 To 12.00

IRIDESCENT
Bowl, Ruffled, 4 1/2 In. .. 3.50 To 6.50
Bowl, Ruffled, 5 In. ...... 6.50 To 7.50
Bowl, Ruffled, 8 In. ...... 8.00 To 9.50
Bowl, Ruffled, 9 1/2 In.
.... 6.50 To 10.00
Bowl, Ruffled, 11 In. ..... 5.00 To 8.00
Bowl, Straight Edge, 5 In. 5.25
Butter, Covered .... 28.00 To 32.00
Candleholder, Pair ..... 17.50 To 24.00
Candy Container, Footed, Covered
.... 10.00
Creamer .... 3.50 To 6.00
Cup .... 5.00 To 7.50
Cup & Saucer .... 9.00 To 12.50
Goblet, Wine, 4 In. .... 12.00 To 16.00
Pitcher, 9 1/2 In. ...... 17.50 To 22.50
Plate, Sherbet, 5 1/2 In. .. 3.00 To 6.50
Plate, 9 In. .... 11.00 To 18.50
Plate, 11 3/4 In. ...... 10.00 To 12.00
Saltshaker 6.00
Sherbet, 2 1/2 In. ...... 6.00 To 6.50
Soup, Dish .... 20.00 To 25.00
Sugar & Creamer, Covered 12.00
Sugar, Covered .... 6.75 To 10.00
Tumbler, Footed, 6 In. ... 7.50 To 12.50
Vase, Ruffled, 5 In. 8.25

PINK
Pitcher, 9 1/2 In. 30.00
Sugar 4.50

RED-YELLOW
Butter 37.50
Pitcher 30.00
Sherbet 3.00
Sugar & Creamer 25.00

Bowl, Ruffled, 9 1/2 In.

Iris & Herringbone, see Iris

Ivex, see Chinex Classic; Cremax

Jadite, see also Jane-Ray

Jadite is a color as well as a pattern. Kitchenware was made in Jadite from 1936 to 1938 by Jeannette Glass Company. A matching set of dinnerware in the same green glass was called Jane-Ray. All of the pieces of kitchenware made of Jadite were also made of a blue glass called Delphite, but it would seem incorrect to call any but the green dishes by the name Jadite.

GREEN

Cup, Measuring	4.00
Pitcher, Pint, Measuring	8.00
Vase	4.50

Jane-Ray, see also Jadite

A plain dinnerware set with ribbed edge was made of Jadite from 1945 to 1963 by Anchor Hocking Glass Company, Lancaster, Ohio. It is called Jane-Ray. The matching kitchenware sets of the same green glass are called Jadite.

JADITE

Bowl, 5 In.	.75
Bowl, 6 In.	2.75
Creamer	2.50
Cup	1.00
Cup & Saucer	2.50
Plate, 7 3/4 In.	1.00
Plate, 9 1/4 In.	1.50 To 2.25
Platter	2.50 To 3.50
Saucer	.50 To 1.00
Sugar & Creamer, Covered	4.00
Sugar, Covered	2.50 To 2.75

Jubilee

In the early 1930s the Lancaster Glass Company, Lancaster, Ohio, made this dinnerware decorated with etched flowers. It was made only in a yellow shade they called topaz.

YELLOW

Goblet, 6 In.	18.00
Plate, 7 In.	4.50
Plate, 8 1/4 In.	7.50

June

June is one of very few patterns that can be dated with some accuracy from the color. Fostoria Glass Company, Fostoria, Ohio, made full dinnerware sets but changed the color. From 1928 to 1944 the glass was azure, green or rose. Crystal was made from 1928 to 1952. If your set is topaz, it dates from 1929 to 1938. Gold-tinted glass was made from 1938 to 1944. Pieces made of color with crystal stems or bases were made only from 1931 to 1944.

BLUE

Goblet, 6 In. .... 22.00 To 26.00
Plate, 7 In. 12.50

Plate, 8 In. 15.00
Plate, 10 In. 60.00

CRYSTAL
Pitcher, 8 1/4 In. 20.00

YELLOW
Goblet, 6 In. .... 25.00 To 32.75
Plate, 6 In. 5.00
Plate, 7 In. 8.00
Plate, 9 In. 14.00
Relish 22.00
Sherbet, Low 19.00
Tumbler, 5 In. 22.00

Knife & Fork, see Colonial

Lace Edge, see also Coronation

To add to the confusion in the marketplace, this pattern, which is most often called Lace Edge, has been called Loop, Open Lace or Open Scallop. The pieces themselves are often confused with other similar patterns, and cups or tumblers may be mixed up with Queen Mary or Coronation. Most of the pieces of Lace Edge were made of pink, although crystal is also found. It was made by Hocking Glass Company, Lancaster, Ohio, from 1935 to 1938.

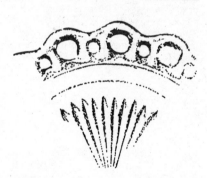

CRYSTAL
Bowl, 6 3/8 In. .... 1.25 To 3.00
Butter 35.00
Candy Container, Covered 33.00
Compote, Covered 22.00
Flower Frog 3.00
Saucer 4.00
Sherbet 32.00
Sugar 10.00
Tumbler, 4 1/2 In. 10.00

PINK
Bowl, Console .... 80.00 To 135.00
Bowl, Flower, Crystal Frog 12.00 To 19.00
Bowl, 6 3/8 In. .... 6.50 To 12.50
Bowl, 7 3/4 In. .... 9.00 To 15.00
Bowl, 9 1/2 In. .... 7.00 To 12.00

Butter, Covered .... 25.00 To 55.00
Candleholder, Pair .... 85.00 To 150.00
Candy Container, Covered, Ribbed 25.00
Compote .... 9.50 To 14.00
Compote, Covered ..... 18.00 To 28.00
Cookie Jar .... 10.00 To 22.50
Cookie Jar, Covered .... 35.00 To 49.75
Creamer .... 10.00 To 12.50
Cup 11.00
Cup & Saucer .... 19.00 To 22.50
Flower Frog 13.50
Plate, Grill, 10 1/2 In. ... 8.50 To 12.50
Plate, Solid Lace, 4 Part, 13 In. .. 19.00
Plate, 7 1/4 In. .... 8.00 To 12.00
Plate, 8 3/4 In. .... 6.50 To 10.00

Plate, 10 1/2 In. ...... 12.00 To 18.00
Platter, 12 3/4 In. ...... 6.50 To 16.50
Relish, Divided, 3 Part, 10 1/2 In.
.... 9.00 To 14.00
Relish, Round, 3 Part, 7 1/2 In.
.... 12.00 To 25.00

Saucer .... 3.00 To 7.50
Sugar .... 8.50 To 14.00
Sugar & Creamer ...... 22.00 To 23.00
Tumbler, Footed, 5 In. .. 25.00 To 37.50
Tumbler, 4 1/2 In. ...... 4.00 To 10.00

Lacy Daisy, see No. 618

Lake Como

Lake Como looks more like a piece of ceramic than a piece of glass at first glance. It is opaque white with decal blue decorations, picturing a lake and part of an ancient ruin. It was made by Hocking Glass Company from 1934 to 1937.

WHITE
Plate, 9 1/4 In. 4.50
Saltshaker 8.25

Laurel

Opaque glass was used by McKee Glass Company, Jeannette, Pennsylvania, to make Laurel dinnerware. The pattern, with a raised band of flowers and leaves as the only decoration, was sometimes called Raspberry Band. A few pieces have decals of a dog in the center, and that group is called Scottie Dog. The dinnerware was made of French ivory, jade green, powder blue or white opal.

BLUE
Platter, 10 3/4 In. 20.00

GREEN
Bowl, Vegetable, 9 3/4 In. 11.25
Bowl, 5 In. .... 3.50 To 4.00
Cup & Saucer .... 5.50 To 6.00
Plate, Sherbet, 6 In. ...... 1.50 To 2.50
Plate, 9 In. .... 4.00 To 7.00
Platter, 10 3/4 In. ...... 9.00 To 12.50
Saucer .... 1.00 To 2.00
Sugar, Child's 14.00
Sugar, Tall 7.50

IVORY
Bowl, Vegetable, 9 3/4 In. 20.00 To 22.00
Bowl, 5 In. 4.00
Bowl, 6 In. .... 5.00 To 7.50
Bowl, 11 In. 17.50
Butter, Covered 35.00
Candleholder, Pair ..... 20.00 To 25.00

Cream & Sugar 15.00
Creamer, Child's .... 14.00 To 16.00
Creamer, Tall .... 7.50 To 12.00
Cup .... 5.50 To 8.00
Cup & Saucer .... 7.00 To 11.00
Dish, Cheese, Covered
.... 33.00 To 45.75
Plate, Child's 12.00
Plate, Sherbet, 6 In. 3.00
Plate, 7 1/2 In. .... 5.00 To 6.50

Plate, 9 In. 4.00
Plate, 9 1/8 In. .... 5.00 To 9.00
Salt & Pepper 30.00
Saucer .... 2.00 To 2.75
Saucer, Child's .... 6.00 To 7.00
Sherbet .... 7.00 To 12.00
Sugar & Creamer, Child's 52.75

Sugar & Creamer, Tall 15.00
Sugar, Child's .... 25.00 To 27.00
Tumbler, 4 1/2 In. 25.00
Tumbler, 5 In. 21.00

WHITE
Saucer 1.75

Leaf

Leaf pattern is not a group of leaf-shaped dishes as has been suggested. The plates are round with an overall design of leaves in the center, a clear ring, then a leaf-decorated rim. It was made by Macbeth-Evans Glass Company in the early 1930s in crystal, green or pink.

GREEN
Plate, 8 In. 5.00

PINK
Plate, 8 In. 5.00

Lily Medallion, see American Sweetheart

Lincoln Drape, see Princess

Lincoln Inn

Lincoln Inn was made by the Fenton Glass Company, Williamstown, West Virginia, in 1928. The ridged dinnerware sets were made of amethyst, black, cobalt, crystal, green, opaque green, pink or red.

COBALT
Goblet, 4 In. 22.50
Goblet, 5 3/4 In. ...... 15.00 To 22.00
Plate, 8 In. 12.00
Sherbet 18.00

CRYSTAL
Goblet, 4 In. 14.00
Sherbet 12.00

GREEN
Sherbet 12.00

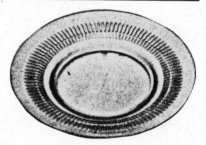

RED
Goblet, 4 In. 12.00
Goblet, 5 3/4 In. .... 9.50 To 15.00
Plate, 8 In. 12.00
Sherbet 15.00
Tumbler, Footed, 3 1/2 In. 12.00 To 15.00

Line No. 300, see Peacock & Wild Rose

Line 191

Line 191 was made by Paden City Glass Company, Paden City, West Virginia. It had many names, including Party Line, Tiered Semi Optic or Tiered Block. It is a durable pattern advertised in 1928 for home, restaurant, hotel and soda fountain. The dishes were made in amber, blue, cheri-glo, crystal, green or mulberry.

GREEN
Sherbet, Footed 3.50
Sugar 3.50

PINK
Sugar 6.00

Line No. 994, see Popeye & Olive

Little Hostess, see Moderntone Little Hostess Party Set

Loop, see Lace Edge

Lorain, see No. 615

Louisa, see Floragold

Lovebirds, see Georgian

Lydia Ray, see New Century

MacHOB

MacHOB is the name devised for the Macbeth-Evans pattern made with a hobnail design. This pattern was made from 1928 of crystal, monax or pink.

CRYSTAL
Tumbler, 5 In. 3.00
Water Set, 6 Tumblers 28.00

Madrid

Madrid has probably had more publicity than any other Depression glass pattern. It was originally made by the Federal Glass Company, Columbus, Ohio, from 1932 to 1939. It was made of amber, blue, crystal, green or pink. In 1976 Federal Glass reworked the molds and made full sets of amber glass called Recollections. These can be identified by a small 76 worked into the pattern. In 1982 crystal pieces of Recollection were made.

AMBER

Ashtray	100.00
Bowl, Console	8.00 To 9.00
Bowl, Deep, 9 1/2 In.	16.00 To 17.50
Bowl, Vegetable, 10 In.	6.50 To 10.00
Bowl, 5 In.	2.50 To 4.25
Bowl, 8 In.	9.00 To 11.50
Bowl, 9 3/8 In.	16.00 To 18.00
Butter, Covered	35.00 To 60.00
Cake Plate, 11 1/2 In.	12.00
Candleholder, Pair	14.00 To 18.75
Coaster, 5 In.	29.00
Cookie Jar, Covered	24.00 To 45.00
Creamer	3.75 To 7.95
Cup & Saucer	4.00 To 7.50
Jar, Jam, 7 In.	10.00 To 12.00
Jello Mold	4.50 To 9.50
Pitcher, Round, 8 1/2 In.	36.00 To 45.00
Pitcher, Square, 8 In.	23.00 To 32.00
Pitcher, 5 1/2 In.	15.00 To 28.00
Plate, Grill, 10 1/2 In.	6.00 To 9.50
Plate, Sherbet, 6 In.	1.50 To 3.00
Plate, 7 1/2 In.	4.50 To 8.50
Plate, 8 7/8 In.	3.50 To 6.00
Plate, 10 1/2 In.	20.00 To 30.00
Platter, 11 1/2 In.	7.00 To 12.00
Relish, 10 1/4 In.	7.50 To 9.50
Salt & Pepper, Flat	35.00 To 40.00
Saucer	1.25 To 2.00
Sherbet	3.75 To 6.00
Soup, Cream	7.00 To 10.50
Soup, Dish	6.50 To 7.50
Sugar	3.75 To 6.00
Sugar & Creamer	7.00 To 12.00
Sugar & Creamer, Covered	26.00 To 34.75
Sugar, Covered	20.00 To 30.00
Tumbler, Footed, 5 1/2 In.	12.00 To 18.75
Tumbler, 3 7/8 In.	9.00 To 16.00
Tumbler, 4 1/4 In.	9.00 To 15.00
Tumbler, 5 1/2 In.	12.00 To 14.50

BLUE

Bowl, Vegetable, 10 In.	19.00 To 35.00
Bowl, 7 In.	16.50
Bowl, 8 In.	37.50
Creamer	12.00
Cup	14.00
Cup & Saucer	15.00 To 20.00
Pitcher, Square, 8 In.	160.00
Plate, Sherbet, 6 In.	6.50
Plate, 7 1/2 In.	15.00
Plate, 8 7/8 In.	12.00 To 16.50
Plate, 10 1/2 In.	60.00
Platter, 11 1/2 In.	22.00
Salt & Pepper	85.00 To 135.00
Sherbet	8.00
Sugar	12.00 To 15.00
Sugar & Creamer	11.50 To 20.00
Tumbler, 3 7/8 In.	20.00 To 21.00
Tumbler, 4 1/4 In.	21.00
Tumbler, 5 1/2 In.	26.00 To 28.00

CRYSTAL

Butter, Covered	55.00
Coaster, Hot Dish	20.00 To 28.00
Cup	4.50
Cup & Saucer	5.00
Jar, Jam	5.00
Plate, Sherbet, 6 In.	2.00
Plate, 8 7/8 In.	3.50
Platter, 11 1/2 In.	7.00
Salt & Pepper, Footed	70.00 To 75.00
Sherbet	3.00 To 4.00
Sugar & Creamer	17.00

Tumbler, 4 In. .... 6.00 To 9.00
Tumbler, 4 1/4 In. .... 6.00 To 9.00

GREEN
Bowl, Vegetable, 10 In.
.... 12.50 To 15.00
Bowl, 5 In. 7.00
Butter, Covered .... 60.00 To 70.00
Cookie Jar, Covered 27.50
Creamer .... 5.00 To 7.50
Cup 5.00
Cup & Saucer .... 8.00 To 8.50
Pitcher, 8 1/2 In. 185.00
Plate, Grill, 10 1/2 In. ... 8.00 To 12.00
Plate, Sherbet, 6 In. 2.50
Plate, 8 7/8 In. .... 2.00 To 8.00
Plate, 10 1/2 In. ...... 27.00 To 28.00
Platter, 11 1/2 In. ...... 9.00 To 16.00
Salt & Pepper .... 52.50 To 54.00

Saucer .... 3.50 To 6.00
Sherbet .... 4.50 To 7.50
Soup, Dish 7.00
Sugar & Creamer 12.50
Sugar, Covered 40.00
Tumbler, 4 In. 3.50
Tumbler, 5 1/2 In. 17.50

PINK
Bowl, Console, 11 In. .... 7.00 To 8.00
Bowl, Deep, 9 1/2 In. 17.00
Bowl, 5 In. 4.50
Bowl, 9 3/8 In. 15.00
Cake Plate .... 8.00 To 15.00
Candleholder, Pair 12.00
Cookie Jar, Covered .... 23.00 To 37.00
Cup .... 5.00 To 6.00
Relish, 3 Part .... 7.50 To 9.00
Tumbler, 4 1/4 In. 9.75

Madrid

Magnolia, see Dogwood

Manhattan

Manhattan is another modern-looking pattern with a design made of molded circles. It was made by Anchor Hocking Glass Company from 1938 to 1941 in crystal or pink. A few green or red pieces are also known. The pattern has been called many names, such as Horizontal Fine Rib, Horizontal Ribbed, Horizontal Rounded Big Rib, Horizontal Sharp Big Rib and Ribbed.

CRYSTAL

Ashtray, Round 5.00
Ashtray, Square 12.00
Bowl, Handled, 7 1/2 In.
.... 5.00 To 9.00
Bowl, 5 3/8 In. .... 3.00 To 5.00
Bowl, 8 In. .... 8.50 To 9.00
Bowl, 9 In. .... 7.00 To 8.50
Candleholder, Double, Pair 9.00
Candleholder, Pair ...... 5.00 To 10.00
Candy Container, Covered 9.50 To 15.00
Compote .... 3.00 To 9.50
Creamer .... 3.00 To 4.75
Cup .... 6.50 To 9.00
Cup & Saucer 8.00
Goblet, 3 1/2 In. .... 2.00 To 6.50
Plate, Sherbet, 6 In. ...... 1.75 To 2.00
Plate, 8 1/2 In. .... 5.00 To 8.25
Plate, 10 1/4 In. .... 4.50 To 10.00
Plate, 14 In. .... 5.00 To 7.75
Relish Insert .... 2.00 To 2.50
Salt & Pepper, Round 8.75
Salt & Pepper, Square 8.75
Saucer 1.00
Sherbet .... 2.25 To 5.00
Sugar .... 1.75 To 4.75
Sugar & Creamer .... 6.50 To 8.00

Tumbler, Footed, 6 In. .... 5.00 To 7.50
Vase .... 3.00 To 7.00

GREEN
Sherbet 2.00
Tumbler, 6 In. 6.00

PINK
Bowl, Handled, 5 3/8 In.
.... 4.25 To 6.00
Candy Container, 3-Footed
.... 3.00 To 6.00
Compote .... 6.00 To 7.00
Cookie Jar .... 35.00 To 39.50
Creamer .... 3.50 To 8.00
Relish Insert .... 2.00 To 4.00
Salt & Pepper .... 25.00 To 35.00
Sherbet .... 3.00 To 5.00
Sugar .... 4.00 To 6.50
Sugar & Creamer .... 5.00 To 12.50
Tumbler, Footed, 6 In. ... 6.00 To 10.00

RED
Relish, Insert .... 2.50 To 3.00

Many Windows, see Roulette

Mayfair, see Rosemary

Mayfair Federal

The Mayfair patterns can easily be recognized, but if you are buying by mail the names are sometimes confusing. Mayfair Federal is the pattern sometimes called Rosemary Arches. It was made in amber, crystal or green by Federal Glass Company from 1934. The other pattern is called Mayfair Open Rose.

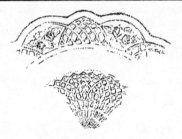

AMBER

Bowl, Oval, 10 In. 12.00
Bowl, 5 In. 4.00
Creamer 9.00
Cup 6.00
Cup & Saucer 7.00
Plate, Grill, 9 1/2 In. 8.50
Plate, 6 3/4 In. 4.00
Plate, 9 1/2 In. . . . . 9.00 To 12.50
Saucer . . . . 2.00 To 3.00
Soup, Cream 16.00
Sugar 6.00
Tumbler, 4 1/2 In. . . . . . 12.00 To 15.00

CRYSTAL

Cup & Saucer 6.50
Plate, 9 1/2 In. . . . . 4.75 To 9.00
Sugar & Creamer 21.00

Mayfair Open Rose

BLUE

Bowl, Vegetable, 7 In. 35.00
Bowl, Vegetable, 9 1/2 In. 39.00
Bowl, Vegetable, 10 In. 35.00
Bowl, 12 In. 45.00
Butter, Covered . . . . . 155.00 To 225.00
Cake Plate, 2-Handled . . 45.00 To 57.00
Candy Container, Covered
    . . . . 135.00 To 145.00
Celery, 2 Part . . . . 30.00 To 35.00
Cookie Jar . . . . 85.00 To 155.00
Creamer 27.00
Cup . . . . 27.00 To 35.00
Cup & Saucer 39.50
Goblet, 7 1/4 In. . . . . . . 88.00 To 98.00
Pitcher, 6 In. 60.00
Pitcher, 8 In. . . . . 80.00 To 85.00
Pitcher, 8 1/2 In. 165.00
Plate, Grill, 9 1/2 In. 22.00
Plate, Off-Center Ring, 6 1/2 In.
    . . . . 18.50 To 22.50
Plate, 8 1/2 In. . . . . 18.00 To 20.00
Plate, 9 1/2 In. . . . . 39.00 To 45.00
Platter, 12 In. 30.00
Relish, Divided . . . . 25.00 To 40.00

Sandwich Server . . . . 37.00 To 57.00
Saucer 12.50
Sherbet, 4 3/4 In. . . . . . 45.00 To 60.00
Sugar 32.00
Tumbler, 4 1/4 In. . . . . . 55.00 To 60.00
Tumbler, 4 3/4 In. . . . . . 85.00 To 87.50
Vase, Sweet Pea . . . . 45.00 To 80.00

CRYSTAL
Salt & Pepper 24.00
Sugar & Creamer ...... 15.00 To 30.00

GREEN
Bowl, Flat, 11 3/4 In. 23.00

PINK
Bowl, Deep, Scalloped, Fruit, 12 In.
.... 18.00 To 35.00
Bowl, Low, Flat, 11 3/4 In. 25.00 To 29.00
Bowl, Vegetable, Covered, 10 In. . 48.00
Bowl, Vegetable, 7 In. .. 12.00 To 20.00
Bowl, 5 In. 11.50
Butter, Covered .... 40.00 To 50.00
Cake Plate .... 14.50 To 26.00
Candy Container, Covered 22.00 To 32.50
Celery 24.00
Cookie Jar .... 22.00 To 35.00
Creamer .... 7.50 To 12.50
Cup .... 8.50 To 12.75
Cup & Saucer .... 16.50 To 22.00
Decanter & Stopper .... 40.00 To 95.00
Goblet, 4 In. 45.00
Goblet, 5 3/4 In. ...... 34.00 To 38.75
Goblet, 7 1/4 In. 89.50

Pitcher, 6 In. .... 22.00 To 26.00
Pitcher, 8 In. .... 27.00 To 45.00
Pitcher, 8 1/2 In. ...... 37.00 To 62.00
Plate, Grill, 9 1/2 In. ... 15.00 To 22.00
Plate, Handled 18.00
Plate, 6 In. .... 3.50 To 8.50
Plate, 6 1/2 In. .... 5.00 To 7.50
Plate, 8 1/2 In. .... 11.00 To 16.50
Plate, 9 1/2 In. .... 25.00 To 36.00
Platter, 12 In. .... 13.00 To 14.00
Relish, 4 Part .... 20.00 To 35.00
Saltshaker 20.00
Sandwich Server .... 20.00 To 26.50
Saucer, Ringed 18.00
Sherbet, Footed, 3 In. ... 9.50 To 15.00
Sherbet, Footed, 4 3/4 In. 45.00
Soup, Cream .... 20.00 To 32.50
Sugar .... 12.00 To 18.00
Sugar & Creamer ...... 22.50 To 35.00
Tumbler, Footed, 3 1/4 In. 20.00 To 45.00
Tumbler, Footed, 5 1/4 In. 22.50 To 30.00
Tumbler, Footed, 6 1/2 In. 20.00 To 26.00
Tumbler, 4 1/4 In. 7.50
Tumbler, 5 1/4 In. ..... 25.00 To 32.50
Vase, Sweet Pea .... 80.00 To 99.50
Whiskey .... 50.00 To 100.00

Meadow Flower, see No. 618

Meandering Vine, see Madrid

Melba, see Hammered Band

Mayfair

Open Rose

Miss America, see also English Hobnail

Miss America or Diamond Pattern was made by Hocking Glass Company from 1933 to 1936. It was made in many colors including amber, crystal, green, ice blue, pink, red and Ritz blue. In 1977 some reproduction butter dishes were made of amberina, crystal, green, ice blue or pink. Saltshakers are also being reproduced.

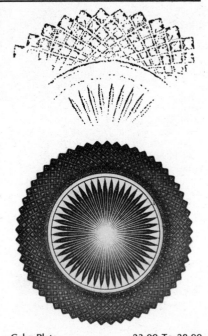

CRYSTAL

Bowl, Vegetable, 10 In. ...	6.00 To 9.00
Bowl, 6 1/4 In.	4.00 To 5.00
Bowl, 8 3/4 In.	16.00 To 22.50
Butter, Covered	150.00
Cake Plate	10.00 To 20.00
Candy Container, Covered	33.50 To 45.00
Celery, 10 1/2 In.	7.00
Compote	6.00 To 8.00
Creamer	4.50
Cup	4.00 To 7.00
Cup & Saucer	6.50 To 10.00
Goblet, 3 3/4 In.	13.00 To 16.50
Goblet, 4 3/4 In.	13.00 To 14.00
Goblet, 5 1/2 In.	13.00 To 15.00
Pitcher, Ice Lip, 8 1/2 In.	55.00
Plate, Grill, 10 1/4 In.	5.00 To 9.00
Plate, Sherbet, 5 3/4 In. ..	2.50 To 3.00
Plate, 8 1/2 In.	3.50 To 4.50
Plate, 10 1/4 In.	7.00 To 10.00
Platter, 12 1/4 In.	6.00 To 12.00
Relish, 4 Part, 8 3/4 In. ..	5.00 To 10.00
Relish, 5 Part, 11 3/4 In.	12.00 To 21.00
Salt & Pepper	14.50 To 20.00
Saucer	1.50 To 2.50
Sherbet	4.50 To 9.00
Sugar	4.50 To 6.00
Sugar & Creamer	9.00 To 10.00
Tumbler, 4 In.	10.00
Tumbler, 4 1/2 In.	10.00
Tumbler, 6 3/4 In.	14.00

GREEN

Plate, 6 3/4 In.	2.00
Tumbler, 4 1/2 In.	16.00

PINK

Bowl, Curved, 8 In.	37.00 To 45.00
Bowl, Straight, 8 3/4 In.	45.00
Bowl, Vegetable, 10 In.	15.00 To 18.00
Bowl, 6 1/4 In.	7.00 To 9.50
Butter	325.00
Cake Plate	23.00 To 28.00
Candy Container, Covered	78.00 To 88.00
Celery	9.00 To 18.00
Coaster, 5 3/4 In.	15.00 To 17.00
Compote	12.00 To 15.00
Creamer	8.50 To 15.00
Cup	6.00 To 13.50
Cup & Saucer	7.00 To 18.50
Goblet, 3 3/4 In.	25.00 To 39.00
Goblet, 4 3/4 In.	42.00
Goblet, 5 1/2 In.	30.00 To 42.00
Pitcher, Ice Lip, 8 1/2 In.	95.00 To 97.50
Plate, Grill, 10 1/4 In. ...	6.00 To 15.00
Plate, Sherbet, 5 3/4 In. ..	4.00
Plate, 8 1/2 In.	8.50 To 12.00
Plate, 10 1/4 In.	12.00 To 20.00
Platter, 12 1/4 In.	11.00 To 22.00
Relish, 4 Part, 8 1/2 In. ..	6.00 To 14.00
Salt & Pepper	30.00 To 45.00
Saucer	2.00 To 4.00
Sherbet	6.50 To 14.00
Sugar	6.50 To 14.00
Sugar & Creamer	20.00 To 25.00
Tumbler, 4 In.	30.00 To 35.00
Tumbler, 4 1/2 In.	14.00 To 19.00
Tumbler, 6 3/4 In.	30.00

Moderne Art, see Tea Room

Moderntone

Moderntone or Wedding Band was made by
Hazel Atlas Glass Company from 1935 to
1942. The cobalt blue and the simple pattern
are popular today with Art Deco enthusiasts.
The pattern was made of amethyst, cobalt
blue, crystal or pink glass. It was also made
of a glass called platonite, which was covered with a variety of bright fired-on colors
including black, light or dark blue, light or
dark green, red, orange, yellow and white
trimmed with a small colored rim.

AMETHYST
Creamer . . . . 5.00 To 6.75
Cup . . . . 3.75 To 5.00
Cup & Saucer 5.00
Plate, 6 In. 2.50
Plate, 7 3/4 In. 4.50
Plate, 9 In. 8.00
Plate, 10 1/2 In. 9.00
Platter, 12 In. 25.00
Salt & Pepper 29.00
Saucer . . . . 1.50 To 2.00
Soup, Cream, Handled 7.50
Sugar 6.75

BLUE
Ashtray, 5 In. . . . . 11.00 To 13.50
Bowl, 5 In. . . . . 11.00 To 15.00
Bowl, 6 1/2 In. 9.50
Bowl, 8 3/4 In. . . . . 18.00 To 25.00
Butter, Covered . . . . 50.00 To 68.00
Creamer . . . . 4.00 To 8.75
Cup . . . . 5.00 To 6.00
Cup & Saucer . . . . 1.25 To 8.75
Jar, Mustard, Covered 15.00
Plate, Sherbet, 5 3/4 In. 2.00
Plate, 6 3/4 In. . . . . 1.00 To 7.50
Plate, 7 3/4 In. . . . . 4.00 To 8.00
Plate, 8 7/8 In. . . . . 5.00 To 6.00
Plate, 10 1/2 In. . . . . . . 12.75 To 18.00
Platter, 11 In. . . . . 10.00 To 25.00
Platter, 12 In. 31.00
Punch Set, 8 Cups, Ladle 175.00
Salt & Pepper . . . . 18.00 To 22.00
Saucer . . . . .50 To 2.50
Sherbet . . . . 2.00 To 7.50
Soup, Cream . . . . 2.00 To 9.50
Sugar . . . . 4.00 To 5.50
Sugar & Creamer . . . . 8.00 To 14.00

Tumbler, 3 In. . . . . 13.00 To 16.00
Tumbler, 5 In. . . . . 8.00 To 16.00
Whiskey, 2 1/2 In. . . . . . 14.00 To 15.00

CRYSTAL
Ashtray, 7 1/2 In. 55.00
Creamer 3.00
Cup . . . . 1.00 To 2.50
Dinner, 7 3/4 In. . . . . 1.75 To 2.50
Salt & Pepper 12.00
Sugar 1.80
Sugar & Creamer . . . . 4.00 To 11.00
Whiskey 3.75

GOLD
Saucer, Child's 2.00

GREEN
Creamer 2.00
Cup 2.25
Cup & Saucer 2.00
Plate, 8 7/8 In. 1.50
Sherbet 2.00
Soup, Cream 2.00
Sugar . . . . 1.25 To 3.00
Tumbler . . . . 4.00 To 4.50

LIGHT BLUE
Bowl, 4 3/4 In. 1.75
Cup & Saucer 2.00
Plate, 8 7/8 In. 2.00
Saucer 75
Sherbet 2.00

LIGHT GREEN
Bowl, 5 In. 1.75
Cup & Saucer 5.50
Plate, 8 7/8 In. 2.00
Saucer 75

PINK
Bowl, 5 In. 2.50
Creamer 2.00
Creamer, Child's 5.00
Cup . . . . 25.00 To 175.00
Cup & Saucer 5.50
Plate, 6 3/4 In. 2.00
Plate, 8 7/8 In. . . . . 1.25 To 2.50
Saucer . . . . .75 To 1.00
Sugar & Creamer 15.00

RED & BLACK STRIPE
Shaker 8.00

WHITE
Creamer 3.00
Sherbet .... 1.00 To 1.50
Sugar 3.00

WHITE & RED
Salt & Pepper .... 7.00 To 12.50

YELLOW
Creamer .... 2.00 To 3.00
Cup & Saucer 2.00
Cup, Child's 4.75
Plate, Child's, 5 1/4 In. 3.50
Plate, 7 In. 2.00
Plate, 8 7/8 In. 1.50
Saucer .... .75 To 2.00
Sherbet 2.00
Soup, Cream 2.00
Sugar 2.00

Moderntone Little Hostess Party Set

The Moderntone Little Hostess Party set was also made by Hazel Atlas in the 1940s. This was a child's set of dishes made in platonite with fired-on colors. We have seen blue, gray, green, maroon, orange, pink, turquoise and yellow, but other colors were probably made.

BLUE
Cup 4.00
Plate, 5 1/4 In. 4.00

GREEN
Plate, 5 1/4 In. 4.00
Saucer, 3 3/4 In. 2.50

PINK
Cup 4.00
Plate, 5 1/4 In. 4.00
Saucer, 3 3/4 In. 2.50
Sugar & Creamer 10.00

YELLOW
Cup 4.00
Saucer, 3 3/4 In. 2.50

Molly, see Imperial Plain Octagon

Moondrops

The New Martinsville Glass Company, New Martinsville, West Virginia, made Moondrops from 1932 to 1940. Collectors like the pieces with the fan-shaped knobs or stoppers. The pattern was made in amber, amethyst, black, cobalt, crystal, dark green, ice blue, medium blue, light green, jadite, pink, red or smoke.

AMBER
Ashtray, 4 In. 12.50
Cup . . . . 4.25 To 5.00
Cup & Saucer . . . . 5.70 To 9.50
Goblet, 2 7/8 In. . . . . 8.75 To 9.50
Goblet, 4 In. . . . . 7.50 To 8.00
Plate, Sherbet, 6 1/4 In. . . 2.50 To 3.25
Plate, 8 1/2 In. . . . . 3.75 To 5.00
Plate, 9 1/2 In. 5.75
Platter, 12 In. 12.00
Relish, 3 Part, 8 In. 15.00
Saucer . . . . 1.75 To 2.00
Sugar 8.00
Whiskey . . . . 5.00 To 6.00

AMETHYST
Bowl, Console, 3-Legged 27.75
Compote, 4 In. 19.75
Cup & Saucer 14.75
Plate, 8 1/2 In. 6.00
Relish, 3 Part, 8 In. 22.50
Soup, Dish 14.75
Whiskey 12.00

COBALT
Cup 7.75
Cup & Saucer 12.00
Sugar 7.75
Tumbler, 4 7/8 In. 13.50

CRYSTAL
Cup 2.50

DARK GREEN
Mug, 5 In. 14.75
Plate, 9 1/2 In. 12.00
Whiskey 6.00

GREEN
Compote 15.00
Goblet, 4 In. 7.50
Goblet, 4 3/4 In. 5.50

JADITE
Cup & Saucer 12.00
Plate, 8 1/2 In. 4.75

LIGHT GREEN
Mug, 5 In. 13.75

PINK
Decanter & Fan, Stopper, 8 1/2 In.
. . . . 40.00

RED
Bowl, 5 1/4 In. 5.00
Butter, Covered, Scalloped, Chrome Holder, 8 In. 350.00
Candleholder, 2 In., Pair 20.00
Cocktail Shaker, Handled 28.00
Cocktail Shaker, 6 Goblets 95.00
Creamer 8.00
Cup . . . . 7.50 To 8.00
Cup & Saucer . . . . 10.00 To 16.50
Goblet, Liqueur 15.00
Goblet, Metal Stem, 5 1/8 In. 9.00
Goblet, 4 In. 12.50
Goblet, 6 1/4 In. 20.00
Pitcher, Ice Lip, 8 In.
. . . . 175.00 To 200.00
Plate, 7 1/8 In. 6.00
Plate, 8 1/2 In. 5.75
Plate, 9 1/2 In. . . . . 8.00 To 15.00
Platter, 12 In. 15.00
Sherbet, 2 5/8 In. . . . . 7.00 To 8.00
Soup, Dish 9.50
Sugar . . . . 6.75 To 11.00
Sugar & Creamer . . . . . . 14.00 To 20.00
Tumbler, 4 7/8 In. 15.00
Tumbler, 5 1/8 In. . . . . . 12.00 To 20.00
Whiskey 10.00

Moonstone

The opalescent hobnails on this pattern gave it the name Moonstone. It was made by Anchor Hocking Glass Company, Lancaster, Ohio, from 1941 to 1946. A few pieces are seen in green.

CRYSTAL
Bottle, Cologne . . . . 8.00 To 15.00
Bowl, Crimped, Handled, 6 1/2 In.
. . . . 6.00 To 8.00
Bowl, Crimped, 9 1/2 In.
. . . . 9.00 To 11.00
Bowl, Divided, 7 3/4 In. . . 5.50 To 8.00
Bowl, Flat, 7 3/4 In. 7.50
Bowl, 5 1/2 In. . . . . 3.00 To 6.00
Box, Cigarette, Covered
. . . . 10.00 To 13.00
Box, Puff . . . . 10.50 To 13.50
Candleholder, Pair . . . . . 11.00 To 13.50

Candy Container, Covered, 6 In.
. . . . 12.50 To 14.00
Candy Container, Cloverleaf-Shaped
. . . . 5.00 To 9.00
Candy Container, Heart-Shaped
. . . . 6.00 To 10.00
Creamer . . . . 4.00 To 6.00
Cup . . . . 4.00 To 5.00
Cup & Saucer . . . . 5.00 To 7.00
Goblet . . . . 10.00 To 14.00
Plate, Sherbet, 6 1/4 In. . . 2.00 To 3.50
Plate, 8 In. . . . . 5.50 To 6.00
Plate, 10 In. . . . . 8.75 To 12.50
Salt & Pepper . . . . 30.00 To 49.50
Sherbet . . . . 3.50 To 5.00
Sugar . . . . 3.00 To 6.00
Sugar & Creamer . . . . 7.00 To 12.00
Vase . . . . 6.00 To 10.00

Mt. Pleasant

Mt. Pleasant, sometimes called Double Shield, was made by L. E. Smith Company, Mt. Pleasant, Pennsylvania, from the mid-1920s to 1934. The pattern was made in black amethyst, a very deep purple that appears black unless held in front of a strong light, or cobalt blue, green or pink. Some pieces have gold trim.

BLACK
Bowl, 3-Footed 8.00
Sherbet 8.50
Sugar 9.50

BLUE
Candleholder, Double 12.00
Creamer 8.50
Cup 8.00
Cup & Saucer . . . . 9.00 To 9.50
Plate, 8 In. 8.50
Soup, Cream 7.50
Sugar 5.00
Sugar & Creamer . . . . . . 20.00 To 22.00

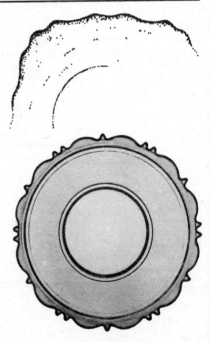

New

New Century, see also Ovide

There is vast confusion about the patterns called New Century, Lydia Ray, Ovide and related pieces. After studying all the available books about Depression glass, the old advertisements and checking with dealers who sell the glass, we have made these decisions.

Most dealers and most people who advertise Depression glass call the pattern pictured here "New Century." It has a series of ribs in the glass design. New Century was made by the Hazel Atlas Glass Company, a firm with factories in Ohio, Pennsylvania and West Virginia, from 1930 to 1935. It is found in amethyst, cobalt, crystal, green or pink.

In 1970 a book listed the pattern by Hazel Atlas with ribs as "Lydia Ray." In this same book, "New Century" was a very plain ware with no impressed or raised pattern. Sometimes it was made in black or white with fired-on colors and was called "Ovide." Research shows that the ribbed pattern was advertised in the 1930s as "New Century" by Hazel Atlas. The plain glassware was also called "New Century." With added enamel designs, it was sometimes called Ovide, Floral Sterling or "Cloverleaf."

In this book, we list no "Lydia Ray" or "Floral Sterling." The plain glass we call "Ovide."

AMETHYST

Pitcher, Ice Lip, 8 In. 20.00
Tumbler, 3 1/2 In. .... 5.00 To 6.00
Tumbler, 4 1/8 In. .... 2.25 To 6.50
Tumbler, 5 In. .... 10.00 To 11.00

COBALT

Pitcher, 8 In. 27.00
Tumbler, 3 1/2 In. .... 2.00 To 6.50
Tumbler, 4 1/8 In. 6.00
Tumbler, 5 In. 8.00

CRYSTAL

Pitcher, 7 3/4 In. 13.00
Saltshaker 14.75
Tumbler, 3 1/2 In. 3.00

GREEN

Bowl, 8 In. 8.00
Creamer 7.50
Decanter & Stopper 38.00
Pitcher, 7 3/4 In. 22.00
Pitcher, 8 In. .... 24.00 To 28.00
Plate, Grill, 10 In. 10.00
Plate, Sherbet, 6 In. 2.00
Plate, 7 1/2 In. 5.00
Plate, 8 1/2 In. .... 5.00 To 6.00
Platter, 11 In. 8.75
Salt & Pepper .... 15.00 To 20.00
Sherbet 4.75
Sugar 4.50
Sugar, Covered 15.00
Tumbler, 3 1/2 In. 7.00

PINK

Pitcher, Ice Lip, 7 3/4 In.
.... 25.00 To 30.00
Pitcher, 8 1/4 In. 30.00
Tumbler, 4 1/8 In. .... 5.00 To 8.00

Newport

Newport or Hairpin was made by Hazel Atlas Glass Company from 1936 to 1940. It is known in amethyst, cobalt blue, pink, platonite white or a variety of fired-on colors.

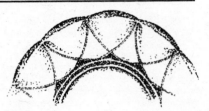

AMETHYST
Bowl, 5 1/4 In. .... 4.00 To 9.00
Butter 20.00
Creamer .... 5.00 To 5.50
Cup & Saucer .... 5.00 To 6.00
Plate, Sherbet, 6 In. ...... 1.00 To 2.50
Plate, 8 1/2 In. .... 2.50 To 8.00
Platter, 11 3/4 In. ...... 9.00 To 14.25
Salt & Pepper 42.50
Saucer .... 1.25 To 2.50
Sherbet 5.50
Soup, Cream .... 5.50 To 8.00
Sugar 5.00
Sugar & Creamer ...... 10.00 To 12.50

COBALT
Bowl, 4 1/4 In. 5.00
Creamer .... 5.00 To 8.00
Cup .... 3.50 To 5.75
Cup & Saucer .... 5.00 To 6.00
Plate, Sherbet, 6 In. ...... 1.50 To 2.50
Plate, 8 1/2 In. .... 4.00 To 5.00
Salt & Pepper .... 32.00 To 32.50

Saucer 1.50
Sherbet .... 5.00 To 6.00
Soup, Cream .... 5.00 To 8.50
Sugar .... 5.00 To 6.75
Sugar & Creamer 11.00
Tumbler 18.00

PINK
Bowl, 5 1/4 In. 4.00

WHITE
Bowl, 6 1/2 In. 10.00
Creamer .... 3.00 To 8.00
Cup & Saucer, Gold Trim 3.00
Plate, Gold Trim, 6 In. 1.00
Plate, 8 1/2 In. 2.50
Salt & Pepper 14.00
Soup, Cream, Gold Trim 2.50
Sugar, Gold Rim 3.50

Normandie

A few Depression glass patterns were made in iridescent marigold color which has been collected as carnival glass. Iridescent Normandie appears in the carnival glass listings as Bouquet and Lattice; when the pattern is in the other known colors it is called Normandie. Look for it in amber, crystal, iridescent or pink. One author also lists green. It was made from 1933 to 1940.

AMBER
Bowl, Vegetable, 10 In.
.... 10.00 To 15.00
Bowl, 5 In. .... 3.50 To 6.50
Bowl, 6 1/2 In. 5.00
Creamer .... 3.50 To 6.50
Cup .... 3.00 To 6.00
Cup & Saucer .... 4.00 To 8.00
Pitcher, 8 In. .... 39.00 To 45.00
Plate, Grill, 11 In. .... 4.00 To 16.75
Plate, Sherbet, 6 In. ...... 1.50 To 2.00

Plate, 8 In. .... 7.00 To 9.00
Plate, 9 1/4 In. 8.50
Plate, 11 In. 16.00
Platter, 11 3/4 In. ...... 8.00 To 15.00
Salt & Pepper .... 29.75 To 31.00
Saucer 2.50
Sherbet .... 3.50 To 7.00
Sugar .... 4.00 To 4.50

Sugar & Creamer 9.00
Sugar, Covered .... 56.50 To 69.75
Tumbler, 4 1/4 In. ...... 9.00 To 10.00
Tumbler, 5 In. 12.25

CRYSTAL
Sherbet .... 2.00 To 4.00

IRIDESCENT
Bowl, Vegetable, 10 In. .. 9.25 To 16.00
Bowl, 5 In. .... 1.75 To 4.50
Bowl, 6 1/2 In. .... 3.50 To 6.50
Creamer .... 2.50 To 4.75
Cup .... 4.00 To 4.25
Cup & Saucer .... 4.50 To 8.00
Plate, Grill, 11 In. .... 4.00 To 9.50
Plate, Sherbet, 6 In. ...... 1.00 To 2.00
Plate, 8 In. 6.00
Platter, 11 3/4 In. ...... 6.00 To 12.00
Saucer .... 1.50 To 2.00
Sherbet .... 2.75 To 6.00
Sugar .... 3.50 To 5.00
Sugar & Creamer .... 9.50 To 11.00

PINK
Bowl, Vegetable, 10 In. 15.00
Bowl, 5 In. .... 3.50 To 5.50

Normandie

Creamer .... 4.50 To 10.00
Cup .... 3.50 To 5.00
Cup & Saucer .... 5.50 To 7.50
Plate, Sherbet, 6 In. ...... 1.50 To 3.00
Plate, 8 In. .... 5.00 To 9.00
Platter, 11 3/4 In. 14.00
Salt & Pepper 50.00
Saucer .... 2.00 To 2.50
Sherbet .... 4.00 To 6.50
Sugar 10.00

No. 601, see Avocado

No. 610

Many patterns are listed both by the original pattern number and by a name. No. 610 is often called Pyramid or Rex. It was made from 1926 to 1932 by the Indiana Glass Company. The pattern was made of crystal, green, pink or yellow. In 1974 and 1975 reproductions were made in black.

CRYSTAL
Saltshaker 30.00

GREEN
Bowl, Oval, 9 1/2 In. .. 18.00 To 40.00
Bowl, 8 1/2 In. 28.00
Creamer 18.00
Dish, Pickle, 9 1/2 In. 40.00
Pitcher 125.00

PINK
Bowl, Oval, 9 1/2 In. .. 35.00 To 40.00

Creamer .... 7.50 To 17.00
Dish, Pickle, 9 1/2 In. .. 25.00 To 40.00
Pitcher 125.00
Relish, 4 Part 30.00
Sugar & Creamer 35.00

YELLOW
Bowl, 4 3/4 In. 20.00
Creamer 19.00

No. 612

Indiana Glass Company, Dunkirk, Indiana, called this pattern No. 612, but collectors call it Horseshoe. It was made from 1930 to 1933 in green, pink or yellow. A sugar and creamer set was made in crystal. Plates came in two styles, one with the center pattern, one plain.

CRYSTAL
Relish, 3 Part 12.50
Saucer 3.00

GREEN
Bowl, Vegetable, 10 1/2 In. 25.00
Bowl, 6 1/2 In. .... 15.75 To 22.50
Bowl, 7 1/2 In. .... 12.00 To 22.00
Bowl, 9 1/2 In. .... 25.00 To 30.00
Candy Container, Covered,
　Handled 175.00
Creamer .... 9.00 To 15.00
Cup .... 6.00 To 15.00
Cup & Saucer .... 6.00 To 12.50
Plate, Sherbet, 6 In. ...... 4.00 To 4.50
Plate, 8 3/8 In. .... 5.00 To 7.50
Plate, 9 3/8 In. .... 4.50 To 6.50
Plate, 11 In. 11.00
Platter, 10 3/4 In. ..... 12.00 To 22.50
Relish .... 12.50 To 16.00
Saucer .... 2.00 To 5.00
Sherbet .... 7.25 To 9.50
Sugar .... 7.50 To 9.50
Sugar & Creamer ...... 17.00 To 22.00
Tumbler, Footed,
　4 3/4 In. .... 10.50 To 19.00

YELLOW
Bowl, Vegetable, Oval, 10 1/2 In.
　................... 16.00 To 25.00
Bowl, 6 1/2 In. 20.00
Bowl, 7 1/2 In. .... 15.00 To 16.50
Creamer .... 10.00 To 11.00
Cup & Saucer .... 8.00 To 17.50
Pitcher 275.00
Plate, Sherbet, 6 In. ...... 2.00 To 3.50
Plate, 8 3/8 In. .... 5.00 To 8.00
Plate, 11 In. .... 8.00 To 10.00
Platter, 10 3/4 In. ..... 12.00 To 20.00
Relish, Footed, 3 Part .. 12.00 To 20.00
Saucer .... 2.50 To 3.50
Sherbet .... 9.00 To 11.00
Sugar .... 8.00 To 10.00
Sugar & Creamer, Footed 24.00
Tumbler, Footed, 4 3/4 In. 20.00

No. 612

No. 615

No. 615 is usually called Lorain or sometimes Basket, Bridal Bouquet, Flower Basket or Hanging Basket. It was made by the Indiana Glass Company from 1929 to 1932 of crystal, green or yellow. Sometimes crystal pieces have red, yellow, blue or green borders. Reproduction pieces were made of milk glass or olive green.

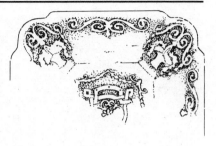

CRYSTAL
Cup & Saucer 7.50
Relish .... 5.50 To 9.00

GREEN
Bowl, Cereal 35.00
Bowl, Vegetable, Oval, 9 3/4
  In. 25.00
Bowl, 7 1/4 In. .... 23.00 To 25.00
Bowl, 8 In. .... 70.00 To 75.00
Cup 6.00
Cup & Saucer 12.50
Plate, Sherbet, 5 1/2 In. .. 3.00 To 6.50
Plate, 7 3/4 In. .... 6.00 To 7.50
Plate, 8 3/8 In. .... 8.00 To 8.50
Plate, 10 In. 29.50
Platter .... 15.00 To 18.50
Sherbet .... 6.50 To 14.00
Sugar & Creamer ...... 20.00 To 24.50
Tumbler, 4 3/4 In.
  .... 13.50 To 15.00

YELLOW
Bowl, Vegetable, 9 3/4 In. 35.00
Bowl, 6 In. .... 20.00 To 40.00
Creamer 15.00
Cup 13.00
Cup & Saucer .... 10.00 To 14.00
Plate, 7 3/4 In. .... 9.50 To 10.00
Plate, 10 1/4 In. ...... 35.00 To 43.00
Plate, 10 3/4 In. ...... 35.00 To 43.00
Platter, 11 1/2 In. ..... 25.00 To 30.00
Relish, 4 Part, 8 1/2 In.
  .... 18.00 To 20.00
Sherbet .... 24.00 To 28.00
Sugar .... 10.00 To 13.50
Tumbler, 4 3/4 In. ..... 15.00 To 18.00

No. 616

No. 616 is called Vernon by some collectors. It was made by Indiana Glass Company from 1930 to 1932. The pattern was made in crystal, green or yellow. Some crystal pieces have a platinum trim.

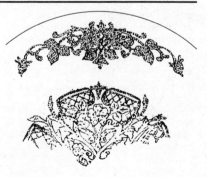

CRYSTAL
Creamer 15.00
Cup 7.00
Cup & Saucer .... 6.25 To 9.50
Plate, 8 In. 5.50
Plate, 11 In. .... 12.00 To 15.00
Sugar 9.50
Sugar & Creamer 17.50

GREEN
Cup & Saucer 17.00
Saucer 3.00
Tumbler, Footed, 5 In. 22.00

YELLOW
Cup & Saucer 14.00
Plate, 8 In. .... 5.50 To 9.50
Saucer .... 2.00 To 3.50
Sugar 17.50

No. 618

Another Indiana Glass Company pattern made from 1932 to 1937 was No. 618 or Pineapple & Floral. It is also called Meadow Flower, Lacy Daisy or Wildflower. The pattern was made of amber, crystal or fired-on green or red. Reproductions were made in olive green in the late 1960s.

AMBER
Bowl, Vegetable, 10 In. 15.00
Creamer . . . . 7.00 To 14.00
Cup & Saucer 8.00
Plate, Sherbet, 6 In. . . . . . . 2.50 To 3.50
Plate, 8 3/8 In. 8.00
Plate, 9 3/8 In. . . . . 7.00 To 10.00
Platter, Handled, 11 In. 12.00
Saucer 2.00
Sugar & Creamer 15.00

CRYSTAL
Ashtray 14.00
Bowl, Vegetable, 10 In. 13.00
Bowl, 6 In. 15.00
Bowl, 7 In. . . . . 2.50 To 5.00
Compote, Diamond-Shaped
. . . . 1.50 To 2.00
Creamer . . . . 5.00 To 8.00
Cup 6.00
Cup & Saucer . . . . 6.50 To 10.00

Plate, Sherbet, 6 In. . . . . . . 1.25 To 2.25
Plate, 8 3/8 In. . . . . 3.00 To 3.50
Plate, 9 3/8 In. . . . . 6.00 To 7.00
Plate, 11 1/2 In. . . . . 6.00 To 12.00
Relish . . . . 10.00 To 12.50
Saucer 1.50
Sherbet 11.00
Soup, Cream 14.50
Sugar . . . . 4.00 To 7.00
Sugar & Creamer . . . . 9.00 To 12.00
Tumbler, 4 1/4 In. . . . . . 19.00 To 22.00

RED
Plate, 8 3/8 In. 5.00

No. 620

No. 620, also known as Daisy, was made by Indiana Glass Company. In 1933 the pattern was made in crystal, in 1940 in amber and in the 1960s and 1970s reproductions were made in dark green or milk glass.

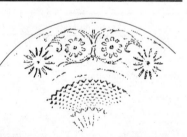

AMBER
Bowl, Vegetable, 10 In. . . 6.50 To 11.50
Bowl, 4 1/2 In. . . . . 5.00 To 7.50
Bowl, 6 In. 16.00
Bowl, 9 3/8 In. . . . . 15.00 To 18.50
Cake Plate . . . . 8.00 To 9.50
Creamer . . . . 4.00 To 7.00
Cup . . . . 2.50 To 4.50
Cup & Saucer . . . . 1.75 To 6.00
Plate, Grill, 10 3/8 In. . . . . 7.50 To 9.00
Plate, Sherbet, 6 In. . . . . . . 2.00 To 2.50
Plate, 7 3/8 In. . . . . 3.50 To 5.50
Plate, 8 3/8 In. . . . . 3.00 To 5.50
Plate, 9 3/8 In. . . . . 3.00 To 6.00

Platter, 10 3/4 In. . . . . . . 6.75 To 10.00
Relish, 3 Part, Footed . . 10.00 To 16.00
Saucer . . . . 1.00 To 1.50
Sherbet . . . . 4.00 To 6.00
Soup, Cream . . . . 4.00 To 5.50
Sugar . . . . 3.50 To 6.00
Sugar & Creamer . . . . 6.50 To 16.00
Tumbler, Footed, 4 1/2 In.
. . . . 14.50 To 15.00

CRYSTAL
Bowl, 4 1/2 In. 1.75
Cup .... 2.00 To 2.50
Plate, Grill, 10 3/8 In. .... 3.00 To 4.00
Plate, Sherbet, 6 In. 2.00
Plate, 8 3/8 In. 2.00

Plate, 9 3/8 In. 3.50
Relish, 3 Part, Footed 5.00
Saucer .... .75
Soup, Cream 2.50
Tumbler, Footed, 4 1/2 In. 4.50
Tumbler, Footed, 6 1/2 In. 8.50

No. 622, see Pretzel

No. 624, see Christmas Candy

Oatmeal Lace Scroll, see Princess Feather

Octagon

Octagon, sometimes called Tiered Octagon or U.S. Octagon, was made by the U.S. Glass Company from 1927 to 1929. It was used by the Octagon Soap Company as premium. The pieces were made of green or pink. Some pieces are found marked with the glass company trademark.

GREEN
Plate, 8 In. 5.00

PINK
Plate, 5 1/2 In. 1.00

Old Cafe

Old Cafe is one of the few patterns with only one name. It was made by the Anchor Hocking Glass Company, Lancaster, Ohio, from 1936 to 1938. Pieces are found in crystal, pink or red.

CRYSTAL
Bowl, 5 In. 3.00
Candy Container, Red Lid 15.00
Relish, Red Insert, 14 In. 24.50

PINK
Bowl, Handled, 5 In. ...... 2.50 To 8.00
Bowl, 3 3/4 In. .... 3.00 To 3.50
Bowl, 5 1/2 In. 5.00
Candy Container 5.00
Cookie Jar, Covered .... 45.00 To 49.50
Cup .... 3.00 To 5.00
Cup & Saucer .... 5.00 To 8.00
Dish, Olive 3.50
Pitcher, 80 Oz. .... 92.00 To 98.00

Plate, Sherbet, 6 In. ...... 3.00 To 4.00
Plate, 10 In. .... 10.50 To 15.00
Saucer .... 2.00 To 4.00
Sherbet .... 3.00 To 5.00
Tumbler, 3 In. 5.00
Tumbler, 4 In. .... 4.50 To 12.50
Vase 8.00

RED
Ashtray 3.00
Bowl, 5 1/2 In. 10.00
Candy Container .... 8.00 To 9.00
Cup .... 3.50 To 6.00
Tumbler, 3 In. .... 5.00 To 6.00

Old English

Old English or Threading was made by the Indiana Glass Company, Dunkirk, Indiana, in the late 1920s and early 1930s. It was first made in amber, crystal, emerald green and light green. Pink was a later color.

CRYSTAL
Tumbler, Footed, 4 1/2 In. 6.00

GREEN
Bowl, Footed, 11 In. 25.00
Candleholder, Pair . . . . .   30.00 To 40.00
Candy Container, Covered 45.00
Pitcher 60.00
Sherbet 12.50

Old Florentine, see Florentine No. 1

Opalescent Hobnail, see Moonstone

Open Lace, see Lace Edge

Open Rose, see Mayfair Open Rose

Open Scallop, see Lace Edge

Optic Design, see Raindrops

Optic Rib, see Imperial Optic Rib

Oregon Grape, see Woolworth

Oriental Poppy, see Florentine No. 2

Ovide, see also New Century

Hazel Atlas made Ovide pattern from 1929 to 1935. It was made in green at first. By 1931-1932 it was black and by 1933-1935 platonite or opaque white glass was used with fired-on colors. A bright fired-on pattern of black, orange, yellow, green and black circles and lines was one of the popular designs. There is great confusion between Ovide and New Century. Read the explanation under New Century.

BLACK
Salt & Pepper 17.50
Sugar 4.50

GREEN
Bowl, Console, 11 In. 6.00
Bowl, Console, 13 1/2 In. 8.50
Bowl, 5 1/2 In. 1.75

Creamer 2.00
Cup .... 1.50 To 2.00
Cup & Saucer 3.00
Sherbet .... 1.50 To 3.00
Sugar .... 2.00 To 3.00
Tumbler, Cone-Shaped, 5 7/8 In. .. 6.75

WHITE
Creamer 5.00
Sugar, Red Band 5.00

Oxford, see Chinex Classic

Oyster & Pearl

Anchor Hocking Glass Company, Lancaster, Ohio, made Oyster & Pearl pattern from 1938 to 1940. It was made in crystal, pink, red or white with fired-on colors. The outside of these fired-on pieces is white, the inside is either pink or green.

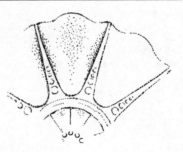

CRYSTAL
Bowl, 10 1/2 In. 12.00
Candy Container, Handled 15.00 To 20.00
Relish, Oval, Divided 4.00

FIRED-ON GREEN
Bowl, Heart-Shaped 5.00
Bowl, 10 1/2 In. 15.75
Candleholder, Pair .... 10.00 To 11.00

FIRED-ON PINK
Bowl, Heart-Shaped 5.00
Bowl, 10 1/2 In. 14.75
Candleholder, Pair 15.75

PINK
Bowl, Round, 5 1/4 In. 3.50
Bowl, 6 1/2 In. 6.50

Bowl, 10 1/2 In. ...... 16.00 To 16.75
Candleholder, Pair 8.00
Plate, 13 1/2 In. ...... 8.00 To 15.00
Relish, Divided .... 4.50 To 6.00

RED
Bowl, Handled, 5 1/4 In.
.... 6.50 To 8.00
Bowl, Round, 5 1/4 In. 8.00
Bowl, 6 1/2 In. .... 5.00 To 9.75
Bowl, 10 1/2 In. ...... 22.00 To 24.75
Candleholder, Pair ..... 22.00 To 27.50
Plate, 13 1/2 In. ...... 20.00 To 21.00

Paneled Aster, see Madrid

Paneled Cherry Blossom, see Cherry Blossom

Pansy & Doric, see Doric & Pansy

Parrot, see Sylvan

Party Line, see Line 191

Patrician

Federal Glass Company, Columbus, Ohio, made Patrician, sometimes called Hinge or Spoke, from 1933 to 1937. Full dinner sets were made. It was made in amber, crystal, green, pink or yellow.

AMBER
Bowl, Vegetable, 10 In.
.... 13.00 To 15.00
Bowl, 5 In. .... 5.00 To 8.00
Bowl, 6 In. .... 11.00 To 16.00
Bowl, 8 1/2 In. .... 15.00 To 25.00
Butter, Covered .... 25.00 To 60.00
Cookie Jar, Covered .... 40.00 To 59.50
Creamer .... 3.00 To 7.50
Cup .... 3.00 To 6.75
Cup & Saucer .... 9.00 To 12.50
Pitcher, 8 In. .... 55.00 To 75.00
Plate, Grill, 10 1/2 In. .... 5.00 To 7.50
Plate, Sherbet, 6 In. ...... 2.50 To 6.00
Plate, 7 1/2 In. .... 6.50 To 8.00
Plate, 9 In. .... 3.50 To 10.00
Plate, 10 1/2 In. .... 3.50 To 6.50
Platter, 11 1/2 In. ...... 9.50 To 18.50
Salt & Pepper .... 20.00 To 37.50
Saucer .... 2.00 To 5.50
Sherbet .... 3.00 To 8.00
Soup, Cream .... 7.00 To 11.50
Sugar .... 3.50 To 5.00
Sugar & Creamer .... 5.00 To 10.00
Sugar & Creamer, Covered 47.00 To 48.00
Sugar, Covered 29.00
Tumbler, Footed, 5 1/4 In. 22.00 To 32.00

Tumbler, 4 In. .... 15.00 To 22.00
Tumbler, 4 1/2 In. ..... 14.00 To 19.00
Tumbler, 5 1/2 In. ..... 20.00 To 25.00

CRYSTAL
Bowl, Vegetable, 10 In. 9.50
Bowl, 6 In. 10.00
Butter, Covered .... 45.00 To 65.00
Cup .... 3.50 To 7.00
Cup & Saucer 8.00
Pitcher, 8 In. 52.00
Pitcher, 8 1/4 In. 75.00
Plate, Grill, 10 1/2 In. .... 3.75 To 7.50
Plate, 7 1/2 In. 7.00
Plate, 9 In. 4.00
Saltshaker 17.50
Saucer 5.00
Sherbet .... 3.50 To 5.00

GREEN

Bowl, 5 In. .... 6.50 To 13.00
Bowl, 6 In. 13.00
Butter, Covered 42.00
Cookie Jar, Covered 100.00
Creamer .... 5.00 To 6.00
Cup .... 3.00 To 6.00
Cup & Saucer .... 8.00 To 13.00
Dish, Jam 25.00
Pitcher, 8 In. .... 76.00 To 90.00
Pitcher, 8 1/4 In. .... 100.00 To 110.00
Plate, Grill, 10 1/2 In. ... 9.50 To 12.00
Plate, Sherbet, 6 In. 5.00
Plate, 7 1/2 In. .... 6.00 To 9.00
Plate, 9 In. .... 5.00 To 9.00
Platter, 11 1/2 In. 12.00
Salt & Pepper .... 19.75 To 45.00
Saucer 4.00
Sherbet .... 5.00 To 10.00
Soup, Cream .... 12.00 To 16.00
Sugar .... 4.00 To 8.00
Sugar & Creamer 12.00
Tumbler, Footed, 5 1/4 In. 35.00 To 37.50
Tumbler, Juice, 4 In. ... 23.00 To 25.00
Tumbler, 4 1/2 In. ..... 17.00 To 20.00
Tumbler, 5 1/2 In. ..... 24.00 To 27.00

PINK

Bowl, 5 In. .... 8.00 To 10.00
Bowl, 8 1/2 In. .... 12.00 To 17.00
Butter, Covered 200.00
Cup & Saucer .... 10.00 To 12.75

Patrician

Plate, Grill, 10 1/2 In. 11.00
Plate, 10 1/2 In. 15.00
Saltshaker 35.00
Soup, Cream .... 14.00 To 15.00
Sugar .... 6.00 To 12.00
Tumbler, 4 In. 19.50
Tumbler, 4 1/2 In. 16.00
Tumbler, 5 1/2 In. 29.75

YELLOW

Plate, 10 1/2 In. 6.00

Peacock & Rose, see Peacock & Wild Rose

Peacock & Wild Rose

Line No. 300 was the name used by Paden City Glass Company, Paden City, West Virginia, for the pattern now called Peacock & Wild Rose. It was made in the 1930s of cobalt blue, green or pink. A few of the lists call this pattern Peacock & Rose.

GREEN

Plate, Footed, 10 1/2 In. 13.00

Vase, 10 In. 65.00

PINK

Ice Bucket, 6 In. 45.00
Vase, 10 In. 45.00

Pear Optic

Pear Optic, sometimes called Thumbprint, was made in 1929 and 1930 by the Federal Glass Company. It was made only in green.

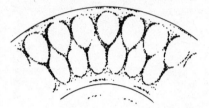

GREEN

Cup	4.00
Cup & Saucer	3.75
Tumbler, 5 In.	4.00
Vase, 9 1/2 In.	18.00

Pebble Optic, see Raindrops

Pebbled Band, see Hammered Band

Penny Line

Paden City Glass Company, Paden City, West Virginia, made Penny Line in amber, cheri-glo, crystal, green, royal blue or ruby. It was No. 991 in the 1932 catalog.

RUBY

Goblet, 3 1/4 In.	5.00
Plate, 6 In.	2.50
Tumbler, 5 1/2 In.	4.50
Tumbler, 6 In.	5.00
Whiskey	4.50

Petal, see Petalware

Petal Swirl, see Swirl

... 1930
... or pink.
... e in monax,
...tern remained
...ral variations were
...ere hand-painted with
...ory, green or pink. Some
...ecorated with a gold rim.
...ruit designs in bright colors were
...n, red or yellow were used to decorate
some wares. All of these patterns have their
own names. These include Aurora, Banded
Petalware, Daisy Petals, Diamond Point,
Petal, Shell or Vivid Bands.

65.00

00

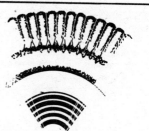

BLUE

Bowl, 8 3/4 In.	12.00
Butter	40.00
Cup	3.50
Cup & Saucer	6.00
Jar, Mustard, Covered; Spoon	9.00
Salt & Pepper	18.00
Soup, Cream	4.00
Tumbler	6.00

CREMAX

Bowl, 5 3/4 In.	4.50
Creamer, Gold Decoration	5.00
Cup	2.50 To 4.00
Cup & Saucer, Gold Decoration	2.50 To 6.50
Plate, Server, 11 In.	5.00
Plate, Server, 11 In., Gold Decoration	11.00
Plate, Sherbet, 6 In.	1.00 To 4.00
Plate, 8 In.	3.00 To 4.00
Plate, 9 In.	3.50 To 4.00
Platter, 13 In.	10.00
Saucer	.50 To 1.25
Soup, Cream	7.00
Sugar	3.50
Sugar, Gold Trim	3.50 To 5.00

CRYSTAL

Bowl, 5 3/4 In.	5.50
Bowl, 8 3/4 In.	6.00
Creamer	7.00
Cup	1.50 To 4.50
Cup & Saucer	3.50 To 6.50
Plate, Gold Trim, 8 In.	5.50
Plate, Server, 11 In.	3.00 To 4.00
Plate, 8 In.	2.00 To 2.50

Plate, 9 In.	5.00
Platter, 13 In.	5.25 To 8.00
Saucer	1.00 To 1.50
Sugar	2.50

FIRED-ON RED

Plate, Server, 11 In.	8.00

MONAX

Bowl, Gold Trim, 8 3/4 In.	4.00
Bowl, 5 3/4 In.	4.00 To 5.50
Creamer	4.00 To 4.75
Cup	2.50
Cup & Saucer	3.75 To 5.75
Cup, Pastel Trim	4.00
Lampshade, 6 In.	7.50 To 12.00
Plate, 6 In.	1.00 To 4.00
Plate, 8 In.	1.00 To 5.00
Plate, 9 In.	3.50 To 6.00
Platter, 13 In.	17.75 To 18.00
Saucer	.50 To 3.50
Sherbet	3.50 To 5.00
Soup, Cream	5.00 To 7.50
Sugar & Creamer	5.00 To 10.00
Sugar, Gold Rim	4.00

PINK

Bowl, 5 3/4 In.	1.00 To 4.50
Bowl, 8 3/4 In.	8.50
Creamer	3.00 To 3.75
Cup	3.50 To 4.00
Cup & Saucer	3.50 To 5.00
Lampshade	10.00
Plate, Server, 11 In.	5.00 To 5.50
Plate, Sherbet, 6 In.	1.00 To 2.00
Plate, 8 In.	1.00 To 3.50
Plate, 9 In.	4.50
Platter, 13 In.	9.00
Saucer	1.00 To 2.50
Sherbet	6.75
Soup, Cream	4.00 To 6.00
Sugar	3.00 To 5.00

Philbe, see also Fire-King

Philbe is a Fire-King Dinnerware made by the Anchor Hocking Glass Company from 1937 to 1940s. It was made in blue, crystal, green or pink. The blue sometimes has platinum trim. Philbe is the dinnerware pattern, the matching kitchenware is called Fire-King Oven Glass.

BLUE
Creamer .... 52.00 To 60.00
Plate, Grill, 10 1/2 In. .. 25.00 To 32.00
Platter, 12 In. .... 47.00 To 53.00
Tumbler, Footed, 5 1/4 In. 55.00

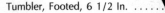

Tumbler, Footed, 6 1/2 In. ......

CRYSTAL
Cup & Saucer 32

GREEN
Creamer .... 35.00 To 39.00
Cup .... 47.00 To 49.00

PINK
Candy Container, Covered
.... 129.00 To 145.00

Pie Crust, see Cremax

Pillar Flute

Pillar Flute was made by Imperial Glass Company, Bellaire, Ohio, in amber, blue, crystal, green and a pink called Rose Marie. It was made about 1930.

LIGHT BLUE
Bowl, 10 In. 9.00
Compote, 7 In. 6.00

Pineapple & Floral, see No. 618

Pinwheel, see Sierra

Pioneer

Pioneer by Federal Glass Company, Columbus, Ohio, was first made in pink in the 1930s. In the 1940s the dishes were made in crystal and the pattern continued to be made into the 1970s.

CRYSTAL
Bowl, 10 1/2 In. 1.50
Bowl, 11 In. 5.00
Plate, 12 In. .... 1.50 To 5.00

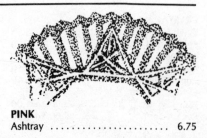

PINK
Ashtray 6.75

Poinsettia, see Floral

Popeye & Olive

Line No. 994 was the original name for this Paden City Glass Company pattern. The popular name today is Popeye & Olive. It was made in cobalt blue, crystal, green or red. The pattern was made in the 1930s and a 1932 ad shows the red as a new color.

BLUE
Bowl, 10 In. 15.00

RED
Bowl, 6 In. 15.00

Poppy No. 1, see Florentine No. 1

Poppy No. 2, see Florentine No. 2

Pretzel

Pretzel, also called No. 622 or Ribbon Candy, was made by Indiana Glass Company, Dunkirk, Indiana, in the 1930s. Only crystal was made. Some reproductions appeared in the 1970s.

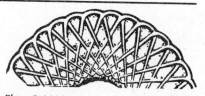

CRYSTAL
Bowl, 7 1/2 In. 2.25
Celery, Oval, 10 1/4 In. .. 1.50 To 3.00
Creamer .... 5.50 To 6.00
Cup & Saucer .... 3.00 To 3.50
Dish, Leaf-Shaped 3.00
Plate, 6 In. .... .75 To 1.50
Plate, 8 In. 2.50
Plate, 9 1/4 In. .... 3.00 To 5.00
Plate, 11 1/2 In. 6.00
Relish, 3-Handled .... 2.00 To 3.00
Saucer .... 1.00 To 1.50
Soup, Dish .... 2.00 To 2.50
Sugar .... 4.00 To 6.00
Sugar & Creamer .... 7.00 To 12.00

Primo

Green and mandarin yellow are the two colors of Primo advertised in the 1932 catalog for U.S. Glass Company.

YELLOW
Bowl, 4 1/2 In. 12.00
Cup .... 3.50 To 4.00
Cup & Saucer .... 5.50 To 6.00
Sugar .... 3.00 To 6.00
Tumbler, 5 In. 8.00

Primus, see Madrid

Princess

Hocking Glass Company, Lancaster, Ohio, made the popular Princess pattern from 1931 to 1935. The first sets were made in green, then in topaz. The amber sometimes came out a rather yellow shade, so if you are assembling a set be careful of the color variations. Pink was added last. There are blue pieces found in the West, but there is a debate about the age or origin of these pieces. Some pieces had a frosted finish, some are decorated with hand-painted flowers. Green is sometimes trimmed with gold, other colors are trimmed with platinum.

AMBER

Cup	6.00 To 9.00
Cup & Saucer	6.00 To 12.50
Grill Plate, 9 1/2 In.	6.00
Plate, 8 In.	6.50 To 8.50
Sherbet	17.50
Tumbler, Footed, 6 1/2 In.	14.00 To 19.00
Tumbler, 4 In.	12.00

BLUE

Creamer	9.75
Cup	4.75
Cup & Saucer	6.75
Pitcher, 8 In.	30.00
Plate, 8 In.	5.50
Plate, 9 1/2 In.	12.50

GREEN

Ashtray	40.00 To 57.75
Bowl, Hat-Shaped, 9 1/2 In.	16.00 To 25.00
Bowl, Octagonal, 9 In.	18.00 To 22.50
Bowl, Vegetable, 10 In.	11.00 To 15.00
Bowl, 4 1/2 In.	14.50 To 18.75
Bowl, 5 In.	12.00 To 20.00
Butter, Covered	60.00 To 75.00
Cake Plate	9.00 To 16.00
Candy Container, Covered	25.00 To 35.00
Coaster	13.00 To 19.00
Cookie Jar, Covered	29.00 To 36.00
Creamer	7.00 To 19.75
Cup	4.50 To 7.50
Cup & Saucer	5.00 To 12.25
Pitcher, 6 In.	24.00 To 32.50
Pitcher, 8 In.	27.00 To 36.00
Plate, Grill, 9 1/2 In.	7.50 To 8.50
Plate, Handled, 11 1/2 In.	13.00 To 18.00
Plate, Sherbet, 5 1/2 In.	3.00

Plate, 8 In.	5.00 To 9.50
Plate, 9 1/2 In.	12.00 To 20.00
Platter, 12 In.	9.00 To 15.00
Relish, Divided	15.00 To 18.75
Salt & Pepper	25.00 To 42.50
Saucer	3.00 To 4.50
Sherbet	8.00 To 12.50
Sugar & Creamer, Covered	18.00 To 30.00
Sugar, Covered	15.00 To 17.50
Tumbler, Footed, 5 1/4 In.	15.00 To 20.00
Tumbler, Footed, 6 1/2 In.	22.00 To 36.00
Tumbler, 3 In.	12.00 To 17.50
Tumbler, 4 In.	17.00 To 18.00
Tumbler, 5 1/4 In.	16.00 To 25.00
Vase	16.00 To 30.00

PINK

Bowl, Hat-Shaped, 9 1/2 In.	14.00 To 15.00
Bowl, Octagonal, 9 In.	25.00
Bowl, Vegetable, 10 In.	10.00 To 10.50
Bowl, 4 1/2 In.	3.50 To 11.00
Bowl, 5 In.	9.50 To 15.00
Butter, Covered	65.00 To 75.00
Cake Plate	12.00 To 12.50
Candy, Container, Covered	30.00 To 38.00
Cookie Jar, Covered	29.50 To 37.50
Creamer	7.00 To 9.00
Cup	2.50 To 7.00
Cup & Saucer	5.00 To 8.50
Grill, 9 1/2 In.	7.00
Pitcher, 6 In.	20.00 To 22.00
Pitcher, 8 In.	25.00 To 28.00
Plate, Grill, Close-Handled, 11 1/2 In.	7.00
Plate, 8 In.	5.00 To 6.50
Plate, 9 1/2 In.	8.00 To 10.00

Platter, 12 In.	9.25 To 10.00
Relish, Divided	22.00
Salt & Pepper, 4 1/2 In.	25.00 To 45.00
Saucer	3.00 To 4.00
Sherbet	8.00 To 10.00
Sugar & Creamer	15.00
Sugar, Covered	17.00
Tumbler, Footed, 4 3/4 In.	9.50 To 10.00
Tumbler, Footed, 5 1/4 In.	9.00 To 15.00
Tumbler, Footed, 6 1/2 In.	20.00 To 28.00
Tumbler, 3 In.	12.50 To 14.50
Tumbler, 4 In.	9.00 To 11.00
Tumbler, 5 1/4 In.	15.00 To 21.00
Vase	15.00 To 20.00

YELLOW

Bowl, Octagonal, 9 In. ...	40.00 To 90.00
Bowl, Vegetable, 10 In.	
....	20.00 To 35.00

Bowl, 5 In.	20.00 To 22.00
Creamer	8.00 To 12.00
Cup	3.50 To 5.50
Cup & Saucer	2.25 To 10.00
Plate, Sherbet, 5 1/2 In. ..	2.00 To 3.50
Plate, 8 In.	4.00 To 8.00
Plate, 9 1/2 In.	8.00 To 12.50
Plate, 12 In.	27.00
Salt & Pepper	55.00
Saucer	3.00
Sherbet	16.00 To 22.00
Sugar	7.00
Sugar & Creamer	20.00 To 40.00
Tumbler, Footed, 5 1/4 In.	
....	12.50 To 17.00
Tumbler, 3 In.	16.00
Tumbler, 4 In.	16.00 To 18.00
Tumbler, 5 1/4 In.	16.00 To 20.00

Princess Feather

Westmoreland Glass Company made Princess Feather pattern in 1939 through 1948. It was originally made in aqua, crystal, green or pink. In the 1960s a reproduction appeared in an amber shade called Golden Sunset. The pattern is sometimes called Early American, Flower, Oatmeal Lace, Scroll & Star or Westmoreland Sandwich.

CRYSTAL

Eye Cup	5.00
Goblet, Water	6.00
Mustard Spoon	7.00

GREEN

Candleholder, Round Base,	
7 1/2 In., Pair	75.00
Sherbet, 3 1/2 In.	12.00

PINK

Bowl, 6 1/2 In.	6.00

Candleholder, Round Base,	
7 1/2 In., Pair	75.00
Compote, 11 In., Dolphin	125.00
Goblet, 5 3/4 In.	16.00
Lamp, Dolphin	125.00
Plate, 5 1/4 In.	3.00
Salt & Pepper, Lids, Mini	10.00
Sherbet, 3 1/2 In.	12.00

Prismatic Line, see Queen Mary

Provincial, see Bubble

Pyramid, see No. 610

Queen Anne

Queen Anne is an Anchor Hocking pattern made in the late 1930s in crystal or pink. It is similar to Bee Hive pattern.

CRYSTAL
Butter, Covered 20.00
Tumbler, 4 In. 4.50

PINK
Bowl, 6 In. 20.00
Butter 17.50
Platter, 13 1/2 In. 40.00

Queen Mary

Queen Mary, sometimes called Prismatic Line or Vertical Ribbed, was made by Anchor Hocking Glass Company from 1936 to 1940. It was made in crystal, pink or red.

CRYSTAL
Ashtray 3.50
Bowl, Handled, 5 1/2 In. . 1.75 To 3.50
Bowl, 5 In. .... 1.50 To 3.00
Bowl, 6 In. .... 2.00 To 5.00
Bowl, 7 In. .... 4.50 To 8.00
Bowl, 8 3/4 In. .... 5.50 To 12.50
Butter, Covered .... 22.50 To 23.00
Candleholder, Pair ..... 10.00 To 20.00
Candy Container, Covered
.... 12.50 To 20.00
Celery, Oval 9.00
Coaster .... 1.50 To 2.00
Compote, Covered 12.50
Creamer 1.50
Cup .... 4.00 To 4.50
Cup & Saucer .... 6.00 To 6.50
Jar, Cigarette, Oval .... 6.00 To 9.00
Plate, 6 In. .... 2.00 To 3.00
Plate, 6 5/8 In. 2.50
Plate, 8 1/2 In. .... 3.50 To 5.00
Plate, 9 3/4 In. .... 7.50 To 8.50
Plate, 12 In. .... 4.50 To 10.00
Relish, 3 Part, 12 In. ..... 6.00 To 8.00
Relish, 4 Part, 14 In. 8.50
Salt & Pepper 30.00
Saucer 1.50
Sherbet .... 2.00 To 3.50
Sugar .... 2.00 To 4.50
Sugar & Creamer .... 7.00 To 12.50

PINK
Bowl, Handled, 5 1/2 In.
.... 3.50 To 4.50
Bowl, 4 In. .... 2.50 To 3.00
Bowl, 5 In. .... 2.00 To 5.00
Bowl, 6 In. .... 2.00 To 5.00
Bowl, 7 In. .... 4.00 To 6.50
Bowl, 8 3/4 In. .... 6.00 To 10.00
Candy Container, Covered
.... 25.00 To 35.00
Compote 5.00
Creamer .... 2.50 To 4.50
Cup .... 2.25 To 5.00
Cup & Saucer .... 4.50 To 7.00
Plate, 6 In. .... 1.00 To 2.75
Plate, 6 5/8 In. 4.00
Plate, 9 3/4 In. .... 12.00 To 18.00
Saucer .... 1.50 To 2.00
Sherbet .... 3.50 To 6.00
Sugar .... 3.50 To 4.00
Sugar & Creamer .... 6.50 To 15.00
Tumbler, Footed, 5 In. .. 14.00 To 18.00
Tumbler, 3 1/2 In. .... 2.50 To 5.00
Tumbler, 4 In. .... 4.00 To 7.00

RUBY RED
Candleholder 14.00

Radiance

New Martinsville Glass Company, New Martinsville, West Virginia, made Radiance pattern from 1936 to 1939. It was made of amber, cobalt, crystal, ice blue or red.

AMBER
Cup & Saucer 9.50

CRYSTAL
Ladle, Punch 18.50

RED
Creamer 15.00
Decanter, Handled, Stopper 90.00
Salt & Pepper 77.50
Sugar 9.00
Tumbler 13.50
Vase, 10 In. 55.00

Raindrops, see also Colony

Watch out for confusion with Raindrops and another pattern called Thumbprint or Pear Optic. The pattern for Raindrops is on the inside of the pieces, the other pattern is on the outside. Federal Glass Company made crystal and green Raindrop dinnerware from 1929 to 1933.

CRYSTAL
Whiskey .... 1.00 To 2.00

GREEN
8 In. 8.00
Cup .... 3.00 To 5.50

Cup & Saucer 3.75
Saucer 2.00
Tumbler .... 3.50 To 3.75
Whiskey, 2 In. 3.25

Raspberry Band, see Laurel

Rex, see No. 610

Ribbed, see Manhattan

Ribbon

Black, crystal, green or pink pieces were made in Ribbon pattern in the 1930s. It was made by the Hazel Glass Company.

CRYSTAL
Bottle, Decanter 8.00
Sugar & Creamer 8.00

GREEN
Bowl, 4 In. 4.50
Bowl, 8 In. 12.50
Candy Container, Covered 15.00 To 23.00

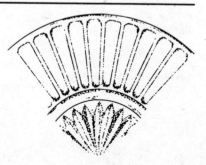

Compote 10.00
Creamer .... 2.75 To 5.50
Cup 4.00
Pitcher 16.00
Plate, Sherbet, 6 1/4 In. .. 2.50 To 2.75
Plate, 8 In. .... 2.50 To 4.50

Saltshaker 18.00
Sherbet .... 2.00 To 3.00
Sugar .... 2.75 To 4.25
Sugar & Creamer .... 5.25 To 12.50
Tumbler, 6 1/2 In. 11.50

Ribbon Candy, see Pretzel

Ring

Hocking Glass Company made Ring from
1927 to 1932. The pattern is sometimes
clear colored glass and sometimes has colored rings added. The clear glass is crystal,
green or pink, which may or may not be
decorated with rings of black, blue, orange,
pink, platinum, red or yellow.

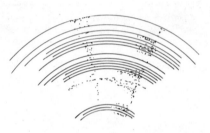

BLUE
Decanter & Stopper .... 21.00 To 30.00
Tumbler, 3 1/2 In. 3.25

CRYSTAL
Butter Tub, Multicolored Rings
.... 6.00 To 10.00
Cocktail Shaker, Multicolored Rings
.... 5.00 To 10.00
Creamer 2.75
Cup .... 2.00 To 2.50
Decanter & Stopper, Multicolored Rings
.... 12.00 To 18.00
Goblet, 7 1/4 In. 4.00
Pitcher, Multicolored Rings, 8 In. .. 8.00
Pitcher, Multicolored Rings, 8 1/2 In.
.... 17.00
Plate, Sherbet, Platinum Rings, 6 1/4 In.
.... 1.50
Plate, 8 In. .... 1.50 To 2.50
Sherbet, Platinum Rings, 4 3/4 In.
.... 4.50
Sherbet, 4 3/4 In. .... 3.50 To 4.00
Sugar, Gold Trim 2.50
Tumbler, Footed, Gold Rings, 6 1/2 In.
.... 3.00 To 7.00
Tumbler, Footed, 3 1/2 In.
.... 2.50 To 3.00
Tumbler, 4 1/4 In. 2.00
Whiskey 2.00

GREEN
Bowl, 5 In. 2.50
Bowl, 8 In. 6.00
Butter Tub 12.00
Cup 2.00
Cup & Saucer .... 3.00 To 4.50
Pitcher, 8 1/2 In. 17.00
Plate, Sherbet, 6 1/4 In. 2.50
Plate, 8 In. .... 2.50 To 3.00
Saucer 1.50
Tumbler, 3 1/2 In. .... 2.00 To 3.50
Tumbler, 4 1/4 In. 3.00
Tumbler, 5 1/8 In. 4.50

Rock Crystal

Rock Crystal was made in many solid colors by McKee Glass Company. Crystal was made in the 1920s. Colors of amber, blue-green, cobalt blue, crystal, green, pink, red or yellow were made in the 1930s.

AMBER

Cake Plate	18.00
Sandwich Server	18.50 To 28.00

CRYSTAL

Bowl, 5 In.	6.50
Candleholder, Double, Pair	20.00
Creamer, Footed	12.00
Cup & Saucer	10.00
Plate, 8 1/2 In.	4.00
Plate, 11 1/2 In.	15.00
Sherbet, Footed	5.00
Tumbler, Concave, 8 1/2 In.	9.25
Vase, Cornucopia	21.00

GREEN

Vase, Footed, 11 In.	37.50

PINK

Bowl, Footed, 12 1/2 In.	60.00
Pitcher, 9 In.	125.00
Sherbet	25.00
Tumbler, Footed, 5 1/2 In.	15.00

RED

Bowl, 5 In.	10.00
Goblet, 5 1/2 In.	7.00
Relish, 11 1/2 In.	7.00
Whiskey	30.00

Rope, see Colonial Fluted

Rose Cameo

Rose Cameo was made by the Belmont Tumbler Company, Bellaire, Ohio, in 1933. It has been found only in green.

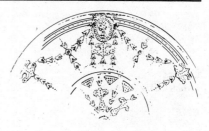

GREEN

Bowl, 4 1/2 In.	6.00
Bowl, 5 In.	3.00 To 6.00
Plate, 7 In.	3.00 To 6.00
Sherbet	3.00 To 5.00
Tumbler, Footed, Cone-Shaped	7.25

Rose Lace, see Royal Lace

Rosemary, see also Mayfair Federal

Rosemary, also called Cabbage Rose with Single Arch or Dutch Rose, was made by Federal Glass Company from 1935 to 1937. It was made in amber, green or pink. Pieces with bases like creamers or cups are sometimes confused with Mayfair Federal. The lower half of the Rosemary pieces are plain, the lower half of Mayfair Federal has a band of arches.

AMBER
Bowl, Vegetable, 10 In. . . 6.50 To 10.00
Bowl, 5 In. . . . . 2.00 To 5.00
Creamer 6.50
Cup . . . . 3.00 To 4.50
Cup & Saucer . . . . 5.00 To 12.75
Plate, Grill, 9 1/2 In. . . . . . 5.00 To 7.00
Plate, 9 1/2 In. . . . . 4.00 To 7.50
Plate, 9 3/4 In. . . . . 2.00 To 5.50
Platter, 12 In. . . . . 5.00 To 8.00
Saucer . . . . 1.25 To 3.00
Soup, Cream . . . . 5.00 To 9.00
Sugar & Creamer . . . . . . 11.00 To 12.75
Tumbler, 4 1/4 In. 14.00

GREEN
Bowl, 5 In. 5.50
Cup 5.00
Cup & Saucer 10.00

Plate, 9 1/2 In. 8.00
Platter, 12 In. 11.50
Saucer 2.00
Sugar . . . . 6.00 To 9.00

PINK
Bowl, Vegetable, 10 In. 15.00
Plate, 6 3/4 In. 4.50
Plate, 9 1/2 In. . . . . 8.00 To 11.50
Platter, 12 In. 14.00
Saucer 2.50
Soup, Cream 12.50
Sugar 10.00
Sugar & Creamer 19.00

Roulette

Anchor Hocking Glass Company made Roulette pattern from 1935 to 1939. It can be found in crystal, green or pink. Collectors originally called the pattern Many Windows.

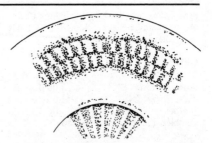

CRYSTAL
Tumbler, Flat, 4 1/4 In. 8.00

GREEN
Bowl, 9 In. . . . . 7.50 To 12.00
Cup . . . . 2.00 To 5.00
Cup & Saucer . . . . 3.00 To 5.00
Pitcher, 8 In. 20.00
Plate, Sherbet, 6 In. . . . . . 1.75 To 2.00
Plate, 8 1/2 In. . . . . 3.00 To 3.75
Plate, 12 In. 8.50
Saucer . . . . 2.00 To 2.50
Sherbet . . . . 1.00 To 4.00
Sugar & Creamer 3.50

Tumbler, Footed, 5 1/2 In.
. . . . 8.50 To 12.00
Tumbler, 5 1/8 In. 10.50

PINK
Pitcher, 8 In. 20.00
Tumbler, 5 1/8 In. 8.00
Whiskey . . . . 6.50 To 7.00

Round Robin

Sometimes a pattern was advertised by the wholesaler, but the manufacturer is unknown today. One of these is Round Robin, sometimes called Accordion Pleats, It was pictured in the catalogs of the late 1920s and 1930s and offered in green, crystal or iridescent marigold.

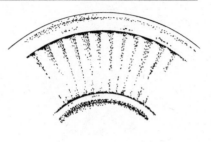

GREEN

Creamer	6.75
Cup & Saucer	3.50
Saucer	1.50 To 11.25
Sherbet	3.00 To 6.00
Sugar	5.00 To 6.00
Sugar & Creamer	9.75

IRIDESCENT

Plate, Sherbet, 6 In.	1.00

Sherbet	1.25 To 2.50
Sugar	2.50
Sugar & Creamer	9.75

Royal Lace

Royal Lace was made from 1934 to 1941. The popular pattern by Hazel Atlas Glass Company was made in amethyst, cobalt blue, crystal, green or pink. It is sometimes called Gladiola or Rose Lace.

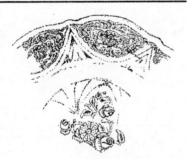

AMETHYST

Cider Set	195.00

BLUE

Bowl, Berry, 10 In.	28.00 To 35.00
Bowl, Rolled Edge, 3-Footed, 10 In.	165.00
Bowl, Ruffled Edge, 3-Footed, 10 In.	75.00
Bowl, Straight Edge, 3-Footed, 10 In.	32.50 To 55.00
Bowl, Vegetable, 11 In.	29.50 To 35.00
Bowl, 5 In.	15.00 To 30.00
Butter, Covered	395.00 To 430.00
Candleholder, Rolled Edge, Pair	90.00 To 130.00
Cider Set	175.00 To 195.00
Cookie Jar, Covered	198.00 To 225.00
Creamer	22.00 To 27.75
Cup	18.00 To 20.00
Cup & Saucer	19.00 To 26.00
Pitcher, Straight Side	69.50 To 95.00
Pitcher, 68 Oz., 8 In.	75.00 To 85.00
Pitcher, 96 Oz., 8 1/2 In.	225.00
Plate, Grill, 9 7/8 In.	17.00 To 21.00
Plate, Sherbet, 6 In.	4.00 To 7.50
Plate, 8 1/2 In.	14.00 To 27.50
Plate, 10 In.	20.00 To 25.00
Platter, 13 In.	30.00 To 35.00
Salt & Pepper	195.00 To 215.00
Saucer	4.00 To 6.00
Sherbet	16.00 To 24.00
Soup, Cream	17.00 To 25.00
Sugar	17.00 To 22.00
Sugar & Creamer, Covered	112.00 To 135.00
Tumbler, 3 1/2 In.	22.00 To 24.00
Tumbler, 4 1/8 In.	17.50 To 28.00
Tumbler, 5 3/8 In.	38.50 To 45.00

CRYSTAL

Bowl, 5 In.	8.50

Royal Lace

Bowl, 10 In. 9.00
Butter, Covered . . . . 30.00 To 50.00
Candleholder, Ruffled, Pair 42.00
Cookie Jar, Covered . . . . 22.00 To 35.00
Creamer . . . . 6.00 To 7.00
Cup . . . . 3.75 To 5.50
Cup & Saucer . . . . 5.50 To 8.50
Pitcher, 68 Oz., 8 In. 40.00
Pitcher, 86 Oz., 8 In. 37.50
Pitcher, 96 Oz., 8 1/2 In. 37.00 To 49.75
Plate, Grill, 9 7/8 In. . . . . . 5.00 To 8.50
Plate, Sherbet, 6 In. . . . . . . 2.00 To 2.50
Plate, 8 1/2 In. 4.50
Plate, 10 In. 5.00
Platter, 13 In. 11.50
Salt & Pepper 32.00
Saucer . . . . 1.50 To 2.00
Sherbet, Metal Holder . . . . 4.50 To 6.50
Soup, Cream 7.00
Sugar . . . . 4.00 To 6.50
Sugar & Creamer, Covered 25.00 To 26.00
Tumbler, 3 1/2 In. . . . . 5.50 To 9.00
Tumbler, 4 1/8 In. . . . . 6.50 To 8.00
Vegetable, 11 In. 12.00

GREEN

Bowl, Ruffled Edge, 3-Legged, 10 In. 45.00
Candle holder, Rolled Edge 20.00 To 27.50
Cookie Jar, Covered . . . . 39.50 To 45.00
Creamer 15.00
Cup 10.00
Cup & Saucer . . . . 17.00 To 18.00
Plate, Grill, 9 7/8 In. 14.50
Plate, Sherbet, 6 In. . . . . . . 3.00 To 5.00
Plate, 8 1/2 In. 12.00
Plate, 10 In. . . . . 14.00 To 16.00
Platter, 13 In. . . . . 20.00 To 22.00

Salt & Pepper . . . . 65.00 To 97.50
Sherbet . . . . 16.00 To 18.00
Soup, Cream . . . . 13.25 To 22.50
Sugar . . . . 10.00 To 15.00
Sugar & Creamer, Covered 55.00
Tumbler, 3 1/2 In. 17.00
Tumbler, 4 1/8 In. . . . . . 16.00 To 18.00

PINK

Bowl, Rolled Edge, 3-Legged, 10 In. 49.75
Bowl, Ruffled Edge, 3-Legged, 10 In.
. . . . 20.00 To 32.50
Bowl, Straight Edge, 3-Legged, 10 In. 14.50
Bowl, Vegetable, 11 In. 15.00
Bowl, 10 In. . . . . 10.00 To 12.00
Butter, Covered 110.00
Candleholder, Rolled Edge, Pair . . 45.00
Candleholder, Ruffled 16.00
Candleholder, Straight 16.00
Cookie Jar, Covered . . . . 30.00 To 45.00
Creamer 12.00
Cup . . . . 8.50 To 9.00
Cup & Saucer . . . . 4.50 To 12.00
Pitcher, 68 Oz., 8 In. . . . 48.00 To 60.00
Pitcher, 96 Oz., 8 1/2 In. 60.00
Plate, Grill, 9 7/8 In. . . . . 8.00 To 12.00
Plate, Sherbet, 6 In. 6.00
Plate, 8 1/2 In. . . . . 4.00 To 8.50
Plate, 10 In. . . . . 6.00 To 14.00
Platter, 13 In. . . . . 10.00 To 16.00
Salt & Pepper . . . . 35.00 To 65.00
Saucer . . . . 3.00 To 4.50
Sherbet . . . . 4.50 To 5.00
Soup, Cream . . . . 8.00 To 12.00
Sugar & Creamer, Covered 30.00
Sugar, Covered 14.00
Tumbler, 3 1/2 In. 14.50
Tumbler, 4 1/8 In. . . . . . . 8.00 To 14.50

Royal Ruby

There is no reason to picture this pattern because it is the plain shape and bright red color that identifies it. Anchor Hocking Glass Company made it in red from 1939 to the 1960s and again in 1977. The same shapes were made in green and called by the pattern name Forest Green.

RED

Ashtray, Round, 4 In.	2.50
Ashtray, Square, 4 1/2 In.	1.50
Bowl, Crimped, 6 1/4 In.	6.00
Bowl, Flared, 11 1/2 In.	20.00
Bowl, Square, 5 In.	1.50
Bowl, 8 1/2 In.	8.50
Creamer, Flat	5.00
Creamer, Footed	3.50 To 5.00
Cup	2.50 To 4.00
Cup & Saucer, Square	3.50 To 4.50
Cup, Punch	2.00 To 4.75
Goblet, Ball Stem	4.00 To 8.00
Jar, Jam, Covered	6.00
Pitcher, Tilted, 3 Qt.	22.50
Pitcher, Upright, 3 Qt.	24.00 To 27.00
Plate, Sherbet, 6 1/2 In.	1.50 To 3.50
Plate, Square, 7 3/4 In.	3.50
Plate, 9 In.	4.00 To 5.00

Punch Set, 6 Cups	32.00
Saucer	1.25 To 1.50
Sherbet	2.00 To 6.00
Soup, Dish	6.00 To 8.00
Sugar & Creamer, Flat	8.75 To 11.00
Sugar & Creamer, Footed	11.00
Sugar, Flat	3.50 To 5.00
Sugar, Footed	3.25 To 5.00
Toothpick	2.50
Tumbler, Collar Base, 4 3/4 In.	4.00
Tumbler, Footed, 3 1/2 In.	7.00
Tumbler, Footed, 4 5/8 In.	4.00
Tumbler, Footed, 5 In.	4.00 To 5.00
Tumbler, Footed, 8 In.	3.50
Tumbler, Twisted Stem, 5 1/8 In.	10.00
Tumbler, 2 1/2 In.	3.00
Tumbler, 5 In.	4.50
Vase, Bulb	4.00
Vase, Coolidge	3.50 To 4.00
Vase, Crimped, 3 In.	2.00
Vase, Globe, 11 X 10 In.	85.00
Vase, Harding, 6 3/8 In.	4.00
Vase, Ivy Ball, 3 3/4 In.	3.00
Vase, Ivy Ball, 5 3/4 In.	4.00
Vase, Ruffled Top, 8 1/2 In.	8.00
Vase, Scalloped Lip, 9 In.	8.00

Russian, see Holiday

S Pattern

Macbeth-Evans Glass Company made S Pattern from 1930 to 1935. It was made before 1932 in crystal, pink, topaz or crystal with gold, blue or platinum trim. The 1934-1935 listing mentions red, green and Monax. Other pieces were made in amber, ruby, Ritz Blue and crystal with many colors of trim including amber, green, rose, platinum, red or white.

AMBER

Cup	3.00
Cup & Saucer	3.75 To 4.25
Plate, Grill, 10 1/2 In.	5.50
Plate, Sherbet, 6 In.	3.75
Plate, 8 In.	2.50
Plate, 9 1/4 In.	5.50
Saucer	1.00

Sugar	3.00	Cup & Saucer	4.50
Tumbler, 4 In.	4.50	Plate, Sherbet, 6 In.	1.50
Tumbler, 5 In.	6.50	Sherbet	4.50

CRYSTAL

Bowl, 5 1/2 In.	2.00 To 3.50
Creamer	3.00
Cup	2.00 To 3.50
Cup & Saucer	3.50 To 4.50
Plate, 8 In.	2.50 To 4.00
Plate, 11 In.	23.00 To 25.00
Saucer	.50 To 1.25
Sugar	1.50 To 5.00
Sugar & Creamer	7.00
Tumbler, 4 In.	3.00 To 6.50
Tumbler, 5 In.	4.00 To 4.50

CRYSTAL WITH AMBER TRIM

Creamer	4.50
Cup	3.00

CRYSTAL WITH GOLD TRIM

Sugar & Creamer	8.00

CRYSTAL WITH PLATINUM TRIM

Sugar & Creamer, Platinum Rim	10.00
Tumbler, 4 1/4 In.	5.50

MONAX

Plate, Sherbet, 6 In.	9.75

PINK

Bowl, 5 1/2 In.	3.50
Sugar	5.00

RED

Plate, 8 In.	45.00

Sail Boat, see White Ship

Sailing Ship, see White Ship

Sandwich Anchor Hocking

Many patterns were called Sandwich. Each company seemed to have one design with that name. The Hocking Glass Company Sandwich pattern was made from 1939 to 1964. Pink and royal ruby were used in 1939-1940; crystal, forest green and opaque white were used in the 1950s and 1960s; amber was used in the 1960s. A reproduction line was introduced in 1977 by another company in amber, blue, crystal or red.

AMBER

Bowl, 4 7/8 In.	2.00 To 2.75
Bowl, 7 In.	5.00
Butter	30.00
Cookie Jar, Covered	25.00 To 27.50
Cup	2.00
Cup & Saucer	3.00 To 5.50
Plate, 9 In.	4.00
Saucer	1.00 To 1.25

CRYSTAL

Bowl, Oval, 8 1/4 In.	3.00 To 4.00
Bowl, Scalloped, 6 1/2 In.	4.00 To 8.00
Bowl, 4 7/8 In.	1.25 To 3.00
Bowl, 5 1/4 In.	4.00
Bowl, 7 In.	3.50 To 5.00
Bowl, 8 In.	12.00
Butter, Covered	22.50 To 30.00
Cookie Jar, Covered	20.00 To 25.00
Creamer	2.00 To 3.00
Cup & Saucer	2.50 To 4.00
Cup, Punch	1.00 To 2.00
Decanter & Stopper	14.00
Pitcher, 1/2 Gal.	38.00 To 40.00
Plate, Cup Ring, 9 In.	2.50 To 5.00
Plate, 8 In.	3.00
Plate, 9 In.	5.00 To 8.50

Punch Bowl 15.00
Punch Set, 12 Cups 25.00
Sherbet .... 3.00 To 4.00
Sugar .... 1.50 To 12.00
Sugar & Creamer .... 5.00 To 8.00
Tumbler, Footed, 5 1/2 In.
.... 8.00 To 10.00
Tumbler, Water, 4 1/2 In.
.... 4.00 To 5.00
Tumbler, 3 1/2 In. .... 2.00 To 4.00

FOREST GREEN
Bowl, 4 7/8 In. .... 2.25 To 3.00
Bowl, 6 1/2 In. 18.50
Cookie Jar .... 12.50 To 21.00

Creamer 12.00
Cup 13.00
Cup & Saucer .... 4.00 To 18.00
Custard .... 2.00 To 2.25
Pitcher, 1/2 Gal. .... 175.00 To 200.00
Pitcher, 6 In. .... 80.00 To 100.00
Plate, 9 In. .... 29.00 To 42.00
Tumbler, 3 1/2 In. .... .75 To 3.00
Tumbler, 4 1/2 In. .... 2.00 To 4.00

GREEN
Cup 13.00

WHITE
Punch Set, 12 Cups .... 25.00 To 40.00

Sandwich Indiana

Another Sandwich pattern was made by the Indiana Glass Company, Dunkirk, Indiana, from the 1920s through the 1980s. Only the colors changed through the years. Amber was made from the late 1920s to the 1970s, crystal in the late 1920s to the 1980s, light green in the 1930s, pink in the late 1920s through the 1930s, red from 1933 to the 1970s and teal blue in the 1950s. The scroll design varies with the size of the plate.

BLUE
Cruet, Stopper 135.00
Cup .... 4.50 To 6.00
Plate, Oval, Indentation, 8 In. 7.50
Sherbet 6.00
Sugar & Creamer, Tray, Diamond
.... 25.00

CRYSTAL
Ashtray, 4-Piece Set ..... 8.00 To 16.00
Bowl, 4 1/4 In. 4.00
Bowl, 6-Sided, 6 In. 3.00
Bowl, 8 1/4 In. 9.50
Butter, Aluminum Cover 40.00
Cake Plate 43.00
Candleholder, 3 1/2 In. .. 8.00 To 12.00
Cruet 29.75
Cup .... 2.00 To 2.50
Cup & Saucer .... 3.75 To 5.00
Cup, Punch 1.50
Plate, Sherbet, Oval, Indentation, 8 In.
.... 3.00

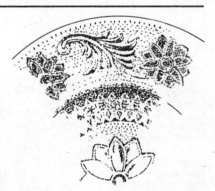

Plate, 7 In. 4.00
Plate, 8 3/8 In. .... 2.50 To 3.50
Plate, 10 1/2 In. 12.00
Sandwich Server 24.50
Sherbet .... 3.50 To 4.00
Sugar & Creamer, Tray
.... 10.00 To 14.25
Sugar, Diamond-Shaped ... 1.00 To 3.00
Tray, Diamond-Shaped 4.00

GREEN
Ashtray, Club-Shaped 1.50
Cup 8.00
Plate, Sherbet, 6 In. 4.00
Plate, 10 1/2 In. 20.00

RED
Sugar 22.00

Sawtooth, see English Hobnail
Saxon, see Coronation

Scroll & Star, see Princess Feather
Shamrock, see Cloverleaf
Sharon

Sharon or Cabbage Rose was made by the Federal Glass Company from 1935 to 1939. The pattern was made in amber, crystal, green or pink. A reproduced version of Sharon made in 1976 was made in amber, blue, dark green, light green and pink.

AMBER
Bowl, Vegetable, 9 1/2 In.
.... 6.00 To 9.00
Bowl, 5 In. .... 4.50 To 5.00
Bowl, 6 In. 9.00
Bowl, 8 1/2 In. .... 4.00 To 8.00
Bowl, 10 1/2 In. ...... 8.00 To 14.50
Butter, Covered .... 20.00 To 35.00
Cake Plate .... 12.00 To 25.00
Candy Container, Covered
.... 20.00 To 37.00
Compote 14.50
Creamer .... 5.00 To 10.00
Cup .... 7.50 To 70.00
Cup & Saucer .... 6.00 To 11.00
Dish, Cheese, Covered
.... 130.00 To 147.50
Pitcher, Ice Lip, 9 In. ... 80.00 To 97.00
Plate, 6 In. .... 2.00 To 3.00
Plate, 7 1/2 In. .... 8.00 To 11.00
Plate, 9 1/2 In. .... 7.00 To 10.00
Platter, 12 1/2 In. ...... 7.00 To 15.00
Relish 10.50
Salt & Pepper .... 17.00 To 35.00
Saucer .... 1.50 To 3.00
Sherbet, Footed .... 6.75 To 8.00
Soup, Cream .... 15.00 To 22.00
Sugar & Creamer, Covered
.... 26.00 To 28.00
Sugar, Covered .... 19.00 To 22.00
Sugar, Open .... 4.50 To 6.00
Tumbler, Footed, 6 1/2 In.
.... 45.00 To 62.50
Tumbler, 4 1/8 In. ..... 16.50 To 22.00
Tumbler, 5 1/4 In. ..... 18.00 To 27.50

CRYSTAL
Cake Plate, Footed, Metal Cover
.... 11.00
Plate, 7 1/2 In. 7.00
Plate, 9 1/2 In. 10.00
Sugar, Covered 26.00

GREEN
Bowl, Vegetable, 9 1/2 In.
.... 14.00 To 22.00
Bowl, 5 In. .... 4.00 To 8.00
Bowl, 8 1/2 In. .... 14.00 To 15.00
Bowl, 10 1/2 In. ...... 16.00 To 22.00
Butter, Covered .... 60.00 To 75.00
Creamer .... 9.00 To 9.50
Cup .... 8.50 To 9.00
Cup & Saucer .... 11.50 To 19.00
Dish, Jam, 7 1/2 In. 20.00
Plate, 6 In. .... 3.00 To 6.50
Plate, 7 1/2 In. .... 10.00 To 12.50
Plate, 9 1/2 In. .... 7.00 To 12.00
Platter, 12 1/2 In. ..... 10.00 To 15.00
Salt & Pepper 60.00
Saucer .... 1.00 To 2.50
Sherbet 7.50
Soup, Cream .... 15.00 To 18.00
Sugar .... 8.00 To 9.50
Sugar, Covered 35.00
Tumbler, 4 1/8 In. 28.00

PINK
Bowl, Vegetable, 9 1/2 In.
.... 10.50 To 13.00
Bowl, 5 In. .... 5.00 To 8.00
Bowl, 6 In. .... 10.00 To 16.00
Bowl, 8 1/2 In. .... 10.00 To 12.50
Bowl, 10 1/2 In. ...... 14.00 To 19.75
Butter, Covered .... 30.00 To 45.00
Cake Plate .... 15.00 To 25.00
Candy Container, Covered
.... 25.00 To 45.00
Creamer .... 6.50 To 10.00
Cup .... 8.25 To 8.50

Cup & Saucer .... 7.00 To 12.50	Sugar .... 7.00 To 8.00
Dish, Jam .... 65.00 To 78.00	Sugar & Creamer, Covered 26.50 To 38.00
Plate, 6 In. .... .50 To 3.50	Sugar, Covered .... 18.75 To 24.50
Plate, 7 1/2 In. .... 8.00 To 12.00	Sugar, Open .... 7.00 To 8.50
Plate, 9 1/2 In. .... 9.00 To 12.00	Tumbler, Footed, 6 1/2 In.
Platter, 12 1/2 In. ..... 12.00 To 22.00	.... 25.00 To 35.00
Salt & Pepper .... 32.00 To 40.00	Tumbler, Thick, 4 1/8 In.
Saucer .... 2.50 To 4.50	.... 17.00 To 24.00
Sherbet .... 7.00 To 10.50	Tumbler, Thin, 5 1/4 In.
Soup, Cream .... 20.00 To 27.00	.... 22.50 To 25.00
Soup, Dish .... 20.00 To 27.00	

Sheffield, see Chinex Classic
Shell, see Petalware
Shirley Temple

Shirley Temple is not really a pattern, but the dishes with the white enamel decoration picturing Shirley have become popular with collectors. They were made as giveaways with cereal from 1934 to 1942. Companies, including Hazel Atlas Glass Company and U.S. Glass, made the dishes. Sugars and creamers, bowls, plates and mugs were made.

COBALT BLUE

Creamer 35.00
Mug .... 40.00 To 60.00

Pitcher .... 25.00 To 27.00

Sierra

Sierra or Pinwheel was made by Jeannette Glass Company from 1931 to 1933. It is found in green or pink.

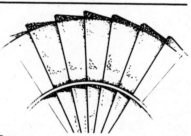

GREEN

Bowl, Vegetable, 9 1/4 In. 25.00
Bowl, 5 1/2 In. .... 6.00 To 10.00
Butter, Covered .... 40.00 To 45.00
Creamer 9.50
Cup .... 7.00 To 8.00
Cup & Saucer .... 8.50 To 10.00
Plate, 9 In. .... 8.00 To 9.50
Platter, 11 In. 18.00
Saltshaker 13.50
Sugar, Covered .... 11.00 To 17.00
Tray, Handled 11.00

Creamer 6.00
Cup 8.00
Cup & Saucer .... 7.00 To 10.00
Pitcher, 6 1/2 In. 32.50
Plate, Dinner .... 5.00 To 8.00
Platter, 11 In. .... 14.50 To 20.00
Salt & Pepper 22.50
Saucer 3.25
Sugar .... 4.50 To 5.50
Sugar & Creamer, Covered 26.00
Tray, Handled .... 7.00 To 11.00
Tumbler, 4 1/2 In. 29.50

PINK

Bowl, Vegetable, 9 1/4 In. 12.00
Bowl, 5 1/2 In. .... 4.00 To 8.00
Bowl, 8 1/2 In. .... 8.75 To 12.00
Butter, Covered .... 40.00 To 42.00

Smocking, see Windsor

Snowflake, see Doric

Sphinx, see Centaur

Spiral

It is easy to confuse Spiral and Twisted Optic Pattern. Ask to be shown examples of each, because even a picture will not be much help. In general the rule is that Twisted Optic spirals to the right or counterclockwise, Spiral goes to the left or clockwise. There are a few pieces that are exceptions. The spiral pattern was made from 1928 to 1930 in green by Hocking Glass Company.

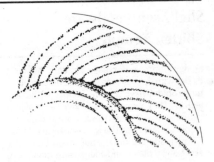

GREEN

Bowl, 4 3/4 In.	4.00
Bowl, 8 In.	15.00
Butter Tub	10.00
Candy Container, Covered	12.00 To 12.75
Creamer	5.00
Cup	3.00 To 4.50
Cup & Saucer	3.75 To 5.00
Pitcher, 7 5/8 In.	17.50 To 35.00
Plate, Sherbet, 6 In.	1.00 To 2.00
Plate, 8 In.	2.00 To 4.50
Preserve, Covered	12.00 To 15.00
Saucer	3.00
Sherbet	2.50 To 4.00
Sugar	4.00 To 5.00

Spiral Flutes

Duncan Miller Glass Company, Washington, Pennsylvania, made Spiral Flutes pattern. It was made of amber, crystal or green glass in 1924, pink in 1926. A few pieces are reported with gold trim and in blue or vaseline-colored glass.

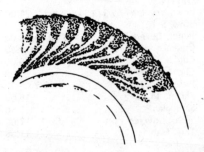

AMBER

Cup & Saucer	6.00
Sherbet	2.50

CRYSTAL

Plate, Gold Rim, 6 In.	1.00

GREEN

Bowl, Flared, 12 In.	18.00
Bowl, 7 1/2 In.	7.50
Plate, 7 5/8 In.	5.00
Plate, 8 5/8 In.	3.50

Spiral Optic, see Spiral

Spoke, see Patrician

Sportsman Series

Hazel Atlas Glass Company made an unusual Depression glass pattern in the 1940s. It was made of cobalt blue, amethyst or crystal with fired-on decoration. Although the name of the series was Sportsman, designs included golf, sailboats, hunting and angelfish and a few strange choices like Windmills. We list Windmill and White Ships separately, although they are sometimes considered part of this pattern.

BLUE & WHITE

Saltshaker, Fish	14.00
Saltshaker, Hunter On Horse, Dogs	16.00
Tumbler, Fish, 4 5/7 In.	4.75
Tumbler, Horse's Head, 4 1/2 In.	8.50

Spun

Spun is an Imperial Glass Company, Bellaire, Ohio, line patented in 1935. It was made in aqua, crystal, red and fired-on colors of orange and pastels.

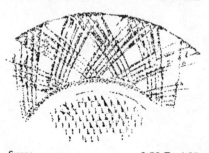

CRYSTAL

Bowl, 10 In.	10.00
Plate, 12 In.	10.00
Tumbler, 5 In.	2.00

Starlight

Hazel Atlas Glass Company made Starlight pattern from 1938 to 1940. Most pieces were made of crystal or pink glass. Some opaque white and a few cobalt pieces are known.

CRYSTAL

Creamer	4.25 To 5.00
Cup	3.75
Cup & Saucer	3.50 To 6.50
Plate, 6 In.	1.50
Plate, 8 1/2 In.	2.00 To 3.00
Plate, 9 In.	5.00
Salt & Pepper	18.00 To 19.50
Sugar	3.50 To 4.25
Sugar & Creamer	6.50 To 7.50

Stippled Rose, see S Pattern

Strawberry, see also Cherry-Berry

Strawberry and Cherry-Berry are similar patterns. The U.S. Glass Company made this pattern in the early 1930s with strawberry decoration. It was made in crystal, green, pink or iridescent marigold.

GREEN
Bowl, 4 In. 16.00
Bowl, 7 1/2 In. 12.50
Butter, Covered ...... 95.00 To 120.00
Pitcher, 7 3/4 In. .... 120.00 To 125.00
Sherbet .... 5.75 To 6.50
Sugar, Large 24.00
Tumbler, 3 5/8 In. 18.00

IRIDESCENT
Bowl, 4 In. 5.00

PINK
Bowl, 4 In. 11.00
Compote, 5 3/4 In. 11.50
Pitcher, 7 3/4 In. .... 120.00 To 135.00
Plate, 7 1/2 In. 10.00
Sherbet 6.00

Sunflower

Sunflower was made by Jeannette Glass Company, Jeannette, Pennsylvania, in the late 1920s and early 1930s. It is found in delphite, pink or one of two shades of green.

GREEN
Ashtray .... 4.00 To 8.00
Cake Plate .... 6.50 To 15.00
Creamer 7.50
Cup .... 7.50 To 8.50
Plate, 9 In. 7.50
Saucer 4.00
Sugar 8.00
Sugar & Creamer 25.00
Tumbler, 4 3/4 In. ..... 12.00 To 13.50

PINK
Ashtray .... 6.50 To 10.50

Cake Plate .... 5.50 To 15.00
Creamer .... 9.00 To 11.00
Cup .... 7.50 To 8.50
Cup & Saucer .... 8.00 To 9.50
Plate, 9 In. .... 7.50 To 11.00
Sugar & Creamer ...... 18.00 To 22.00
Tumbler, 4 3/4 In. ...... 9.00 To 15.00

Sweet Pear, see Avocado

Swirl

Swirl, sometimes called Double Swirl or Petal Swirl, was made by Jeannette Glass Company during 1937 and 1938. It was made of amber, delphite, ice blue, pink or a green-blue color called ultramarine.

AMBER
Candleholder, Pair 10.00
Candy Container, Covered 57.50
Candy Container, Footed 6.50
Plate, 9 1/4 In. 8.00
Salt & Pepper 20.00

DELPHITE
Bowl, 5 1/4 In. 7.50
Bowl, 9 In. . . . . 9.50 To 15.00
Creamer 8.00
Plate, Sherbet, 6 1/2 In. . . 3.00 To 3.50
Plate, 9 1/4 In. . . . . 5.00 To 6.00
Platter, 12 In. 22.50
Sugar . . . . 7.00 To 8.00

PINK
Ashtray, Embossed, Pennsylvania Tire
. . . . 16.75
Butter 55.00
Butter, Covered . . . . . . 90.00 To 125.00
Candy Container, Covered 30.00 To 55.00
Candy Container, Footed . . 5.25 To 7.50
Coaster . . . . 4.50 To 5.00
Creamer . . . . 4.00 To 5.25
Cup 6.50
Plate, Sherbet, 6 In. 2.25
Plate, 9 1/4 In. . . . . 4.50 To 9.50
Saucer 1.50
Sherbet 4.00
Sugar & Creamer 11.00
Tumbler, 4 In. 5.00
Tumbler, 4 5/8 In. 8.00
Tumbler, 4 3/4 In. 7.50
Vase, 6 1/2 In. 7.00
Vase, 8 1/2 In. 10.00

ULTRAMARINE
Bowl, Closed-Handled, 10 In.
. . . . 16.00 To 22.50
Bowl, Console, 10 1/2 In.
. . . . 14.50 To 16.00
Bowl, 5 1/4 In. . . . . 4.00 To 7.50

Bowl, 9 In. . . . . 10.00 To 14.50
Butter . . . . 185.00 To 220.00
Candleholder, Double, Pair
. . . . 17.25 To 25.00
Candy Container, Covered
. . . . 50.00 To 85.00
Candy Container, Footed . . 5.00 To 9.00
Console 10.00
Creamer . . . . 5.00 To 8.50
Cup . . . . 4.50 To 5.50
Cup & Saucer . . . . 5.50 To 8.50
Plate, Sherbet, 6 1/2 In. . . 2.00 To 3.50
Plate, 7 1/4 In. 4.00
Plate, 8 In. . . . . 4.00 To 7.75
Plate, 9 1/4 In. . . . . 6.00 To 9.75
Salt & Pepper . . . . 18.00 To 30.00
Sandwich Server, 12 1/2 In.
. . . . 8.00 To 12.00
Saucer . . . . 1.00 To 2.50
Sherbet . . . . 5.00 To 8.50
Sugar . . . . 5.00 To 6.00
Sugar & Creamer . . . . 6.00 To 15.50
Tumbler, 4 In. 12.00
Vase, 8 1/2 In. . . . . 9.00 To 16.50

Swirled Big Rib, see Spiral

Swirled Sharp Rib, see Diana

Sylvan

Sylvan is often called Parrot or Three Parrot because of the center pattern on the plates. It was made by Federal Glass Company in 1931 and 1932 in amber, blue, crystal or green.

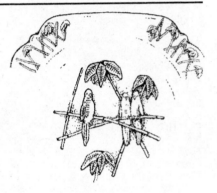

AMBER
Cup 28.00
Sherbet .... 2.00 To 10.50

GREEN
Bowl, Vegetable, 10 In.
.... 30.00 To 40.00
Bowl, 5 In. 12.00
Bowl, 8 In. .... 50.00 To 60.00
Butter, Covered ..... 245.00 To 250.00
Creamer .... 15.00 To 25.00
Cup .... 16.00 To 19.00
Cup & Saucer .... 22.00 To 35.00
Plate, Grill, 10 1/2 In. 20.00
Plate, 7 1/2 In. .... 12.00 To 20.00
Plate, 9 In. .... 20.00 To 35.00
Platter, 11 1/4 In. 27.50
Salt & Pepper 175.00
Saucer .... 7.00 To 8.00
Sherbet, Footed, Cone-Shaped
.... 15.00 To 20.00

Sugar 14.00
Sugar & Creamer ...... 25.00 To 35.00
Sugar, Covered .... 40.00 To 60.00
Tumbler, Footed, 5 3/4 In.
.... 65.00 To 75.00
Tumbler, 5 1/2 In. 65.00

Tassell, see Princess

Tea Room

The very Art Deco design of Tea Room has made it popular with a special group of collectors; it is even called Moderne Art by some. The Indiana Glass Company, Dunkirk, Indiana, made it from 1926 to 1931. Dinner sets were made of amber, crystal, green or pink glass.

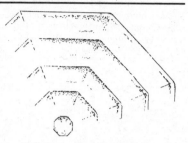

CRYSTAL
Bowl, Vegetable, 9 1/2 In. 30.00
Salt & Pepper 69.50
Tumbler, Footed, 6 3/4 In. 12.00
Vase, Ruffled Edge, 9 In.
.... 17.00 To 23.00

GREEN
Candleholder, Pair 42.00
Creamer 11.00
Ice Bucket 42.50
Lamp, Electric, 9 In. .... 35.00 To 45.00
Pitcher .... 115.00 To 125.00
Plate, 8 1/4 In. 18.00
Relish, Oval, 8 1/2 In. 12.50
Saltshaker 24.00
Sandwich Server .... 25.00 To 30.00
Saucer 13.00
Sherbet 16.00
Sugar .... 9.00 To 11.00

Sugar & Creamer, Tray, Rectangular
.... 34.00 To 60.00
Vase, Ruffled Edge, 9 In.
.... 25.00 To 35.00
Water Set, 6 Tumblers 225.00

PINK
Bowl, Vegetable, 9 1/2 In.
.... 32.00 To 42.50
Bowl, 8 3/4 In. 28.50
Candleholder, Pair ..... 27.50 To 34.00
Creamer, 4 In. .... 9.00 To 11.00
Sugar & Creamer, Rectangular, Tray
.... 35.00
Sugar & Creamer, 4 In. 19.00
Sugar, 4 In. 9.50
Tumbler, 5 1/4 In. 15.75

Tear Drop

Tear Drop, a pattern made in full dinnerware sets, was made by Duncan & Miller Glass Company, Washington, Pennsylvania, from 1934 to at least 1943. It was made in crystal.

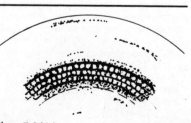

CRYSTAL
Bowl, Handled, 11 3/4 In. 15.00
Compote, 3 1/4 X 5 1/4 In. 10.00
Cup 6.00
Cup & Saucer 9.00
Goblet, Champagne ...... 8.00 To 9.00
Plate, Handled, 11 In. 18.00
Plate, 7 3/4 In. 6.50
Relish, 10 In. 10.00
Tumbler, Cocktail 6.00

Thistle

Thistle pattern was made by Macbeth-Evans Glass Company from 1929 to 1930. The pattern pictured large thistles on the pink, green, crystal or yellow dishes.

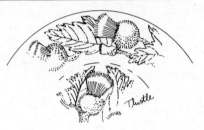

CRYSTAL
Butter, Covered 30.00

PINK
Bowl, 5 1/2 In. 12.00
Butter, Covered 30.00
Cake Plate, 13 In. 70.00
Cup . . . .   9.00 To 12.50
Plate, 8 In. . . . .   5.00 To 8.00
Saucer 7.00

Threading, see Old English

Three Parrot, see Sylvan

Thumbprint, see Pear Optic

Tiered Block, see Line 191

Tiered Octagon, see Octagon

Tiered Semi Optic, see Line 191

Twisted Optic

Twisted Optic is the pattern sometimes confused with Spiral. Be sure to look at the information about that pattern. Imperial Glass Company made Twisted Optic from 1927 to 1930 in amber, blue, canary yellow, green or pink.

GREEN
Candleholder, 3 In. 9.00
Plate, Sherbet, 6 In. . . . . . .   1.50 To 1.75
Plate, 8 In. . . . .   2.00 To 4.00
Vase, Crimped, 8 1/4 In. 12.50

PINK
Bowl, 7 In. 5.00
Creamer 9.00
Cup & Saucer . . . .   3.50 To 6.00
Pitcher, 64 Oz. 15.00
Plate, Sherbet, 6 In. 1.75
Sherbet . . . .   4.00 To 4.75
Soup, Cream 7.50
Sugar 3.00
Sugar & Creamer 9.00

U.S. Octagon, see Octagon

Vernon, see No. 616

Versailles

Versailles by Fostoria Glass Company was made in many colors during the years of production 1928 to 1944. Azure, green or rose were made from 1928 to 1944, topaz from 1929 to 1938, gold-tinted glass from 1938 to 1944 and crystal bases with colored glass from 1931 to 1944.

GREEN
Bowl, 12 In. 30.00

YELLOW
Bowl, 6 In. 22.50
Bowl, 12 In. 30.00

Vertical Ribbed, see Queen Mary

Victory

The Diamond Glass-Ware Company, Indiana, Pennsylvania, made Victory pattern from 1929 to 1932. It is known in amber, black, cobalt blue, green or pink. A few pieces have gold trim.

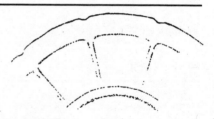

AMBER
Cup . . . . 2.00 To 5.00
Plate, 7 In. 9.00
Saucer 3.00

GREEN
Candleholder, Gold Trim, Pair
. . . . 15.00 To 17.50
Cup 4.75
Cup & Saucer 6.00

PINK
Bowl, Vegetable, 9 In. 15.00
Cup & Saucer 5.50
Plate, 8 In. 4.00
Plate, 9 In. 6.00
Platter, 12 In. 15.00

Sylvan

Windsor

Vitrock

Vitrock is both a kitchenware and a dinner-ware pattern. It has a raised flowered rim and so is often called Floral Rim or Flower Rim by collectors. It was made by Hocking Glass Company from 1934 to 1937. It was made of white with fired-on colors, solid red or green, or decal-decorated centers.

FIRED-ON BLUE
Vase, 7 1/2 In. 6.00

WHITE
Bowl, 4 In. 2.00
Bowl, 6 In. 2.00
Creamer . . . .   3.00 To 4.00
Cup & Saucer 2.50
Plate, 7 1/4 In. 2.50

Saucer . . . .   .50 To 2.00
Soup, Cream 2.00
Sugar 3.00

Vivid Bands, see Petalware

Waffle, see Waterford

Waterford

Waterford or Waffle pattern was made by Anchor Hocking Glass Company from 1938 to 1944. It was made in crystal, pink, yellow or white. In the 1950s some forest green pieces were made.

CRYSTAL
Ashtray 3.00
Bowl, 4 3/4 In. . . . .   2.50 To 7.50
Bowl, 8 1/4 In. . . . .   4.75 To 8.50
Butter, Covered . . . .   14.00 To 17.50
Cake Plate, Handled . . . . .   3.00 To 6.00
Coaster . . . .   1.00 To 4.00
Cup . . . .   3.50 To 4.00
Cup & Saucer 8.00
Goblet, 5 1/4 In. 9.75
Lamp 18.00
Pitcher, Tilted, 42 Oz. . .   10.00 To 12.50
Pitcher, Tilted, 80 Oz. . .   15.00 To 22.50
Plate, Sherbet, 6 In. . . . . . .   1.00 To 2.75
Plate, 7 1/8 In. . . . .   1.25 To 3.00
Plate, 9 5/8 In. . . . .   3.00 To 5.00
Plate, 13 3/4 In. . . . .   4.50 To 6.00
Relish . . . .   8.00 To 15.00

Saucer . . . .   1.25 To 2.00
Sherbet . . . .   2.25 To 6.00
Sugar, Covered . . . .   4.50 To 6.00
Tumbler, Footed, 4 7/8 In.
. . . .   6.00 To 6.75

GREEN
Plate, 13 3/4 In. . . . .   6.00 To 8.00
Relish 14.75

PINK
Bowl, 4 3/4 In. . . . .   3.00 To 6.00
Bowl, 5 1/2 In. 7.50
Bowl, 8 1/4 In. . . . .   9.50 To 12.00
Butter, Covered . . . . .   125.00 To 160.00
Cake Plate, Handled, 10 1/4 In. . . .   5.00
Cup & Saucer . . . .   8.50 To 12.50
Plate, 7 1/8 In. 8.00
Plate, 9 5/8 In. . . . .   8.00 To 10.00
Plate, 13 1/2 In. . . . .   7.50 To 9.00
Saucer . . . .   1.50 To 3.50
Sherbet . . . .   5.00 To 6.00
Sugar, Covered 10.50
Tumbler, Footed, 4 7/8 In. 9.00

Wedding Band, see Moderntone

Westmoreland Sandwich, see Princess Feather

White Sail, see White Ship

White Ship

White Ship, also called Sailing Ship, Sail Boat or White Sail, is really part of the Sportsman series made by Hazel Atlas in 1938. The ships are enamel decorations on cobalt blue glass.

BLUE
Cocktail Shaker . . . . 15.00 To 26.50
Pitcher, Ice Lip, 80 Oz. 25.00
Plate, 9 In. . . . . 10.00 To 15.00
Tumbler, 3 1/4 In. 4.25
Tumbler, 5 1/2 In. . . . . 3.00 To 5.00
Water Set, 5 Tumblers 70.00

Wildflower, see No. 618

Wildrose with Apple Blossom, see Flower Garden with Butterflies

Wild Rose, see Dogwood

Windmill

Windmill or Dutch is also a part of the Sportsman series by Hazel Atlas made in 1938. Of course it pictures a landscape with a windmill.

BLUE
Cocktail Shaker . . . . 10.00 To 15.00
Tumbler, 3 1/2 In. 5.00
Tumbler, 4 1/2 In. . . . . 5.00 To 6.00
Tumbler, 5 1/2 In. 6.00

Windsor

Windsor pattern, also called Diamond, Smocking or Windsor Diamond, was made by Jeannette Glass Company, Jeannette, Pennsylvania, from 1936 to 1946. The pattern is most easily found in pink, green and crystal, although pieces were made of delphite, amberina, red or blue.

BLUE
Ashtray 39.50

CRYSTAL
Bowl, Boat-Shaped 9.00
Bowl, Footed, 7 In. 3.00
Bowl, 4 3/4 In. .... 2.00 To 3.50
Bowl, 10 1/2 In. 6.00
Butter, Covered .... 13.00 To 20.00
Cake Plate 5.00
Candleholder, 3 In. ..... 10.00 To 12.00
Creamer .... 2.00 To 4.50
Creamer, Holiday Style 3.00
Cup .... 1.50 To 2.00
Cup & Saucer .... 3.50 To 4.00
Pitcher, 4 1/2 In. ...... 12.00 To 17.00
Pitcher, 6 3/4 In. 9.50
Plate, Chop, 13 5/8 In. 8.00
Plate, Handled, 10 1/4 In.
     .... 3.50 To 5.00
Plate, Sherbet, 6 In. 1.50
Plate, 9 In. .... 3.00 To 4.00
Relish, Divided, 11 1/2 In.
     .... 3.00 To 5.00
Saltshaker 6.00
Sugar 2.25
Sugar & Creamer, Covered 11.00
Tray, 4 X 4 In. 2.00
Tumbler, Flat, 3 1/2 In. ... 3.50 To 4.00
Tumbler, Footed, 4 In. 4.50
Tumbler, 5 In. 6.00

GREEN
Ashtray .... 19.50 To 42.50
Bowl, Boat-Shaped 19.50
Bowl, Vegetable, 9 1/2 In.
     .... 9.00 To 12.50
Bowl, 4 3/4 In. 3.00
Bowl, 5 1/8 In. 10.00
Bowl, 8 1/2 In. 8.50
Cake Plate 25.00
Coaster 5.50
Creamer .... 6.00 To 14.00
Cup 6.50

Cup & Saucer .... 7.75 To 8.50
Pitcher, 6 3/4 In. ...... 30.00 To 65.00
Plate, Chop, 13 5/8 In. 10.00
Plate, Handled, 10 1/4 In. 7.00
Plate, 7 In. 8.00
Plate, 9 In. .... 7.00 To 9.50
Platter, 11 1/2 In. 10.00
Salt & Pepper .... 28.00 To 32.00
Saucer .... 1.75 To 3.00
Sherbet 6.50
Soup, Cream 16.00
Sugar & Creamer 18.00
Tumbler, 3 1/4 In. 20.00
Tumbler, 4 In. .... 12.50 To 13.00
Tumbler, 5 In. 20.00

PINK
Ashtray .... 25.50 To 30.00
Bowl, Boat Shape ...... 15.00 To 18.00
Bowl, 4 3/4 In. .... 2.75 To 5.00
Bowl, 5 1/8 In. .... 8.00 To 9.50
Bowl, 8 1/2 In. 8.00
Bowl, 12 1/2 In. ...... 45.00 To 48.50
Butter .... 32.50 To 36.75
Cake Plate 10.00
Candleholder, Pair ..... 50.00 To 55.00
Coaster .... 4.00 To 7.50
Creamer .... 5.00 To 7.00
Cup .... 4.00 To 5.50
Cup & Saucer .... 6.50 To 22.50
Pitcher, 6 3/4 In. ...... 13.50 To 25.00
Plate, Chop, 13 5/8 In.
     .... 10.00 To 15.00

Plate, Handled, 10 1/4 In.
.... 5.00 To 9.00
Plate, Sherbet, 6 In. ...... 1.50 To 3.50
Plate, 7 In. .... 5.00 To 8.50
Plate, 9 In. .... 5.00 To 8.00
Platter, 11 1/2 In. ...... 9.00 To 15.00
Relish, Divided, 11 1/2 In.
.... 60.00 To 69.50
Salt & Pepper .... 18.00 To 22.00
Saucer .... 1.00 To 3.75

Sherbet .... 4.00 To 6.00
Soup, Cream .... 13.50 To 14.00
Sugar & Creamer, Covered 22.50
Sugar, Covered .... 8.00 To 12.50
Tray, Handled, 8 1/2 X 9 3/4 In.
.... 22.00
Tumbler, 3 1/4 In. .... 7.00 To 8.50
Tumbler, 4 In. .... 7.00 To 9.25
Tumbler, 5 In. .... 9.00 To 15.00

Windsor Diamond, see Windsor

Winged Medallion, see Madrid

Woolworth, see also Grape

Woolworth was made by Westmoreland Glass Company, Grapeville, Pennsylvania, in the early 1930s. The design showing bunches of grapes was also called Oregon Grape, but it is not the same as the pattern called just Grape. It was made of crystal, blue, green or pink glass.

GREEN
Pitcher, 80 Oz. 25.00
Tumbler, 5 1/2 In. 12.00

X Design

X Design or Criss Cross was another Hazel Atlas pattern made from 1928 to 1932. The name indicates that the pattern has rows of x's in grids. It was made in crystal, green, pink or white opaque glass. Only a breakfast set was made.

BLUE
Butter, Covered, 1/4 Pound 12.00

CRYSTAL
Bowl, Mixing, 6 3/4 In. 2.50
Butter, Covered, 1 Pound 4.50
Plate, 8 In. 2.50
Reamer 3.00

GREEN
Refrigerator Jar, Covered 5.50

Swankyswigs

In October, 1933, Kraft Food Company began to market cheese spreads in decorated, reusable glass tumblers. The tumbler was made in 5-ounce size and was designed with a smooth beverage lip and a permanent color decoration. The designs were tested and changed as public demand indicated. Hazel-Atlas Glass Company made the glasses, which were decorated by hand by about 280 girls, working in shifts around the clock. In 1937 a silk screen process was developed and the tulip design was made by this new, faster method. The glass was also thinner and lighter in weight.

The decorated Swankyswigs were discontinued from 1941 to 1946, the war years. They were made again in 1947 and were continued through 1958. Then plain glasses were used for most of the cheese, although a few special decorated Swankyswigs have been made since that time.

Antique No.1, Black, 3 3/4 In. 1.50
Antique No.1, Blue, 3 1/4 In. 1.50
Antique No.1, Blue, 3 3/4 In. 2.00
Antique No.1, Brown, 3 3/4 In. ... 1.50
Antique No.1, Green, 3 3/4 In. ... 1.50
Antique No.1, Orange, 3 1/4 In. .. 1.50
Antique No.1, Orange, 3 3/4 In. ... 2.00
Antique No.1, Red, 3 1/4 In. 1.50
Antique No.1, Red, 3 3/4 In. 2.00
Band No.1, Red & Black, 3 3/8 In.
.... 3.00 To 4.00
Band No.2, Red & Black, 4 3/4 In.
.... 4.50
Band No.3, Blue & White, 3 3/8 In.
.... 2.00 To 2.50
Band No.4, Blue Bands, 3 3/8 In.
.... 3.00 To 4.00
Bustlin' Betsy, Blue, 3 1/4 In. 1.50
Bustlin' Betsy, Brown, 3 1/4 In.
.... 1.50 To 2.00
Bustlin' Betsy, Green, 3 1/4 In. ... 1.50
Bustlin' Betsy, Orange, 3 1/4 In. .. 1.50
Bustlin' Betsy, Red, 3 1/4 In. 1.50
Bustlin' Betsy, Yellow, 3 1/4 In. ... 1.50
Carnival, Blue, 3 1/2 In. 4.00
Carnival, Green, 3 1/2 In. 8.00
Carnival, Red, 3 1/2 In. 4.00
Carnival, Yellow, 3 1/2 In. 8.00

Checkerboard, White & Blue, 3 1/2 In.
.... 14.00
Checkerboard, White & Red, 4 5/8 In.
.... 18.00
Circle & Dot, Black, 3 1/2 In.
.... 3.00 To 4.50
Circle & Dot, Black, 4 3/4 In. 6.00
Circle & Dot, Blue, 3 1/2 In.
.... 3.00 To 4.50
Circle & Dot, Blue, 4 3/4 In. 6.00
Circle & Dot, Green, 3 1/2 In.
.... 3.00 To 4.50
Circle & Dot, Green, 4 3/4 In.
.... 6.00
Circle & Dot, Red, 3 1/2 In. 4.50
Cornflower No.2, Dark Blue, 3 3/16 In.
.... 1.50
Cornflower No.2, Dark Blue, 3 1/2 In.
.... 2.00
Cornflower No.2, Light Blue, 3 1/2 In.
.... 1.50
Cornflower No.2, Red, 3 3/16 In.
.... 1.50
Cornflower No.2, Red, 3 1/2 In. .. 2.00
Cornflower No.2, Yellow, 3 3/16 In.
.... 1.50
Cornflower No.2, Yellow, 3 1/2 In.
.... 2.00
Daisy, Red, White & Green, 3 1/4 In.
.... 1.50
Daisy, Red, White & Green, 3 3/4 In.
.... 1.50
Forget-Me-Not, Blue, 3 1/2 In.
.... 1.50 To 2.00
Forget-Me-Not, Dark Blue, 3 1/2
In. .... 1.50 To 2.00
Forget-Me-Not, Red, 3 1/2 In.
.... 1.50 To 2.00
Forget-Me-Not, Yellow, 3 1/2 In.
.... 1.50 To 2.00
Galleon, Black, 3 1/8 In. 3.00
Kiddie Cup, Black, 3 3/4 In. 2.00
Kiddie Cup, Blue, 3 1/4 In. 1.50
Kiddie Cup, Blue, 3 3/4 In. 2.00
Kiddie Cup, Brown, 3 1/2 In. 2.00
Kiddie Cup, Green, 3 3/4 In. 2.00
Kiddie Cup, Orange, 3 1/4 In. 1.50
Kiddie Cup, Orange, 3 3/4 In. 2.00
Kiddie Cup, Red, 3 1/4 In. 2.00
Kiddie Cup, Red, 3 3/4 In. 2.00

...ject	Color	Year Reproduction First Reported
...eese dish	Green, pink	1977
...t & pepper shak-	Green, pink and other colors	1980
...gar & creamer, ...vered	Pink, green	1982
...lk pitcher, mug	Cobalt blue	1982

Glass Factories

	Location	Dates
	Clarksburg, West Virginia	1914–1951
	Sapulpa, Oklahoma	1914–present
...ompany	Bellaire, Ohio	c. 1920–1952
...ompany	Cambridge, Ohio	1901–1958
...s	Wheeling, West Virginia	1860s–1939
...& Glass	Coraopolis, Pennsylvania	1894–1933, 1936–1967
...Glass	Beaver Falls, Pennsylvania	1879–1934
...y	Millville, New Jersey	1930s
...re	Indiana, Pennsylvania	1891–1931
...ar Glass	Dunbar, West Virginia	1913–1953
...ass	Washington, Pennsylvania	1893–1955
...pany	Columbus, Ohio	1900–1979?
...ompany	Williamstown, West Virginia	1906–present
...pany	Fostoria, Ohio: Moundsville, West Virginia	1887–present
...ompany	Washington, Pennsylvania; Zanesville, Ohio; Clarksburg, West Virginia; Wheeling, West Virginia	1902–1956
...pany	Newark, Ohio	1893–1956
...Hocking	Lancaster, Ohio	1905–present; Anchor Hocking—1937 on

Lattice & Vine, Red & White, 3 1/2 In. .... 8.00 To 10.00
Posy Cornflower No.1, Blue, 3 1/2 In. 2.00
Posy Cornflower No.1, Green, 3 1/2 In. 2.25
Posy Jonquil, Yellow & Green 3.00
Posy Jonquil, 3 1/2 In. 2.50
Posy Tulip, 3 3/16 In. 3.00
Posy Tulip, 3 1/2 In. 2.50
Posy Violet, 3 3/16 In. 3.00
Posy Violet, 3 1/2 In. 2.50
Sailboat No.1, Blue, 3 1/2 In. .... 5.00 To 6.50
Sailboat No.2, Blue, Red & Green 15.00
Sailboat No.2, Blue, 3 1/2 In. ... 15.00
Sailboat No.2, Green, 3 1/2 In. .. 15.00
Star No.1, Black, 3 1/2 In. 4.50
Star No.1, Green, 3 1/2 In. 4.50
Star No.1, Green, 4 3/4 In. 8.00
Star No.1, Red .... 3.00 To 4.50
Star No.2, Orange, 4 5/8 In. 3.00
Texas Centennial, Cobalt Blue, 4 3/4 In. 20.00

Texas Centennial, Green, 3 1/2 In. 5.50
Tulip No.1, Black, 3 1/2 In. 3.00
Tulip No.1, Blue, 3 1/4 In. 3.00
Tulip No.1, Dark Blue, 3 1/2 In. .. 3.00
Tulip No.1, Green, 3 1/4 In. 3.00
Tulip No.1, Green, 3 1/2 In. 3.00
Tulip No.1, Red, 3 1/4 In. 3.00
Tulip No.1, Red, 3 1/2 In. 3.00
Tulip No.2, Black, 3 1/2 In. 5.50
Tulip No.2, Blue, 3 1/2 In. 5.50
Tulip No.2, Green, 3 1/2 In. 5.50
Tulip No.2, Red, 3 1/2 In. 5.50
Tulip No.3, Blue, 3 1/2 In. .... 1.00 To 2.50
Tulip No.3, Dark Blue, 3 1/2 In. .. 2.00
Tulip No.3, Light Blue, 3 1/2 In. .. 2.00
Tulip No.3, Light Blue, 3 7/8 In. .. 2.50
Tulip No.3, Red, 3 1/2 In. 2.00
Tulip No.3, Red, 3 7/8 In. 2.50
Tulip No.3, Yellow, 3 1/2 In. 2.00
Tulip No.3, Yellow, 3 7/8 In. 2.50
Tulip 1975, Red & White 3.50

Reproductions

(List based on information from *Depression Glass Daze* and other sources)

Pattern	Object	Color	Year Reproduction First Reported
Adam	Butter dish	Green, pink	1981
Avocado	Cream & sugar, cup & saucer, handled dish, nappy, pickle, pitcher	Blue, burnt honey, frosted pink, pink, red amethyst, yellow	1974
Avocado	Pitcher	Green	1979
Avocado	Tumbler	Blue, frosted pink, green, pink, red amethyst, yellow	1974
Bubble	Ashtray, bowl, ivy ball, punch cup, vase	Red	1977–1978
Cape Cod	Dinner set		1978
Cherry Blossom	Berry bowl, 8½ in.	Green, pink	1982
Cherry Blossom	Butter dish	Cobalt, dark green, light blue, light green, pink, red	1976
Cherry Blossom	Butter dish, child's size	Cobalt blue, iridescent, light green, pink	1973
Cherry Blossom	Cereal bowl, 6 in.	Green, pink	1982
Cherry Blossom	Child's set, plate, cup, saucer, sugar & creamer	Cobalt, green, pink	1973
Cherry Blossom	Dinner set, cookie jar	Green, pink	1982
Cherry Blossom	Cup	Delphite, green, pink, red	1977
Cherry Blossom	Pitcher	Blue, green, pink, red	1979
Cherry Blossom	Salt & pepper shaker	Cobalt, delphite, green, pink	1977
Cherry Blossom	Sandwich tray, open handled	Green, pink	1982
Cherry Blossom	Saucer	Blue, green, pink, red	1973

Pattern	Object	Col
Cherry Blossom	Tumbler, footed	Cob
Cherry Blossom	Vegetable dish, 8⅜ in.	Gre
Early American Sandwich	Ashtray, berry set, bowl, bridge set, napkin holder, platter, pitcher, snack set, 3 part relish, tidbit, tumbler, vase, basket, boxes, candleholder	Am
English Hobnail	18 pieces available	R
English Hobnail	26 pieces	P
Iris	Candy dish (bottom only), vase	N
Madrid (called Recollection)	Various items	(
Madrid	Dinner set	
Mayfair	Cookie jar	
Mayfair	Shot glass	
Miss America	Butter dish	
Miss America	Pitcher, tumbler	
Miss America	Salt & pepper	
Royal Ruby	Tumbler, 7 oz., 9 oz., 12 oz., 16 oz.	
Sandwich Anchor Hocking	Cookie jar, covered	
Sandwich Indiana	Basket, bridge set, candleholder, goblets, napkin holder, nappy, punch set, snack set, tidbit, vase, wine set	
Sandwich Indiana	Basket, candleholder snack set, wine set	
Sandwich Indiana	Dinner set	
Sharon	Butter dish	

Pattern
Sharon
Sharon
Sharon
Shirley Temple

Name
Akro Agate
Bartlett-Collins
Belmont Tumble
Cambridge Glass
Central Glass Wo
Consolidated Lam Company
Co-Operative Flin Company
Dell Glass Compa
Diamond Glass-W Company
Dunbar Flint Glas Corporation/ Dun Corporation
Duncan & Miller Company
Federal Glass Com
Fenton Art Glass
Fostoria Glass Com
Hazel-Atlas Glass
A.H. Heisey & Com
Hocking Glass Company/ Anchor Glass Corporation

Name	Location	Dates
Imperial Glass Company	Bellaire, Ohio	1904–present
Indiana Glass Company	Dunkirk, Indiana	1907–present
Jeannette Glass Company	Jeannette, Pennsylvania	c. 1900–present
Jenkins Glass Company	Kokomo, Indiana; Arcadia, Indiana	1901–1932
Lancaster Glass Company	Lancaster, Ohio	1908–1937
Libbey Glass Company	Toledo, Ohio	1892–present
Liberty Works	Egg Harbor, New Jersey	1903–1932
Louie Glass Company	Weston, West Virginia	?–present
Macbeth-Evans Glass Company	Indiana (several factories); Toledo, Ohio; Charleroi, Pennsylvania; Corning, New York	1899–present
McKee Glass Company	Jeannette, Pennsylvania	1853–1961
Morgantown Glass Works	Morgantown, West Virginia	late 1800s–1972
New Martinsville Glass Manufacturing Company	New Martinsville, West Virginia	1901–1944
Paden City Glass Manufacturing Company	Paden City, West Virginia	1916–1951
Seneca Glass Company	Fostoria, Ohio; Morgantown, West Virginia	1891–present
Silex (division of Macbeth-Evans)	Corning, New York	mid-1930s
L.E. Smith Glass Company	Mt. Pleasant, Pennsylvania	1907–present
Standard Glass Manufacturing Company (subsidiary of Hocking/ Anchor Hocking)	Lancaster, Ohio	1924–present
United States Glass Company	Pennsylvania (several factories); Tiffin, Ohio; Gas City, Indiana	1891–1966
Westmoreland Glass Company	Grapeville, Pennsylvania	1890–present

Depression Glass Pattern List

(R) = has been reproduced
* = Prices & paragraph in body of book

Pattern Name	Cross-References	Manufacturer and Dates	Colors and Description
ABC Stork		Belmont	Crystal or green; child's plate
Accordion Pleats	See Round Robin		
* Adam (R)	Chain Daisy; Fan & Feather	Jeannette, 1932–1934	Crystal, green, pink or yellow
Aero Optic		Cambridge, 1929	Crystal, emerald, Peach-blo, Willow Blue
Afghan & Scottie Dog		Hazel Atlas, 1938	Blue with white decorations
* Akro Agate		Akro Agate, 1932–1951	Marbleized colored glass
* Alice		Anchor Hocking, 1940s	Jadite or opaque white; blue or pink borders
* Alpine Caprice	See also Caprice	Cambridge	Blue, crystal or pink; satin finished
* American	Fostoria	Fostoria, 1915	Crystal
American Beauty	See English Hobnail		
* American Pioneer		Liberty Works, 1931–1934	Amber, crystal, green or pink
* American Sweetheart	Lily Medallion	Macbeth-Evans, 1930–1936	Blue, cremax, crystal, monax, pink, red or smoke
Angel Fish		Hazel Atlas, 1938	Blue with white decorations
* Anniversary		Jeannette, 1947–1949	Amethyst, milk glass or pink; 1970–1972—crystal or iridescent amber
Apple Blossom	See Dogwood		
Apple Blossom Border	See Blossoms & Band		
April		Macbeth-Evans	Pale pink
Aramis		Dunbar, 1936	Luster colors
Arcadia Lace		Jenkins, c. 1930	

Pattern Name	Cross-References	Manufacturer and Dates	Colors and Description
Arctic		Hocking, 1932	Red & white decorations
Art Moderne		Morgantown, 1929	Rose or green with black stem & foot
Artura		Indiana, c. 1930	Crystal, green or pink
Athos		Dunbar, 1936	Colored stripes
* Aunt Polly		U.S. Glass, late 1920s	Amber, blue, green, iridescent or pink
Aurora	See Petalware		
Autumn		McKee, 1934	French ivory, jade green
* Avocado (R)	No. 601; Sweet Pear	Indiana Glass, 1923–1933	Crystal, green or pink; reproductions in amber amethyst, blue, frosted pink, green or pink
B Pattern	See Dogwood		
Ballerina	See Cameo		
Bamboo Optic	See also Octagon Bamboo Optic	Liberty, 1929	Green or pink; luncheon set
Bananas		Indiana, c. 1930	Green or pink
Banded Cherry	See Cherry Blossom		
Banded Fine Rib	See Coronation		
Banded Petalware	See Petalware		
Banded Rainbow	See Ring		
Banded Ribbon	See New Century		
Banded Rings	See Ring		
Barbra		Dunbar, 1928	Pink
Basket	See No. 615		
* Beaded Block	Frosted Block	Imperial, 1927–1930s	Amber, crystal, green, ice blue, iridescent, pink or red
* Bee Hive	See also Queen Anne	U.S. Glass, 1926	Crystal with amber, green or pink trim
Belmont Ship Plate		Belmont	Amber, crystal, green or iridescent
Berwick	See Boopie		
Beverage with Sailboats	See White Ship		

Pattern Name	Cross-References	Manufacturer and Dates	Colors and Description
Bibi		Anchor Hocking, 1940s	Forest green or red
Big Rib	See Manhattan		
Blackberry Cluster	See Loganberry		
Blaise		Imperial, c. 1930	Amber, crystal, green or Rose Marie
Blanche		Standard, c. 1930	Crystal
Block	See Block Optic		
* Block Optic	Block	Hocking, 1929–1933	Crystal, green, pink or yellow
Block with Rose	Rose Trellis	Imperial	Crystal, green or pink
Block with Snow-flake	Snowflake on Block		Green or pink; plates only
Block with Wind-mill	See Windmill & Checkerboard		
* Blossoms & Band	Apple Blossom Border	Jenkins, 1927	Crystal, green, iridescent marigold or pink
* Boopie	Berwick	Anchor Hocking, late 1940s–1950s	Crystal, forest green or royal ruby; glasses
Bordette	See also Chinex Classic; see also Cremax	Macbeth-Evans, 1930–1940	Chinex or cremax
Bouquet & Lattice	See Normandie		
* Bowknot		Late 1920s	Crystal or green
Bridal Bouquet	See No. 615		
Bridget		Jeannette, 1925	Green or topaz; bridge set
* Bubble (R)	Bullseye; Provincial	Anchor Hocking, 1934–1965	Crystal, dark green, pale blue or pink; 1960s—milk white or ruby red
Bullseye	See Bubble		
* Burple		Anchor Hocking, 1940s	Forest green or ruby red
Butterflies & Roses	See Flower Garden with Butterflies		
Buttons & Bows	See Holiday		
* By Cracky		Smith, late 1920s	Amber, canary or green

Pattern Name	Cross-References	Manufacturer and Dates	Colors and Description
Cabbage Rose	See Sharon		
Cabbage Rose with Single Arch	See Rosemary		
Camellia		Jeannette, 1947–1951	Crystal
* Cameo	Ballerina; Dancing Girl	Hocking, 1930–1934	Crystal with platinum, green, pink or yellow
Candlewick		Imperial, 1936	Crystal
* Cape Cod (R)		Imperial, 1932	Amber, blue, crystal or ruby
* Caprice	See also Alpine Caprice	Cambridge, 1936	Amber, amethyst, blue, crystal or pink
Carolyn	See Yvonne		
Caribbean	Wave	Duncan & Miller, 1936	Crystal, crystal trimmed with ruby or sapphire blue
Catalonian		Consolidated, 1927–1936	Amethyst, emerald green, Honey, jade, Spanish Rose
* Centaur	Sphinx	Lancaster, 1930s	Green or yellow
Chain Daisy	See Adam		
* Chantilly		Jeannette, 1960s	Crystal or pink
Charade			Amethyst, dark blue or pink
Chariot		Hocking, 1932	Red & white decorations
Cherry	See Cherry Blossom		
* Cherry-Berry	See also Strawberry	U.S. Glass, early 1930s	Amber, crystal, green or pink
* Cherry Blossom (R)	Banded Cherry; Cherry; Paneled Cherry Blossom	Jeannette, 1930–1939	Crystal, delphite, green, jadite, pink or red; reproductions— blue, delphite, green or pink
Chesterfield		Imperial, c. 1930	Amber, green or Rose Marie; iced tea set
Chico		Louie, 1936	Black, green, pink, royal blue, ruby or topaz; crystal handles; beverage set

Pattern Name	Cross-References	Manufacturer and Dates	Colors and Description
* Chinex Classic	See also Classic; see also Cremax; see also Ivex; see also Oxford; see also Pie-Crust; see also Sheffield	Macbeth–Evans, c. 1938–1942	Ivory; decal decorated; colored edges
* Christmas Candy	Christmas Candy Ribbon; No. 624	Indiana, 1937	Crystal, emerald green, seafoam green or teal blue
Christmas Candy Ribbon	See Christmas Candy		
* Circle	Circular Ribs	Hocking, 1930s	Crystal, green or pink
Circular Ribs	See Circle		
Classic	See also Chinex Classic; see also Cremax	Macbeth–Evans, 1930–1940	Chinex or cremax
Cleo		Cambridge, 1929	Emerald green, Peach-blo or Willow blue
Clico		McKee, 1930	Crystal with black or green feet, jade green transparent green or rose pink
* Cloverleaf	Shamrock	Hazel Atlas, 1930–1936	Black, crystal, green, pink or topaz
* Colonial	Knife & Fork	Hocking, 1934–1938	Crystal, green, opaque white or pink
* Colonial Block		Hazel Atlas	1930s—green or pink; 1950s—white
* Colonial Fluted	Rope	Federal, 1928–1933	Crystal or green
Colony	Elongated Honey-comb; Hexagon Tri-ple Band	Hazel Atlas, 1930s	Crystal, green or pink; beverage sets
* Columbia		Federal 1936–1942	Crystal or pink
Columbus		Anchor Hocking	Amber; plate only
Comet	Scroll	U.S. Glass, mid-1920s	Crystal, green or pink
Corded Optic		Federal, 1928	Crystal or green
* Coronation	Banded Fine Rib; Saxon; see also Lace Edge	Anchor Hocking, 1936–1940	Crystal, pink or ruby red
Cosmos		Jeannette, 1950	Crystal or golden iri-descent; water set

Pattern Name	Cross-References	Manufacturer and Dates	Colors and Description
Cracked Ice		Indiana, 1930s	Green or pink
Crackled	See Craquel		
Craquel	Crackled; Stippled; Tree of Life	U.S. Glass, 1924	Crystal with green trim
* Cremax	See also Bordette; see also Chinex classic; see also Classic; see also Ivex; see also Oxford; see also Pie-Crust; see also Sheffield	Macbeth–Evans, 1930–1940	Cream; decal decorated; colored edges
Criss Cross	See X Design		
Crossbar		Federal, mid-1930s	Crystal, Golden Glow, Green or Rose Glow
Crystal Leaf		Macbeth–Evans, 1928	Crystal, green or pink
Cube	See Cubist		
* Cubist	Cube	Jeannette, 1929–1933	Crystal, green, pink or ultramarine; reproductions—amber or avocado
Cupid		Paden City, late 1920s	Green, light blue or pink
Daisy	See No. 620		
Daisy J		Jeannette, 1926	Amber or green
Daisy Petals	See Petalware		
Daisy Spray & Lattice		Federal, 1928	Crystal or green
Dance of the Nudes		Consolidated, 1920s	Crystal or pink
Dancing Girls	See Cameo		
D'Artagnan		Dunbar, 1936	Lusters
Dear		Jeannette, 1930s	
Debbra		Hocking, 1931–1933	Green, rose or topaz
Della Robbia		Westmoreland, 1920s–1930s	Amber, crystal, green or pink
* Dewdrop		Jeannette, 1954–1955	Crystal
Diamond	See Windsor		
Diamond Arch	Diamond Lattice	Federal, 1938–1940	Crystal, green or pink

Pattern Name	Cross-References	Manufacturer and Dates	Colors and Description
Diamond Dart		Macbeth–Evans, 1928	Crystal or emerald green
Diamond Lattice	See Diamond Arch		
Diamond Panel	See Diamond Point Columns		
Diamond Pattern	See Miss America		
Diamond Point	See Petalware		
Diamond Point Columns	Diamond Panel	Hazel Atlas?, late 1920s–1930s	Crystal, green, iridescent or pink
* Diamond Quilted	Flat Diamond	Imperial, 1920s–1930s	Amber, black, blue, crystal, green, pink or red
Diamond Squat		Federal, 1928	Water set
* Diana	Swirled Sharp Rib	Federal, 1937–1941	Amber, crystal, green or pink
Diner		U.S. Glass, 1927	Amber, green or pink
Dixie		Macbeth–Evans 1931	Green or pink; water set
* Dogwood	Apple Blossom; B Pattern; Magnolia; Wildrose	Macbeth–Evans, 1930–1934	Cremax, crystal, green, monax, pink or yellow
Doreen		Westmoreland, 1924	Amber, blue, crystal, green or rose
* Doric	Snowflake	Jeannette, 1935–1938	Crystal, delphite, green, pink or yellow
* Doric & Pansy	Doric with Pansy; Pansy & Doric	Jeannette, 1937–1938	Crystal, pink or ultramarine
Doric with Pansy	See Doric & Pansy		
Do-Si-Do		Smith, 1930s	Black or black with crystal
Double Shield	See Mt. Pleasant		
Double Swirl	See Swirl		
Drape & Tassel	See Princess		
Dutch Rose	See Rosemary		
Early American	See Princess Feather		
Early American Hobnail	See also Hobnail	Imperial, 1930s	Amber, black, blue, crystal, green, pink or red

Pattern Name	Cross-References	Manufacturer and Dates	Colors and Description
Early American Lace		Duncan & Miller, 1932	Amber, crystal, green, rose or ruby
Early American Rock Crystal	See Rock Crystal		
Early American Sandwich (R)		Duncan & Miller, 1925–1949	Amber, chartreuse, crystal, green, pink or ruby
Early American Scroll		Heisey, 1932	
Early American Thumbprint		Heisey, 1932	Crystal, golden yellow, green or rose
Egg Harbor		Liberty, 1929	Green or rose
Elongated Honeycomb	See Colony		
* English Hobnail (R)	American Beauty; Sawtooth; see also Miss America	Westmoreland, 1920–1970	Amber, blue, cobalt, crystal, green, pink or turquoise; 1980s—red
Everglades		Cambridge, 1933–1934	Amber, Carmen, crystal, Eleanor Blue or forest green
* Fairfax		Fostoria, 1927–1944	Amber, black, blue, green, orchid, pink, ruby or topaz
Fan & Feather	See Adam		
Fanfare		Macbeth-Evans	Pale pink
Feather Scroll	See Scroll Fluted		
Fieldcrest		Jenkins	Crystal, green or iridescent amber
Fine Rib	See Homespun		
Fire-King Dinnerware	See Philbe		
* Fire-King Oven Glass	See also Philbe	Anchor Hocking, 1942–1950s	Crystal or pale blue
Flanders		U.S. Glass, 1927	Pink or pink with crystal trim
Flat Diamond	See Diamond Quilted		
Flora		Imperial, c. 1925	Amber, green or Rose Marie
Floradora	Floral Bouquet	Imported, 1929	Amber, amethyst or green

Pattern Name	Cross-References	Manufacturer and Dates	Colors and Description
* Floragold	Louisa	Jeannette, 1950s	Crystal, ice blue, iridescent, red-yellow or shell pink
* Floral	Poinsettia	Jeannette, 1931–1935	Amber, crystal, delphite, green, jadite, pink, red or yellow
* Floral & Diamond Band		U.S. Glass, 1920s	Black, green or pink
Floral Bouquet	See Floradora		
Floral Rim	See Vitrock		
Floral Sterling		Hazel Atlas, early 1930s	
* Florentine No. 1	Old Florentine; Poppy No. 1	Hazel Atlas, 1932–1935	Cobalt, crystal, green, pink or yellow
* Florentine No. 2	Oriental Poppy; Poppy No. 2	Hazel Atlas, 1932–1935	Amber, cobalt, crystal, green, ice blue or pink
Flower	See Princess Feather		
Flower & Leaf Band	See Indiana Custard		
Flower Band		McKee, 1934	French Ivory, jade green or Poudre Blue
Flower Basket	See No. 615		
Flower Garden	See Flower Garden with Butterflies		
* Flower Garden with Butterflies	Butterflies & Roses; Flower Garden; Wildrose with Apple Blossom	U.S. Glass, late 1920s	Amber, black, blue, crystal, green, pink or yellow
Flower Rim	See Vitrock		
Forest		Co-Operative Flint, 1928	Blue, green or pink
* Forest Green		Anchor Hocking, 1950–1957	Green
* Fortune		Anchor Hocking, 1937–1938	Crystal or pink
Fostoria	See American		
Fountain Swirl		Imperial, 1928–1930	Crystal, green or pink
Franklin		Fenton, 1934	Amber, crystal or ruby; beverage glasses
Frosted Block	See Beaded Block		
Frosted Ribbon		Anchor Hocking, 1940	Red

Pattern Name	Cross-References	Manufacturer and Dates	Colors and Description
* Fruits		Hazel Atlas, 1931–1933	Crystal, green, pink or iridized
Full Sail		Duncan Miller, 1925	Amber or green
Garland		Indiana	Crystal—1935; decorated milk glass—1950s
Georgian		Hocking, 1935	Crystal or green; beverage sets
* Georgian	Lovebirds	Federal, 1931–1936	Crystal or green
Georgian		Duncan & Miller, 1928	Amber, crystal, green or rose
* Georgian Fenton		Fenton, c. 1930	Amber, black, crystal, green, royal blue, ruby or topaz
Gladioli	See Royal Lace		
Gloria		Cambridge, c. 1930	
Gothic Arches	Romanesque	L. E. Smith, 1920s	Amber, crystal, green or yellow
Grand Slam		Federal, 1930	Crystal; bridge set
* Grape	See also Woolworth	Standard, 1930s	Green, rose or topaz
Groucho		Louie, 1936	Black, green, pink, royal blue, ruby or topaz; crystal handles; beverage set
Hairpin	See Newport		
* Hammered Band	Melba; Pebbled Band	L. E. Smith, early 1930s	Black, green or pink
Hanging Basket	See No. 615		
* Harp		Jeannette, 1954–1957	Crystal, crystal with gold trim, light blue or pink
Harpo		Louis, 1936	Black, green, pink, royal blue, ruby or topaz; crystal handles; beverage set
Hazel Atlas Quilt		Hazel Atlas, 1937–1940	Amethyst, cobalt blue, green or pink
Hazen		Imperial, c. 1930	
* Heritage		Federal, late 1930s–1960s	Crystal, blue, light green or pink

122

Pattern Name	Cross-References	Manufacturer and Dates	Colors and Description
Hex Optic	See Hexagon Optic		
* Hexagon Optic	Hex Optic	Jeannette, 1928–1932	Green or pink; c. 1960—blue-green or iridized
Hexagon Triple Band	See Colony		
High Point		Anchor Hocking	Ruby; water set
Hinge	See Patrician		
Hob		Jenkins, 1927–1931	Crystal or green
* Hobnail	See also Early American Hobnail	Hocking, 1934–1936	Crystal or pink; red rims; black base
Hobstars Intaglio		Imperial, c. 1930	Crystal, green or pink
* Holiday	Buttons & Bows; Russian	Jeannette, 1947–1949	Crystal, iridescent, pink or shell pink opaque
* Homespun	Fine Rib	Jeannette, 1939–1940	Crystal, light blue or pink
		Hazel Atlas	Cobalt blue or crystal
* Homestead		Smith, 1930s	Amber, black, green or pink
Honeycomb	See Hexagon Optic		
Horizontal Fine Rib	See Manhattan		
Horizontal Ribbed	See Manhattan		
Horizontal Rounded Big Rib	See Manhattan		
Horizontal Sharp Big Rib	See Manhattan		
Horseshoe	See No. 612		
Huck Finn		Jenkins, c. 1930	
Huckabee		Imperial, c. 1930	
Hughes		Morgantown, 1932	Black, crystal, green, Ritz Blue or ruby; beverage set
Ida		Imperial, c. 1930	Blue, crystal, green or ruby
Imperial Hunt		Cambridge, 1932	
* Imperial Optic Rib	Optic Rib	Imperial, 1927	Amberina, blue, crystal, green or iridized
* Imperial Plain Octagon	Molly	Imperial, 1927	Crystal, green or pink

Pattern Name	Cross-References	Manufacturer and Dates	Colors and Description
Indian		Federal, c. 1930	Green
* Indiana Custard	Flower & Leaf Band; see also Orange Blossom	Indiana, 1930s–1950s	Custard or ivory; bands of pastel colors
* Iris (R)	Iris & Herringbone	Jeannette, 1928–1932, 1950s, 1970s	Crystal, iridescent or pink; later wares—blue-green or red-yellow
Iris & Herringbone	See Iris		
Ivex	See also Chinex Classic; see also Cremax	Macbeth–Evans, 1930–1940	Chinex or cremax
Jack Frost		Federal, 1928	Crackled; water, iced tea & lemonade sets
* Jadite	See also Jane-Ray	Jeannette, 1936–1938	Jadite
Jamestown	See Tradition		
Jane		Lancaster, c. 1930	Green, pink or topaz
* Jane-Ray	See also Jadite	Anchor Hocking, 1945–1963	Jadite
Jenkins' Basket		Jenkins	Crystal, green or iridescent amber
John		Federal, mid-1930s	Crystal, Golden Glow, green or Rose Glow
* Jubilee		Lancaster, early 1930s	Yellow
* June (R)		Fostoria, 1928–1952	Azure blue, crystal, gold tinted, green, rose or topaz
Kimberly		Duncan & Miller, 1931	Amber, crystal, green or rose
King Arthur		Indiana, c. 1930	Green or pink
Knife & Fork	See Colonial		
Krinkle		Morgantown, 1924	
* Lace Edge	Loop; Open Lace; Open Scallop; see also Coronation	Anchor Hocking, 1935–1938	Crystal or pink
Lacy Daisy	See No. 618		
* Lake Como		Hocking, 1934–1937	White with blue decoration

Pattern Name	Cross-References	Manufacturer and Dates	Colors and Description
Langston		Morgantown, 1932	Black, crystal, green, Ritz Blue or ruby
Lariette		U.S. Glass, 1931	
* Laurel	Raspberry Band; see also Scottie Dog	McKee, 1930s	Ivory, jade, powder blue or white opal
* Leaf		Macbeth–Evans, early 1930s	Crystal, green or pink
Lenox		McKee, 1930s	Crystal, green, Ritz blue or rose pink
Lido		Federal, mid-1930s	Crystal, Golden Glow, green or Rose Glow
Lily Medallion	See American Sweetheart		
Lily Pons		Indiana, c. 1930	Green
Lincoln Drape	See Princess		
* Lincoln Inn		Fenton, 1928	Amethyst, black, cobalt, crystal, green, jadite, pink or red
Lindburgh	Scalloped Panels	Imperial, c. 1930	Crystal, green or rose pink
Line 92	See Twitch		
* Line 191	Party Line; Tiered Block; Tiered Semi-Optic	Paden City, 1928	Amber, blue, Cheri-Glo, crystal, green or mulberry
Line 300	See Peacock & Wild Rose		
Line 412	See Peacock Reverse		
Line 550	See Sheraton		
Line 994	See Popeye & Olive		
Little Bo Peep		Anchor Hocking, 1940	Green & orange on ivory; child's line
Little Hostess	See Moderntone Little Hostess		
Little Jewel	See also New Jewel	Imperial, late 1920s–1930	Crystal, green, pink or white
Loganberry	Blackberry Cluster	Indiana, c. 1930	Green or pink
Lombardi		Jeannette, 1938	Light blue; bowl only
Loop	See Lace Edge		

Caprice

Bubble

Daisy

Colonial

Cubist

American Sweetheart

Coronation

Fire King

Moderntone

Floral

Florentine No. 2

Fine Rib

Rosemary

Sierra

Sandwich Anchor Hocking

English Hobnail

Ruby Red

Swirl

Windsor, "Windsor Diamond"

Colonial

Floragold

Autumn Leaf

Amberstone

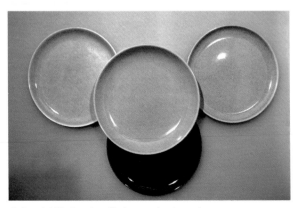

Left and right, American Modern; *center*, Iroquois

Blueberry, Stangl

Cat-tail

Betty

No. 620

Corn King

Fiesta

Hacienda

Little Red Riding Hood

Bittersweet

Hilda

Harlequin

Hall teapots

Mardi Gras   Patio

Riviera

Red Poppy

Rosebud

Tulip

Wild Rose

Pattern Name	Cross-References	Manufacturer and Dates	Colors and Description
Lorain	See No. 615		
Lorna		Cambridge, 1930	Amber, crystal, emerald, Gold Krystol or Peach-Blo
Lotus		Westmoreland, 1920s–1930s	Amber, blue, crystal, green or rose
Louisa	See Floragold		
Lovebirds	See Georgian		
Lydia Ray	See New Century		
* MacHOB		Macbeth–Evans, 1928	Crystal, monax or pink
* Madrid (R)	Meandering Vine; Paneled Aster; Primus; Winged Medallion	Federal, 1932–1939	Amber, blue, crystal, green or pink
Magnolia	See Dogwood		
* Manhattan	Horizontal Fine Rib; Horizontal Ribbed; Horizontal Rounded Big Rib; Horizontal Sharp Big Rib; Ribbed	Anchor Hocking, 1938–1941	Crystal, green, pink or red
Manor		Fostoria, 1931–1944	Crystal, green or topaz
Many Windows	See Roulette		
Mapleleaf		Westmoreland, 1923	Plate only
Marguerite		Westmoreland, 1924	Amber, blue, crystal, green or rose
Marilyn		Morgantown, 1929	Green or pink
Martha Washington		Cambridge, 1932	Amber, crystal, forest green, Gold Crystol, Heatherbloom, royal blue or ruby
Mary		Federal, mid–1930s	Crystal, Golden Glow, green or Rose Glow
Mayfair	See Mayfair Open Rose		
* Mayfair Federal	Rosemary Arches	Federal, 1934	Amber, crystal or green
* Mayfair Open Rose (R)	Mayfair; Open Rose	Hocking, 1931–1937	Crystal, green, ice blue, pink or yellow

Pattern Name	Cross-References	Manufacturer and Dates	Colors and Description
Meandering Vine	See Madrid		
Meadow Flower	See No. 618		
Melba	See Hammered Band		
Melon		Morgantown, 1932	Black, blue, green, ruby or opal with colors; beverage set
Memphis		Central, 1923	Amethyst, black, blue, canary or green
Millay		Morgantown, 1932	Black, blue, crystal, green or ruby; beverage set
* Miss America (R)	Diamond Pattern; see also English Hobnail	Hocking, 1933–1936	Amber, crystal, green, ice blue, pink, red, Ritz blue
Moderne Art	See Tea Room		
* Moderntone	Wedding Band	Hazel Atlas, 1934–1942	Amethyst, cobalt blue, crystal, pink or platonite fired-on colors
* Moderntone Little Hostess	Little Hostess	Hazel Atlas, 1940s	Fired-on colors
Molly	See Imperial Plain Octagon		
Monarch		Anchor Hocking	Ruby
Monticello		Imperial	Crystal
* Moondrops		New Martinsville, 1932–1940	Amber, amethyst, black, cobalt blue, crystal, dark green, ice blue, jadite, light green, medium blue, pink, red or smoke
* Moonstone	Opalescent Hobnail	Anchor Hocking, 1941–1946	Crystal with opalescent hobnails or green
* Mt. Pleasant	Double Shield	L. E. Smith, 1920s–1934	Black amethyst, cobalt blue, green or pink
Mt. Vernon		Cambridge, 1933	Amber, blue, Carmen, crystal or green
Mt. Vernon		Imperial, c. 1930	Crystal
Mutt 'N Jeff		Federal, 1928	Crystal or green; water set
Naomi		Seneca, mid-1930s	Blue or crystal

Pattern Name	Cross-References	Manufacturer and Dates	Colors and Description
Nautilus		Cambridge, 1933–1934	Amber, crystal or royal blue
* New Century	Banded Ribbon; Lydia Ray; see also Ovide	Hazel Atlas, 1930–1935	Amethyst, cobalt blue, crystal, green or pink
New Jewel	See also Little Jewel	Imperial, 1931	Crystal, green, pink or white
* Newport (R)	Hairpin	Hazel Atlas, 1936–1940	Amethyst, cobalt blue, fired-on monax, pink or platonite white
No. 601	See Avocado		
* No. 610	Pyramid; Rex	Indiana, 1926–1932	Crystal, green, pink or yellow; reproductions (1974–1975)—black
* No. 612	Horseshoe	Indiana, 1930–1933	Green, pink or yellow
* No. 615	Basket; Bridal Bouquet; Flower Basket; Hanging Basket; Lorain	Indiana, 1929–1932	Crystal, crystal with colored borders, green or yellow; reproductions—milk glass or olive green
* No. 616	Vernon	Indiana, 1930–1932	Crystal, crystal with platinum trim, green or yellow
* No. 618	Lacy Daisy; Meadow Flower; Pineapple & Floral; Wildflower	Indiana, 1932–1937	Amber, crystal or fired-on green or red; 1960s—olive green
* No. 620	Daisy	Indiana	1933—crystal; 1940—amber; 1960s–1970s—dark green or milk glass
No. 622	See Pretzel		
No. 624	See Christmas Candy		
Nora Bird		Paden City, 1929	Amber, blue, Cheri-Glo or green
* Normandie	Bouquet & Lattice	Federal, 1933–1940	Amber, crystal, green, iridescent or pink
Oatmeal Lace	See Princess Feather		
Ocean Wave	Ripple	Jenkins, c. 1930	
* Octagon	Tiered Octagon; U.S. Octagon	U.S. Glass, 1927–1929	Green or pink

Pattern Name	Cross-References	Manufacturer and Dates	Colors and Description
Octagon Bamboo Optic	See also Bamboo Optic	Liberty, 1929	Green or pink
Octagon Edge		McKee	Green or pink
* Old Cafe		Anchor Hocking, 1936–1938	Crystal, pink or red
Old Central Spiral		Central, 1925	
* Old English	Threading	Indiana, late 1920s–early 1930s	Amber, crystal, emerald green, light green or pink
Old Florentine	See Florentine No. 1		
Opalescent Hobnail	See Moonstone		
Open Lace	See Lace Edge		
Open Rose	See Mayfair Open Rose		
Open Scallop	See Lace Edge		
Optic Design	See Raindrops		
Optic Rib	See Imperial Optic Rib		
Orange Blossom	See also Indiana Custard	Indiana, 1957	Milk glass
Orchid		Paden City, early 1930s	Cobalt blue, green, pink or yellow
Oregon Grape	See Woolworth		
Oriental Poppy	See Florentine No. 2		
Orphan Annie		Westmoreland, 1925	Amber, blue, crystal or green; breakfast set
* Ovide	See also New Century	Hazel Atlas, 1929–1935	Black, green, platonite trimmed with fired-on colors or white
Oxford	See also Chinex Classic; see also Cremax	Macbeth–Evans, 1930–1940	Chinex or cremax
* Oyster & Pearl		Anchor Hocking, 1938–1940	Crystal, pink, red or white with fired-on green or pink
Palm Optic		Morgantown, 1929	Green or pink
Panel	See Sheraton		
Paneled Aster	See Madrid		

Pattern Name	Cross-References	Manufacturer and Dates	Colors and Description
Paneled Cherry Blossom	See Cherry Blossom		
Panelled Ring-Ding		Hocking, 1932	Black, green, orange, red, yellow or painted bands
Pansy & Doric	See Doric & Pansy		
Pantryline		Hocking, 1920s–1930s	
Parrot	See Sylvan		
Party Line	See Line 191		
* Patrician	Hinge; Spoke	Federal, 1933–1937	Amber, crystal, green, pink or yellow
Patrick		Lancaster, c. 1930	Rose or topaz
Peacock & Rose	See Peacock & Wild Rose		
* Peacock & Wild Rose	Line 300; Peacock & Rose	Paden City, 1930s	Cobalt blue, green or pink
Peacock Optic		Morgantown, 1929–1930	Green or pink
Peacock Reverse	Line 412	Paden City, 1930s	Cobalt blue, red or yellow
* Pear Optic	Thumbprint	Federal, 1929–1930	Green
Pebble Optic	See Raindrops		
Pebbled Band	See Hammered Band		
* Penny Line		Paden City, 1932	Amber, Cheri-Glo, crystal, green, royal blue or ruby
Petal	See Petalware		
Petal Swirl	See Swirl		
* Petalware	Aurora; Banded Petalware; Daisy Petals; Diamond Point; Petal; Shell; Vivid Bands	Macbeth–Evans 1930–1940	Cremax, crystal, monax or pink; gold trim; hand-painted fruit designs; fired-on blue, green, red or yellow
* Philbe	Fire-King Dinnerware; see also Fire-King Oven Glass	Anchor Hocking, 1937–1940s	Blue, blue with platinum trim, crystal, green or pink
Pie-Crust	See also Chinex Classic; see also Cremax	Macbeth–Evans, 1930–1940	Chinex or cremax

Pattern Name	Cross-References	Manufacturer and Dates	Colors and Description
* Pillar Flute		Imperial, c. 1930	Amber, crystal, green or pink
Pillar Optic		Hocking, 1935	Green
Pineapple & Floral	See No. 618		
Pineapple Optic		Morgantown, 1929	Green or rose
Pinwheel	See Sierra		
* Pioneer		Federal, 1930s–1970s	Crystal or pink
Plymouth		Fenton, 1933	Amber, green or ruby
Poinsettia	See Floral		
Polar Bear		Hocking, 1932	Red & white decorations
Polo		Hazel Atlas, 1938	Blue with white decorations
* Popeye & Olive	Line 994	Paden City, early 1930s	Cobalt blue, crystal, green or red
Poppy No. 1	See Florentine No. 1		
Poppy No. 2	See Florentine No. 2		
* Pretzel	No. 622; Ribbon Candy	Indiana, 1930s	Crystal
* Primo		U.S. Glass, 1932	Green or yellow
Primrose Lane		Morgantown, 1929	Green or pink
Primus	See Madrid		
* Princess	Drape & Tassell; Lincoln Drape; Tassell	Hocking, 1931–1935	Amber, blue, pink or topaz; frosted finish; gold or platinum trim or painted flowers
* Princess Feather	Early American; Flower; Oatmeal Lace; Scroll & Star; Westmoreland Sandwich	Westmoreland, 1939–1948	Aqua, crystal, green or pink; 1960s—amber
Prisma		Anchor Hocking	
Prismatic Line	See Queen Mary		
Provincial	See Bubble		
Punties		Duncan & Miller, 1931	Amber, crystal, green or rose
Puritan		Duncan & Miller, 1929	

Pattern Name	Cross-References	Manufacturer and Dates	Colors and Description
Pyramid	See No. 610		
Pyramid Optic		Hocking	Crystal or green
* Queen Anne	See also Bee Hive	Anchor Hocking, late 1930s	Crystal or pink; beverage set
* Queen Mary	Prismatic Line; Vertical Rib	Anchor Hocking, 1936–1940	Crystal, pink or red
* Radiance		New Martinsville, 1936–1939	Amber, cobalt blue, crystal, ice blue or red
* Raindrops	Optic Design; Pebble Optic	Federal, 1929–1933	Crystal or green
Raspberry Band	See Laurel		
Rex	See No. 610		
Ribbed	See Manhattan		
* Ribbon		Hazel Atlas, 1930s	Black, crystal, green or pink
Ribbon Candy	See Pretzel		
Ried		Federal, Fry, 1930	Crystal with blue or green trim
* Ring	Banded Rainbow; Banded Rings	Hocking, 1927–1932	Crystal, green or pink; rings of black, blue, orange, pink, platinum, red or yellow
Ring-Ding		Hocking, 1932	Painted bands of green, orange, red or yellow
Ringed Target		Macbeth–Evans, 1931	Crystal, green or pink; iced tea set
Ripple	See Ocean Wave		
* Rock Crystal	Early American Rock Crystal	McKee, 1920s–1930s	Amber, blue-green, cobalt blue, crystal, green, pink, red or yellow
Romanesque	See Gothic Arches		
Rope	See Colonial Fluted		
Rose		Standard, c. 1930	Topaz
Rose & Thorn	See Thorn		
* Rose Cameo		Belmont Tumbler, 1933	Green
Rose Lace	See Royal Lace		
Rose Trellis	See Block with Rose		

Pattern Name	Cross-References	Manufacturer and Dates	Colors and Description
* Rosemary	Cabbage Rose with Single Arch; Dutch Rose	Federal, 1935–1937	Amber, green or pink
Rosemary Arches	See Mayfair Federal		
* Roulette	Many Windows	Anchor Hocking, 1935–1939	Crystal, green or pink
* Round Robin	Accordion Pleats	Late 1920s–1930s	Crystal, green or iridescent marigold
Roxana		Hazel Atlas, 1932	Crystal, white or yellow
* Royal Lace	Gladioli; Rose Lace	Hazel Atlas, 1934–1941	Amethyst, cobalt blue, crystal, green or pink
* Royal Ruby (R)		Anchor Hocking, 1939–1960s, 1977	Red
Russian	See Holiday		
* S Pattern	Stippled Rose Band	Macbeth–Evans, 1930–1935	Crystal, green, monax, pink, red, ritz blue or topaz; amber, blue, gold, green, pink, platinum, red or white trim
Sail Boat	See White Ship		
Sailing Ship	See White Ship		
* Sandwich Anchor Hocking (R)		Anchor Hocking, 1939–1964	Amber, crystal, forest green, pink, red or white
* Sandwich Indiana (R)		Indiana, 1920s–1980s	Amber, crystal, light green, pink, red or teal blue
Saturn		Heisey, 1937	Crystal or pale green
Sawtooth	See English Hobnail		
Saxon	See Coronation		
Scallop Edge		McKee	Green or pink
Scalloped Panels	See Lindburgh		
Scottie Dog	See also Laurel	McKee, 1930s	Children's set
Scrabble		Macbeth–Evans, 1931	Crystal, green or pink; iced tea set and tumblers
Scramble		Westmoreland, 1924	Amber, blue, crystal, green or rose
Scroll	See Comet		
Scroll & Star	See Princess Feather		

Pattern Name	Cross-References	Manufacturer and Dates	Colors and Description
Scroll Fluted	Feather Scroll	Imperial, c. 1930	Crystal, green or pink
Seafood Buffet		McKee, 1936	
Sea-Side		Jenkins	Crystal, green or iridescent amber
Semper		Louie, 1931	Green, pink or topaz; refreshment set
Shaeffer		Imperial, c. 1930	Amber, blue, crystal or green
Shamrock	See Cloverleaf		
* Sharon (R)	Cabbage Rose	Federal, 1935–1939	Amber, crystal, green or pink
Sheffield	See also Chinex Classic; see also Cremax	Macbeth–Evans, 1930–1940	Chinex or cremax
Shell	See Petalware		
Sheraton	Line 550; Panel	Bartlett Collins, 1930s	
* Shirley Temple (R)		Hazel Atlas; U.S. Glass, 1934–1942	Cobalt blue & white
* Sierra	Pinwheel	Jeannette, 1931–1933	Green or pink
Simplicity		Morgantown	Green or pink
Smocking	See Windsor		
Snowflake	See Doric		
Snowflake on Block	See Block with Snowflake		
Soda Fountain		Indiana, c. 1930	Green or pink
Soda Shop		Smith, mid-1920s	
Sommerset		Morgantown, 1932	Black, blue, crystal, green or ruby; beverage set
Spanish Fan	Spanish Lace		Crystal or green
Spanish Lace	See Spanish Fan		
Sphinx	See Centaur		
* Spiral	Spiral Optic; Swirled Big Rib	Hocking, 1928–1930	Green
* Spiral Flutes		Duncan & Miller, 1924–early 1930s	Amber, crystal, crystal with gold trim, green, light blue, pink or vaseline

Pattern Name	Cross-References	Manufacturer and Dates	Colors and Description
Spiral Optic	See Spiral		
Spoke	See Patrician		
* Sportsman Series	See also White Ship; see also Windmill	Hazel Atlas, 1940s	Amethyst, cobalt blue or crystal with fired-on decorations
Spring Flowers		Imperial, 1920s	Plate only
* Spun		Imperial, 1935	Aqua, crystal, fired-on orange, pastel colors or red
Square		Morgantown, 1928	
Squat Optic		Federal, 1928	Water set
Squirt		Macbeth–Evans, 1931	Crystal or emerald green; water sets
* Starlight		Hazel Atlas, 1938–1940	Cobalt blue, crystal, pink or white
Stippled	See Craquel		
Stippled Rose Band	See S Pattern		
* Strawberry	See also Cherry-Berry	U.S. Glass, 1930s	Crystal, green, iridescent marigold or pink
Strawflower		Imperial, c. 1930	Amber, crystal, green or Rose Marie
Stripe		Hocking, 1932	Red and white bands
Sunburst		Jeannette, 1938–1940	Crystal
* Sunflower		Jeannette, late 1920s–early 1930s	Delphite, emerald green, light green or pink
Sweet Pear	See Avocado		
* Swirl	Double Swirl; Petal Swirl	Jeannette, 1937–1938	Amber, delphite, ice blue, pink or ultramarine
Swirled Big Rib	See Spiral		
Swirled Sharp Rib	See Diana		
* Sylvan	Parrot; Three Parrot	Federal, 1931–1932	Amber, blue, crystal or green
Tall Boy		Federal, 1928	Green; iced tea sets
Tassell	See Princess		
* Tea Room	Moderne Art	Indiana, 1926–1931	Amber, crystal, green or pink

Pattern Name	Cross-References	Manufacturer and Dates	Colors and Description
* Tear Drop		Duncan & Miller, 1934–1943	Crystal
Terrace		Duncan & Miller, 1935	Amber, blue, crystal or ruby
Thistle		Macbeth–Evans, 1929–1930	Crystal, green, pink or yellow
Thorn	Rose & Thorn	U.S. Glass, 1930s	Black, crystal, green or pink
Threading	See Old English		
Three Bands	Vitrock	Hocking, 1930s	Opaque white with three enameled bands
Three Parrot	See Sylvan		
Thumbprint	See Pear Optic		
Tiered Block	See Line 191		
Tiered Octagon	See Octagon		
Tiered Semi-Optic	See Line 191		
Tom & Jerry		Hazel Atlas, 1930s	Opaque white, enameled decorations
Tom & Jerry		McKee, 1940s	Black, ivory or white with black, gold, green or red decorations
Tradition	Jamestown	Imperial, 1936–1940	
Tree of Life	See Craquel		
Trojan		Fostoria, 1929–1944	Gold tint, green, rose pink or topaz yellow
Trudy		Standard, c. 1930	Green or pink
Truman		Liberty, 1930	Green or pink
Trump Bridge		Federal, 1928	Colored enamel decorations; luncheon set
Tudor Ring		Federal, 1928	Crystal or green; water set
Tulip		Dell, 1930s	Amber, amethyst, blue, crystal or green
Twentieth Century		Hazel Atlas, 1928–1931	Crystal, green or pink
Twin Dolphin		Jenkins	Crystal, green or iridescent amber
Twisted Optic		Imperial, 1927–1930	Amber, blue, canary yellow, green or pink

Pattern Name	Cross-References	Manufacturer and Dates	Colors and Description
Twitch	Line 92	Bartlett-Collins, early 1930s	Green
U.S. Octagon	See Octagon		
Vernon	See No. 616		
* Versailles		Fostoria, 1928–1944	Azure, crystal bases with colored glass, gold tinted, green, rose or topaz
Verticle Rib	See Queen Mary		
* Victory		Diamond Glass, 1929–1932	Amber, black, cobalt blue, green or pink; gold trim
Victory Model		Silex, 1938–1942	Amber, cobalt, green or pink; coffee pot
Viking		Imperial, 1929	Green or rose
* Vitrock	Floral Rim; Flower Rim	Hocking, 1934–1937	Green, red, or white with fired-on colors; decal decorations
Vivid Bands	See Petalware		
Waffle	See Waterford		
Wagner		Westmoreland, 1924	Amber, blue, green or rose
Wakefield		Westmoreland, 1933–1960s	Crystal
Washington Bi-Centennial		1932	Topaz; tumbler
* Waterford	Waffle	Anchor Hocking, 1938–1944	Crystal, pink, white or yellow; 1950s—forest green
Wave	See·Caribbean		
Weatherford		Cambridge, 1926	Amber-Glo, emerald or Peach-Blo
Wedding Band	See Moderntone		
Westmoreland Sandwich	See Princess Feather		
Wheat		Federal, early 1930s	Crystal, green or pink
Whirly-Twirly		Anchor Hocking, 1940s	Forest green or red
White Sail	See White Ship		

Pattern Name	Cross-References	Manufacturer and Dates	Colors and Description
* White Ship	Beverages with Sailboats; Sail Boat; Sailing Ship; White Sail	Hazel Atlas, 1938	Blue with white decorations
Wiggle		McKee, 1925	Amethyst, amber, blue, canary or green
Wildflower	See No. 618		
Wildrose	See Dogwood		
Wildrose with Apple Blossom	See Flower Garden with Butterflies		
* Windmill		Hazel Atlas, 1938	Blue
Windmill & Checkerboard	Block with Windmill		Crystal or green
* Windsor	Diamond; Smocking; Windsor Diamond	Jeannette, 1936–1946	Amberina, blue, crystal, delphite, green, pink or red
Windsor Diamond	See Windsor		
Winged Medallion	See Madrid		
Woodbury		Imperial, c. 1930	Amber, crystal, green or Rose Marie
* Woolworth	Oregon Grape; see also Grape	Westmoreland, early 1930s	Blue, crystal, green or pink
Wotta Line		Paden City, 1933	Amber, amethyst, Cheri-Glo, crystal, ebony, green, royal blue, ruby or topaz
* X Design	Criss Cross	Hazel Atlas, 1928–1932	Crystal, green, pink or white; breakfast set
Yankee		Macbeth–Evans, 1931	Crystal, green or pink; water set
Yoo-Hoo		Jenkins, c. 1930	
Yo-Yo		Jenkins, c. 1930	
Yvonne	Carolyn	Lancaster, mid-1930s	Green or yellow
Zeppo		Louie, 1936	Black, green, pink, royal blue, ruby or topaz; crystal handles; beverage set

We welcome any additions or corrections to this chart. Please write to us c/o Crown Publishers, Inc., One Park Avenue, New York, N.Y. 10016.

American Dinnerware

Introduction

Many patterns of ceramic dinnerware were made in America from the 1930s through the 1950s. Some refer to it as "Depression dinnerware," but the name used by the manufacturers was "American dinnerware" and that is the name used by most collectors and dealers.

Pottery, porcelain, semiporcelain, ironstone, and other ceramic ware are included in the category of dinnerware. Most were made in potteries located in Southern Ohio, and in West Virginia near the Ohio River. Each factory made many patterns for sale to gift shops and department stores. They also made special patterns for use as premiums and free give-aways or to sell for low prices as store promotions.

American dinnerware patterns fall into six categories. The first to be rediscovered by collectors and the first to be reproduced have been the solid-colored pottery lines such as "Fiesta" or "Harlequin." Some of this type of dinnerware was also made in California potteries before 1950.

Many manufacturers preferred hand-painted decorations on their dinnerware. Included in this group are the pieces made by Southern Potteries under the name "Blue Ridge" and the pottery by Stangl picturing fruit, flowers, or birds.

An unusual type of dinnerware made by Harker, and others, was "Cameo Ware": a solid-color plate embellished with a white decoration that appears to be cut into the colored glaze.

Realistically shaped pieces resembling corn were produced by several makers; the most important was "Corn King" by the Shawnee Pottery Company. Green and yellow dishes were made in full sets. Other sets of dishes in three-dimensional shapes include the "Little Red Riding Hood" line, and many cookie jars and salt and pepper shakers.

Some of the dishes were made in very modern shapes with solid-color decorations. The innovative shapes and subtle earth-tone colorings made them a favorite in the 1940s and 1950s—e.g., wares designed by Russel Wright and made by several firms, and the "Lu-Ray" pattern by Taylor, Smith, and Taylor.

Most of the dinnerware was decorated with decal designs: colored, printed patterns applied to the dishes. The most famous of these designs, "Autumn Leaf," was made for and sold by the Jewel Tea Company. Mexican-inspired designs such as "Mexicana" by Homer Laughlin were popular during the late 1930s. The Hall China Company made many decal-decorated wares, including "Poppy," "Red Poppy," and "Crocus." Black silhouette designs against light-colored dishes were popular in the 1930s—e.g., "Silhouette" by the Crooksville China Company and "Taverne" by the Hall China Company.

Because the dishes were made by so many manufacturers there is a problem with variations in vocabulary. We have arbitrarily decided that a demitasse cup and saucer or set is to be called an "after dinner" cup and saucer. Most sugar bowls made for these dinnerware sets had covers. Today many have lost the original cover and are sold as open sugars. We have indicated if the sugar is open or covered when it was priced for sale.

The terms "kitchenware" and "dinnerware" are used in the original sense. A dinnerware set includes all the pieces that might have been used on a dinner table, including dishes, bowls, platters, tumblers, cups, pitchers, etc. A kitchenware set has bowls and storage dishes of the type used in a kitchen and does not include dinner plates or cups.

Colors often were given romantic names and whenever necessary we have used more ordinary language so that although we may describe a set as "surf green" or "Persian Cream" we will list it as green or ivory. Some colors, like camellia (rose), cadet (light blue), Indian red (orange), or Dresden (deep blue), are explained in the paragraph descriptions.

Be sure to look at the Glossary on page 251. This explains the size—e.g., a 10-inch plate is a dinner plate, a 7-ounce tumbler is from 4 to 4½ inches high—as well as special names, such as *nappy*, and other terms. A list of known patterns and makers starts on page 192.

It is important to remember that the descriptions of dinnerware may include many strange names. Some are the factory names, some names refer to the pattern (decorations applied to the piece), and many of the names were used by the factory to describe the shape: e.g., "Taverne" is a pattern, "Laurel" is the shape of the dish used to make that pattern, and "Taylor, Smith, and Taylor" is the name of the company that made the dinnerware.

Pieces of American dinnerware are constantly being discovered in attics, basements, garage sales, flea markets, and antique shops. The publications that offer them through the mail use descriptions that often include both the pattern and the shape name. Learn to recognize the shapes that were used by each maker.

Although hundreds of patterns are included in this book, many patterns were not seen at sales this year and were not included. Prices listed in this book are actual prices asked by dealers at shows, shops, and through national advertising. It is not the price you would pay at a garage sale or church bazaar. Prices are not estimates. If a high and low are given, we have recorded several sales. There is a regional variation in the prices, especially for the solid-color wares. In general, these pieces are higher priced in the West, lower in the center of the country.

There have been a few reissues of dinnerwares. Harlequin was put back into production in 1979; the Woolworth Company was the sole distributor. Complete dinner sets are being made in the original colors. The only difference is that the salmon now being produced is a deeper color than the original. The sugar bowls are being made with closed handles. A Fiesta look-alike has been made by Franciscan since 1978 under the name "Kaleidoscope."

If you plan to collect dinnerwares, be sure to do further research into your patterns in the books listed in the Bibliography below.

Collector Clubs and Publications

DEPRESSION GLASS DAZE
Box 57
Otisville, MI 48463

THE GLASS COLLECTOR
P.O. Box 27037
Columbus, OH 43227

GLASS REVIEW
P.O. Box 542
Marietta, OH 45750

NATIONAL DEPRESSION GLASS ASSOCIATION
NEWS & VIEWS
8337 Santa Fe Lane
Shawnee Mission, KS 66212

THE NATIONAL JOURNAL
P.O. Box 3121
Wescosville, PA 18106

THE PADEN CITY PARTY LINE
13325 Danvers Way
Westminster, CA 92683

Bibliography

Bougie, Stanley J., and Newkirk, David A. *Red Wing Dinnerware*. Privately printed, 1980 (Rte. 3, Box 141, Monticello, MN 55362).

Chipman, Jack, and Stangler, Judy. *Bauer Pottery 1982 Price Guide*. Privately printed, 1982 (16 East Holly St., Pasadena, CA 91003).

Cunningham, Jo. *The Collector's Encyclopedia of American Dinnerware*. Paducah, Kentucky: Collector Books, 1982.

————. *Hall China Price Update*. Privately printed, 1982 (Box 4929, G.S., Springfield, MO 65808).

————. *Update: The Autumn Leaf Story Price Guide, 1979/1980*. Privately printed, 1979 (Box 4929, G.S., Springfield, MO 65808).

Duke, Harvey. *Superior Quality Hall China: A Guide for Collectors*. Privately printed, 1977 (Box HB, 12135 N. State Rd., Otisville, MI 48463).

Enge, Delleen. *Franciscan Ware*. Paducah, Kentucky: Collector Books, 1981.

Fridley, A. W. *Catalina Pottery: The Early Years 1927–1937*. Privately printed, 1977 (P.O. Box 7723, Long Beach, CA 90807).

From Kiln to Kitchen: American Ceramic Design in Tableware. Springfield, Illinois: Illinois State Museum, 1980.

Hayes, Barbara, and Bauer, Jean. *The California Pottery Rainbow.* Privately printed, 1975 (1629 W. Washington Blvd., Venice, CA 90291).

Huxford, Sharon & Bob. *The Collectors Encyclopedia of Fiesta.* Revised Fourth Edition. Paducah, Kentucky: Collector Books, 1981.

————. *The Collectors Encyclopedia of Roseville Pottery.* Paducah, Kentucky: Collector Books, 1976.

Kerr, Ann. *Russel Wright and His Dinnerware.* Privately printed, 1981 (P.O. Box 437, Sidney, OH 45365).

————. *The Steubenville Saga.* Privately printed, 1979 (P.O. Box 437, Sidney, OH 45365).

Klein, Benjamin. *The Collector's Illustrated Price Guide to Russel Wright Dinnerware.* Smithtown, New York: Exposition Press, Inc., 1981.

Lehner, Lois. *Complete Book of American Kitchen and Dinner Wares.* Des Moines, Iowa: Wallace-Homestead Book Company, 1980.

Nelson, Maxine Feek. *Versatile Vernon Kilns.* Privately printed, 1978 (P.O. Box 1686, Huntington Beach, CA 92647).

Newbound, Betty. *The Gunshot Guide to Values of American Made China & Pottery.* Privately printed, 1981 (4567 Chadsworth, Union Lake, MI 48085).

———— & Bill. *Southern Potteries Inc. Blue Ridge Dinnerware.* Paducah, Kentucky: Collector Books, 1980.

Newkirk, David A. *A Guide to Red Wing Prices.* Privately printed, 1982 (Rte. 3, Box 146, Monticello, MN 55362).

Pottery 1880-1960. Encino, California: Orlando Gallery, 1973.

Rehl, Norma. *Abingdon Pottery.* Privately printed, 1981 (P.O. Box 556, Milford, NJ 08848).

————. *The Collectors Handbook of Stangl Pottery.* Privately printed, 1979 (P.O. Box 556, Milford, NJ 08848).

————. *Stangl Pottery Part II.* Privately printed, 1982 (P.O. Box 556, Milford, NJ 08848).

Riederer, LaHoma, and Bettinger, Charles. *Fiesta III, A Collector's Guide to Fiesta, Harlequin, and Riviera Dinnerware.* Privately printed (P.O. Box 2733, Monroe, LA 71201) (1980).

Roberts, Brenda. *The Collectors Encyclopedia of Hull Pottery.* Paducah, Kentucky: Collector Books, 1980.

Simon, Dolores. *Red Wing Pottery with Rumrill.* Paducah, Kentucky: Collector Books, 1980.

————. *Shawnee Pottery.* Paducah, Kentucky: Collector Books, 1977.

Tefft, Gary & Bonnie. *Red Wing Potters & Their Wares.* Privately printed, 1981 (W174 N9422 Devonwood Rd., Menomonee Falls, WI 53051).

Amberstone

Fiesta is a popular pattern found in solid colors. In 1967 Amberstone was made by the Homer Laughlin China Company, Newell, West Virginia, using the Fiesta shapes. The pieces were glazed a rich brown. Some pieces had black machine-stamped underglaze patterns. The pieces were sold for supermarket promotions and were called Genuine Sheffield dinnerware. Full sets of dishes were made.

Bowl, 5 1/2 In.	2.00 To 3.00
Plate, Bread & Butter	2.00 To 3.00
Plate, Dinner	3.00 To 4.00
Plate, Pie	25.00
Plate, 6 In.	2.50
Plate, 10 In.	5.00
Platter	4.00
Salt & Pepper	7.50
Saucer	1.00
Server	12.00

Server, Tidbit, Tray With Handles	12.50
Sugar, Covered	4.50

American Modern

Russel Wright was a designer who made dinnerware in modern shapes for many companies. American Modern was made by the Steubenville Pottery Company, Steubenville, Ohio, from 1939 to 1959. The original dishes were made in Seafoam (blue-green), Coral, Chartreuse, Granite Gray and Bean Brown (a shaded brown). The brown was replaced with Black Chutney (dark brown) during World War II. Canteloupe, Glacier Blue and Cedar Green were added in the 1950s. Matching linens and glassware were made.

BLUE

Saucer	1.00 To 3.00

BROWN

Bowl, Cereal	5.00
Bowl, Fruit, 5 1/2 In.	5.00
Creamer	10.00
Cup & Saucer	5.00
Dish, Serving, 7 X 10 In.	5.00
Plate, 6 In.	2.00
Plate, 6 1/2 In.	2.00
Plate, 8 In.	2.00
Plate, 10 In.	3.00

CANTELOUPE

Cup	3.00
Plate, 6 1/2 In.	2.00

CEDAR GREEN

Bowl, Handled, 5 1/2 In.	3.00
Cup & Saucer	4.50 To 5.00
Plate, 6 In.	1.25
Plate, 10 In.	4.50

Saltshaker 2.00	Gravy Boat 15.00
Saucer 2.00	Gravy Boat, Handled 6.00
	Pickle 7.00
CHARTREUSE	Plate, Chop 20.00
Bowl, Oval, 10 In. 3.00	Plate, 6 1/2 In. 2.00
Bowl, Vegetable, 9 In. 7.50	Plate, 10 In. .... 3.00 To 6.00
Coaster 2.50	Platter 15.00
Cup 5.50	Platter, 9 X 13 In. 7.00
Cup & Saucer 4.00	Salt & Pepper 10.00
Gravy Boat 5.00	Saucer 1.00
Pitcher 25.00	Sugar, Covered 10.00
Plate, 8 In. 3.50	Teapot 35.00
Plate, 10 In. .... 4.00 To 5.00	Vegetable, Divided 45.00
Platter, 13 In. 9.00	
Salt & Pepper 3.50	**SEAFOAM BLUE**
Sugar & Creamer, Covered 15.00	Bowl, Fruit 8.00
Tray, Square, Curled Corner, 12 In.	Bowl, Salad 25.00
.... 7.00	Bowl, Vegetable, Open 15.00
	Bread & Butter 3.00
CORAL	Casserole, Covered 30.00
Casserole, Covered 21.00	Celery 20.00
Cup & Saucer 4.00	Coaster-Ashtray 12.00
Plate, 8 In. 3.50	Coffeepot, After Dinner 35.00
Salt & Pepper 5.00	Creamer 8.00
	Cup .... 7.00 To 15.00
GRANITE GRAY	Cup & Saucer .... 8.50 To 20.00
Bowl, Fruit 8.00	Cup & Saucer, After Dinner 9.00
Bowl, Soup 6.00	Dish, Pickle 10.00
Bowl, Vegetable, Open 15.00	Gravy Boat 15.00
Casserole, Covered 30.00	Pitcher 35.00
Casserole, Covered, Handled, 12 In.	Plate, Chop 20.00
.... 25.00	Plate, 6 In. .... 2.50 To 5.00
Celery, 13 In. 6.00	Plate, 10 In. .... 4.00 To 6.00
Coffeepot 75.00	Platter 15.00
Creamer 8.00	Relish, Rosette 35.00
Cup .... 3.00 To 5.00	Salt & Pepper 12.00
Cup & Saucer 8.00	Soup, Dish 6.00
Cup & Saucer, After Dinner	Sugar 10.00
.... 10.00 To 25.00	Teapot 35.00
Fork & Spoon, Salad 35.00	

Autumn Leaf

One of the most popular American dinner-ware patterns is Autumn Leaf. It was made for the Jewel Tea Company, a grocery chain, from 1936. Hall China Company, East Liverpool, Ohio, Crooksville China Company, Crooksville, Ohio, Harker Potteries, Chester, West Virginia, and Paden City Pottery, Paden City, West Virginia, made dishes with this design. The Autumn Leaf pattern is always the same shades of dark yellow and rust leaves. The shape of the dish varied with the manufacturer. Several special terms are used to describe these shapes, such as the word bud-ray, which describes a bowl lid with a knob surrounded by raised rays.

Collectors can find Autumn Leaf pattern tinware, plastic tablecloths, glassware, clocks, even painted furniture. There are several books about Autumn Leaf and a collector club listed on page 140 in this book.

Baker, Fluted	8.00 To 11.00
Bean Pot, Two Handles	50.00
Bowl, Custard, Large	10.00
Bowl, Divided, Oval	30.00
Bowl, Fruit, 5 1/2 In.	2.50 To 4.50
Bowl, Fruit, 8 3/4 In.	8.00
Bowl, Salad, 9 In.	8.00 To 12.00
Bowl, Set Of 3; 6 1/4, 7 1/2 & 9 In.	29.00 To 40.00
Bowl, Souffle, 8 In.	10.00
Bowl, Sunshine, No.3	7.00
Bowl, Sunshine, No.4	8.00
Bowl, Sunshine, No.5	15.00
Bowl, Utility, 7 1/2 In.	9.00
Bowl, Utility, 9 In.	15.00
Bowl, Vegetable, Oval	10.00 To 18.00
Bowl, 5 In.	3.00 To 4.50
Bowl, 6 In.	4.00 To 7.00
Bowl, 6 1/2 In.	8.00 To 9.00
Bowl, 7 In.	8.00
Butter, Pound	150.00 To 225.00
Butter, 1/4 Pound	75.00 To 100.00
Cake Saver	25.00 To 47.50
Casserole & Lid, Deep	15.00 To 25.00
Clock	300.00
Coaster	3.50 To 5.00
Coffee Server, 96 Oz.	18.00 To 24.00
Coffeepot, Drip, 8 Cup	18.00 To 34.00
Coffeepot, Electric	115.00 To 145.00
Coffeepot, Satin-Ray Top, 8 Cup	15.00 To 35.00
Coffeepot, Sunshine	22.00
Cookie Jar, Big Ear	57.00 To 68.00
Creamer, 1940	4.00 To 6.00
Cup	3.00 To 5.00
Cup & Saucer	7.75 To 10.00
Cup, Custard	2.50 To 4.50
Cup, St.Dennis	12.00
Dish, Sauce	3.00
Dish, Souffle, Individual	5.00
Drip Jar	3.50 To 8.00
Drip Jar, Salt & Pepper	25.00
Gravy Boat & Underplate	20.00
Hot Plate, Oval, 10 3/4 In.	6.25 To 8.00
Hot Plate, Round, 7 1/4 In.	5.00 To 7.00
Jar, Marmalade, Plate	13.00 To 25.00
Lid, Steam Hole, Bud-Ray, 6 In.	5.00 To 6.00
Mug, Cone-Shaped	25.00 To 32.00
Mug, Irish	60.00 To 69.50
Mustard Set, 3 Piece	35.00
Nappy, 5 1/2 In.	1.00
Pie Baker, French, Flute	7.00 To 13.00
Pie Plate, 8 In.	7.00
Pie Plate, 9 1/2 In.	9.00
Pitcher, Milk, 6 In.	6.00 To 20.00
Plate, Bread & Butter, 6 In.	.75 To 3.00
Plate, Cake, Footed	95.00
Plate, 6 In.	2.50
Plate, 7 1/4 In.	4.00 To 6.50

Plate, 8 In. 3.50
Plate, 9 In. .... 3.00 To 7.75
Plate, 10 In. .... 4.50 To 11.00
Platter, 11 In. .... 6.00 To 10.00
Platter, 13 In. 14.00
Salt & Pepper, Casper .. 10.00 To 13.50
Salt & Pepper, Range ... 12.00 To 16.50
Saucer .... 1.25 To 2.00
Souffle 3.00
Soup, Coupe .... 7.00 To 12.00
Soup, Cream .... 4.00 To 14.00
Stack Set, Mary Lou .... 32.50 To 40.00
Sugar & Creamer, Covered, Sunshine
.... 16.00

Sugar & Creamer, Ruffled, Open .. 10.00
Sugar, Covered .... 8.00 To 13.50
Teapot, Aladdin .... 20.00 To 32.00
Teapot, Aladdin/infuser 31.00
Teapot, Long Spout, 7 In.
.... 30.00 To 48.00
Teapot, Sunshine 30.00
Vase 115.00
Warmer, Oval .... 77.50 To 110.00
Warmer, Round ...... 90.00 To 110.00
Water Jug, Sunshine .... 10.00 To 15.00

Ballerina

Solid-colored pottery was popular in the 1950s. The Universal Potteries, Cambridge, Ohio, made Ballerina from 1947 to 1956. Ballerina was very modern in shape, had solid-colored glazes. A later line was decorated with abstract designs. The original Ballerina solid-colored dinnerware was offered in Dove Gray, Jade Green, Jonquil Yellow and Periwinkle Blue. In 1949 Chartreuse and Forest Green were added. By 1955 Burgundy, Charcoal and Pink were added, while some other colors have been discontinued.

There was also a line called Ballerina Mist which was a pale blue-green with decal decorations.

BLUE
Plate, 6 In. 1.25
Plate, 10 In. 2.50
Saltshaker 5.00

BURGUNDY
Plate, 6 In. 1.25
Plate, 8 In. 1.75
Plate, 10 In. 2.50

Saucer, 8 In. 1.00

CHARTREUSE
Plate, 8 In. 1.75

FOREST GREEN
Creamer .... 3.50 To 6.00
Eggcup .... 8.00 To 10.00
Plate, 6 In. 1.25

GRAY
Plate, 10 In. 2.50
Saucer, 8 In. 1.00

GRAY WITH DECAL
Plate, 6 In. 3.00

JADE GREEN
Cake Plate 3.00
Soup, Dish 3.00

YELLOW
Cake Plate 4.00
Plate, 6 In. 1.25
Plate, 10 In. 2.50

Banded

Banded is a kitchenware pattern made by the Hall China Company, East Liverpool, Ohio, from 1937. Ridges forming a band are molded into the pieces. Banded is the name of both a solid color line and the shape for some decal-decorated pieces. The solid pieces are usually found in Chinese Red.

CADET BLUE
Cookie Jar 15.00

CHINESE RED
Bowl, Batter 15.00
Carafe 20.00
Teapot 16.00

Betty

Betty is a Blue Ridge pattern made on the Candlewick shape. It features a red flower, a yellow flower and green leaves.

Plate, 6 In. 1.25
Saucer 1.25

Blue Ridge

Blue Ridge, Hall, Universal and Stangl potteries made patterns by the name Bittersweet. Listed here is the Universal Bittersweet pattern made from 1942 to 1949. It has bright orange and yellow decal decoration.

Casserole, Covered 14.75
Plate, 9 In. 3.00
Salt & Pepper Shaker 5.00
Shaker & Cover, Drip Jar Set 15.00
Stack Set, 3 Piece 20.00

Blue Bouquet

Standard Coffee of New Orleans, Louisiana, gave Blue Bouquet pattern dinnerware and kitchenware as a premium from the early 1950s to the early 1960s. Although it was made by the Hall China Company, East Liverpool, Ohio, it is most easily found in the South. The pattern is very plain with a thin blue border interrupted by roses.

Baker, French 7.00
Bowl, Salad .... 8.00 To 15.00
Coffeepot, Large 25.00
Lid, Coffee, Banded 5.00
Shaker, Handled 5.00

Blue Garden

Blue Garden is a line of Hall dishes made in 1939. The body is cobalt blue, the design is a decal floral pattern.

Bowls, Nested, 8, 9, 10 In. 15.00
Salt & Pepper 32.00

Blue Parade, see Rose Parade

Blueberry

Stangl Pottery, Trenton, New Jersey, made Blueberry (pattern No. 3770) before 1942. The heavy red pottery dishes were glazed with a yellow border and a sgraffito decoration of blueberries in the center.

Bowl, 5 1/2 In. 4.00
Cup 3.50

Bob White

Bob White was made by Red Wing Potteries from 1956 to 1967. It was one of the most popular dinnerware patterns made by the factory. The pattern, a modern hand-painted design, shows a stylized bird and background.

Beverage Server 15.00
Cup & Saucer . . . . 7.00 To 12.50

Lid, Cookie 10.00
Pitcher, Tall 37.50
Platter 42.50
Relish, 3 Part 32.50
Salad 6.50
Salt & Pepper 22.50
Sugar & Creamer, Covered 17.00

Brown-Eyed Susan

Brown-Eyed Susan was first made by the Vernon Kilns, Vernon, California, in the 1940s.

Bowl, 9 In.   8.00
Plate, 10 In. 4.00

Cactus

Cactus is a Mexican-inspired pattern made by Hall China, first made in 1937. It is not made in dinnerware pieces.

Coffeepot 30.00
Platter, 12 In. 15.00

Calico Fruit

Dinnerware and kitchenware were made in Calico Fruit pattern in the 1940s. It was made by Universal Potteries, Cambridge, Ohio; matching tinware and glass pieces were also made by other firms. The design of the fruit is a vivid red and blue on a plain white dish. Unfortunately the decals often fade.

Bowl, Covered, 8 In. .... 6.00 To 10.00
Pitcher 12.50
Pitcher, Covered 27.50
Plate, 9 In. 4.00
Shaker, 9 In. 15.00

Caliente

Every pottery company seemed to make a solid color dinnerware in the 1940s. Paden City Glass Company, Paden City, West Virginia, made Caliente, a semi-porcelain, in blue, green, tangerine and yellow. There is also matching ovenproof cooking ware.

BLUE
Bowl, 6 In. 3.00
Cup 3.00
Plate, 6 In. 1.50
Plate, 10 In. 3.00
Saucer 1.50

GREEN
Bowl, 6 In. 3.00
Cup 3.00

TANGERINE
Bowl, 6 In. 3.00
Cup 3.00
Plate, 6 In. 1.50
Plate, 10 In. 3.00
Saucer 1.50

YELLOW
Plate, 10 In. 3.00
Teapot, Covered 35.00

Cameo Rose Hall

Cameo Rose made by Hall China Company has gray and white leaf decorations. It was not made by the cameo process used for cameo shellware and other designs.

Cup & Saucer 8.00
Plate, 5 3/4 In. .... 2.50 To 3.00
Plate, 7 3/4 In. .... 2.00 To 3.00
Plate, 10 In. .... 4.00 To 6.00
Salt & Pepper .... 12.00 To 15.00
Sugar, Covered .... 8.00 To 12.00
Teapot 35.00

BLUE
Platter, Oval, 15 1/2 In. 18.00

Cameo Rose, see Rose; Cameo Shellware

Cameo Rose Harker, see also Cameo Shellware; White Rose

The names of the various cameo ware shapes and designs are confusing. One pattern is Cameo Rose, made by Harker China Company, Chester, West Virginia, from about 1940. The design is of solid white roses against a colored blue, pink, gray or yellow background.

BLUE
Bowl, Fruit, 5 1/4 In. 4.50
Plate, 6 1/4 In. 3.00

Plate, 9 In. 6.00
Plate, 10 In. 8.50
Platter, Oval, 15 1/2 In. 18.00
Platter, 10 1/2 In. 12.00

PINK
Cup & Saucer 5.00
Plate, 9 In. 6.00

Cameo Shellware

Another cameo pattern is Cameo Shellware, the same design as Cameo Rose but the dishes are fluted.

BLUE
Cup & Saucer . . . . 6.00 To 8.00
Plate, 6 In. 3.00
Plate, 10 In. 5.00

Carnival

Carnival is a pottery decorated with abstract star-like patterns, made by Stangl Pottery, Trenton, New Jersey, from 1954 to 1957.

Bowl, 5 1/4 In. 1.50
Casserole, Bottom, Handled 5.00
Plate, 9 1/2 In. 25.00
Plate, 10 In. 6.00
Plate, 14 In. 5.00
Soup, Dish, 8 In. 2.50
Sugar 8.00

Casualstone

Casualstone is another of the family of Fiesta dinnerwares. Homer Laughlin Company, Newell, West Virginia, made the dishes for supermarket promotions under the trade name Coventry in 1970. Antique Gold Fiesta Ironstone dishes were decorated with a gold-stamped design on some pieces. Small, deep dishes were left in solid colors.

Bowl, 5 1/2 In.	2.50
Cup	2.50
Cup & Saucer, Set	3.00
Plate, Decal, 6 In.	1.00
Plate, 6 In.	1.50
Plate, 10 In.	2.50 To 5.00
Saucer	.75 To 2.00
Server, Tidbit	10.00

Cat-Tail

Cat-Tail pattern dishes must have been found in most homes in America in the 1940s. Sears, Roebuck and Company featured the pattern from 1934 to 1956. It was made by the Universal Potteries, Cambridge, Ohio. The red and black cat-tail design was used for the dinnerwares and matching tinware, kitchenware, glassware, furniture and table linens.

Berry Bowl	4.00
Bowl, Mixing, 9 In.	7.50
Bowl, Set Of 3, Covered	30.00 To 35.00
Bowl, 5 In.	3.25
Bowl, 7 1/2 In.	7.00
Bowl, 8 3/4 In.	9.00
Butter, Covered	20.00 To 30.00
Carafe, Stopper	12.00
Casserole, Covered, 8 1/2 In.	12.00 To 18.00
Coffeepot, Small	20.00
Cookie Jar, 9 In.	40.00
Creamer	4.00
Jar, Refrigerator, Small	8.00
Jug, Batter, Metal Lid, Celluloid-Handled	40.00
Pie Dish, 10 In.	10.00
Pitcher, Milk, 64 Oz.	20.00
Plate, Cake, 12 1/2 In.	8.00
Plate, 6 In.	1.50 To 2.00
Plate, 10 In.	2.50 To 7.00
Platter, 11 3/4 In.	7.00
Platter, 12 In.	4.00
Platter, 13 3/4 In.	7.00
Reamer, 2 Part	175.00
Saltshaker, Flat, 4 1/4 In.	4.00
Saucer	1.00 To 1.50
Sugar & Creamer	20.00
Sugar, Covered	6.00
Syrup, 6 In.	35.00
Teapot	20.00 To 25.00
Water Jug, Stopper	10.00
Water Server, Covered	7.50

Chinese Red, see also Banded; Saf-Handle

Chinese Red is a color used by Hall China Company, East Liverpool, Ohio. This bright red was used on many shapes of dishes. A few are listed here that are not included in the more recognizable sets.

Bean Pot, Tab-Handled 25.00
Casserole, Oval, Handle 16.00

Jug, Ball, No.2 .... 10.00 To 17.50
Jug, Ball, No.3 .... 12.00
Jug, Classic 15.00
Shaker, Handle, Salt & Pepper 9.50
Teapot, Morning 15.00

Cock O' the Morn

Cock O' the Morn was made by Southern Potteries, Erwin, Tennessee. The hand-painted pattern shows a rooster crowing at the sun, just rising over a distant barn. Another similar pattern by Southern Potteries is called Rooster.

Plate, 6 In. 3.00
Plate, 10 In. 4.00

Colonial

Colonial was the first kitchenware line made by Hall China Company, East Liverpool, Ohio. It was first made in 1932. The first pieces were made in ivory or ivory with lettuce-colored exteriors. Later pieces were made in Chinese Red, Delphinium (blue), Golden Glo or with decal decorations. Some are still being made.

Stangl pottery had a modern dinnerware shape called Colonial. Salem China Company, Salem, Ohio, made a pattern called

Colonial that was decorated with red and green decorations reminiscent of a wall stencil design.

DAFFODIL
Jug, No.4, 5 1/2 In. 10.00

LETTUCE
Creamer, 3 1/2 In. 8.00
Cup & Saucer, After Dinner, Set ... 8.00

Conchita

Mexican-inspired designs became the rage for dinnerwares in the late 1930s. Conchita was one of several made by Homer Laughlin Company, Newell, West Virginia. The dinnerware was a decal-decorated ware made on the Century shape line. The decoration pictured three pots of cactus in one corner and if it is a large flat piece like a plate, a group of hanging gourds and peppers. There

is a thin red border trim. Conchita decals were also used on kitchenwares made on the Kitchen Kraft shapes.

Cup & Saucer .... 7.00 To 8.00
Plate, Deep, 8 In. 4.50
Plate, 5 In. .... 3.00 To 4.00
Plate, 9 In. .... 3.00 To 4.00

Conchita Kitchen Kraft

Conchita pattern decals of three pots of cactus were used to decorate the Oven-Serve and Kitchen Kraft oven-to-table kitchenwares made by Homer Laughlin Company, Newell, West Virginia, in the 1930s.

Bowl, Mixing, 10 In. 22.50
Plate, Cake, 10 1/2 In.
.... 15.00 To 17.50

Coors, see Rosebud

Corn King

Dishes shaped like ears of corn? This novel idea became a popular reality when Corn King pattern was sold by Shawnee Pottery Company, Zanesville, Ohio, before 1954. The green and yellow dishes, three-dimensional representations of ears of corn, ranged from dinner plates to small salt and pepper shakers. Corn King has darker yellow corn kernels and lighter green leaves than a later pattern called Corn Queen.

Butter, 1/4 Pound 15.00
Creamer 5.00
Plate, 7 1/2 In. 4.00
Plate, 10 In. 7.00

Shaker, Large 6.00
Shaker, Pair, Small 7.00
Sugar With Lid 10.00

Corn Queen

Corn King was redesigned slightly by Shawnee Pottery Company, Zanesville, Ohio, and continued to be marketed from 1954 to 1961. The kernels of the new line were lighter yellow and the foliage was a deeper green. It was called Corn Queen.

Casserole, Covered, Medium 25.00
Creamer 12.00
Mug 20.00
Pitcher, Milk, 8 1/2 In. 30.00
Sugar, Covered .... 12.00 To 20.00

Country Garden

Buttercups, bluebells and jonquils are pictured on the Country Garden dinnerware, at least according to the advertisements. The flowers are stylized. The pattern was made by Stangl Pottery, Trenton, New Jersey, from 1956 to 1974.

Cup 3.00
Lazy Susan, 10 In., No.3943 ..... 12.00
Plate, 9 1/2 In. 3.50

Crab Apple

One of the most popular patterns made by Southern Potteries, Inc., Erwin, Tennessee, under the name Blue Ridge was Crab Apple. This brightly colored hand-painted dinnerware was decorated with groups of red apples and green leaves. A thin red spatter border was used. Matching glassware was made. The pattern was in production after 1930 and was discontinued when the factory went out of business in 1957.

Bowl, Salad 2.00
Bowl, 5 1/4 In. . . . . 2.00 To 2.50
Bowl, 6 1/4 In. 3.00
Bowl, 9 1/2 In. 4.50
Cup 3.00
Plate, 9 1/4 In. 2.50
Plate, 10 In. 3.50
Platter, Small 6.00

Platter, 11 3/4 In. 4.50
Saucer . . . . 1.50 To 2.00
Sugar, Covered 4.25

Crocus

Crocus was a popular name for dinnerware patterns. Prices listed are for Crocus pattern by Hall China Company, East Liverpool, Ohio, in the 1930s. The decal-decorated dinnerware was sometimes called Holland. The design was a border of oddly shaped crocuses in black, lavender, red, green and pink. Most pieces had platinum trim. Other firms, including Stangl pottery and Blue Ridge, had very different-looking dinnerwares called Crocus.

Bean Pot, Lid 15.00
Bottle & Stopper, Sunshine, Water
. . . . 85.00
Bowl, Mixing, No.3 . . . . 7.50
Bowl, No.4, Sunshine, 7 1/2 In. . . 12.00
Bowl, No.5, Sunshine, 9 In. 15.00
Bowl, Salad 12.00
Bowl, 5 1/2 In. . . . . 4.50 To 6.00
Casserole, Covered 27.50
Coffeepot, Banded 15.00
Coffeepot, Colonial . . . . 30.00 To 33.00
Coffeepot, Drip-O-Later, With Dripper
Marked 35.00
Coffeepot, Stepdown, Large 25.00
Cup & Saucer 7.75
Pepper, Shaker, 4 In. 8.00
Plate, 6 In. 3.00

Plate, 10 In. 7.75
Platter, 11 In. 9.00
Salt & Pepper, Handled 17.50
Soup, Tureen, Big Lip 85.00
Sugar & Creamer, Lid, Art Deco . . 37.50
Sugar, Lid, Art Deco 22.50
Teapot, Colonial 20.00
Teapot, Covered, Colonial 36.00

Cumberland

Large hand-painted blue and white flowers with green leaves and reddish flowerlets are centered on the plates of Cumberland pattern. The pattern was made by Southern Potteries, Inc., Erwin, Tennessee, about 1948.

Cup & Saucer 5.00
Plate, 10 In. 3.00

Daffodil

Daffodil is a pattern made by Southern Potteries, Inc., Erwin, Tennessee, under the trademark Blue Ridge. It pictures a large single yellow and orange daffodil realistically painted on each plate. The dinnerware used has the piecrust edge.

Bowl, Salad 5.00
Bowl, Vegetable 7.75

Daisy

Daisy or Hawaiian 12-point Daisy is a Fiesta Casual pattern. Two designs, Daisy and Yellow Carnation, were made by the Homer Laughlin Company, Newell, West Virginia. They were both first made in 1962, discontinued in 1968. Daisy pattern has turquoise and brown daisies in the center and a turquoise rim, on the familiar Fiesta shape.

Plate, 8 In. 3.50
Plate, 10 In. 3.50

Delicious

Delicious pattern pictures two Delicious apples with green and yellow leaves, it has a beaded edge. The hand-painted pattern was made by Southern Potteries, Inc., Erwin, Tennessee, under the trade name Blue Ridge before 1957, when the firm went out of business.

Plate, 6 In. 1.50
Plate, 10 In. 3.50
Saucer 1.50

Dogwood

Dogwood pattern was made by Homer Laughlin China Company, Newell, West Virginia. It is a decal-decorated line of dinnerware. The edges are gold, the pattern realistic pink and white sprays of dogwood. It was made in the 1960s. Another pattern named Dogwood was made by Stangl Pottery Company, Zanesville, Ohio, in 1965, it is a heavy pottery dinnerware.

Creamer .... 4.00 To 5.00
Cup & Saucer 7.00
Plate, 10 In. .... 3.00 To 4.00
Teapot 15.00

Dutch Boquet

A large red tulip with green leaves and a fanciful sprig of green leaves and red berries is the center decoration for a pattern called Dutch Boquet. The Southern Potteries, Inc., Erwin, Tennessee, made this dinnerware on the Candlewick-shaped dishes with a beaded edge.

Bowl, Vegetable, 9 In. 7.00
Plate, 10 In. 3.00

Early California

In the late 1930s Vernon Kilns, Vernon, California, made a solid color line of dinnerware called Early California. The dishes made in blue, brown, green, orange, pink, turquoise or yellow were made to be used as mix-and-match sets. The dishes are marked with the name of the pattern.

BLUE

Plate, Salad 1.25
Saucer 2.00

GREEN

Plate, Dinner 3.00

Fiesta, see also Amberstone; Casualstone; Daisy; Fiesta Ironstone; Fiesta Kitchen Kraft; Yellow Carnation

Fiesta ware was introduced in 1936 by the Homer Laughlin China Company, Newell, West Virginia, redesigned in 1969 and withdrawn in 1973. The design was characterized by a band of concentric circles, beginning at the rim.

Cups had full-circle handles until 1969, when partial-circle handles were made. The original Fiesta colors were bright green, dark blue, Fiesta red and yellow. Later old ivory, turquoise, gray, rose, forest green, light green and chartreuse were added. The redesigned Fiesta Ironstone, made from 1969 to 1973, was made only in mango red, antique gold and turf green (medium green).

Most Fiesta ware was marked with the incised word Fiesta. Some pieces were hand-stamped before glazing.

The Fiesta shape was also made with decal decorations, but these are not considered Fiesta by collectors, rather they are collected by the pattern names.

There is also a Fiesta Kitchen Kraft line, a group of kitchenware pieces made in the early 1940s in blue, green, red or yellow. These were bake-and-serve wares. Glassware and linens were made to match the Fiesta colors.

BLUE

Coddler, Egg 30.00
Cup & Saucer, After Dinner 20.00
Relish 49.75
Salt & Pepper 5.00

CHARTREUSE

Bowl, 4 3/4 In. 8.00
Bowl, 5 1/2 In. 10.00
Bowl, 6 In. 15.00

Coffeepot 65.00
Creamer 4.50
Cup & Saucer . . . . 15.00 To 19.00
Gravy Boat . . . . 16.50 To 18.00
Mug . . . . 28.00 To 34.00
Mug, Tom & Jerry . . . . . 13.00 To 25.00
Plate, Chop, 12 In. 12.00
Plate, 6 In. . . . . 2.00 To 5.00
Plate, 7 In. 3.00
Plate, 9 In. 2.25
Plate, 10 In. 12.00
Platter, Oval 8.00
Salt & Pepper 17.50
Saucer . . . . .50 To 3.00
Soup, Cream 15.00
Soup, Dish . . . . 15.00 To 17.00
Sugar 2.00

DARK BLUE

Bowl, Fruit, Flat 85.00

Bowl, Fruit, 11 3/4 In. 18.00
Bowl, Mixing, 10 In. 49.50
Bowl, Nesting, No.2 .... 25.00
Bowl, Nesting, No.4 .... 70.00
Bowl, Salad 33.00
Bowl, 4 3/4 In. .... 6.00 To 7.50
Bowl, 5 1/2 In. .... 6.50 To 10.00
Bowl, 5 3/4 In. 6.50
Bowl, 6 In. .... 11.00 To 12.50
Bowl, 6 1/4 In. 15.00
Cake Plate 29.00
Candleholder, Bulb ..... 10.00 To 17.00
Coffee, Covered, After Dinner 26.50
Coffeepot, After Dinner Set,
    4 Cup & Saucer 175.00
Compote, Footed 30.00
Compote, Sweet .... 20.00 To 24.00
Cookie & Lid, Large 130.00
Creamer 6.00
Cup .... 14.00 To 16.00
Cup & Saucer .... 10.00 To 17.50
Cup & Saucer, After Dinner 25.00
Eggcup .... 17.00 To 20.00
Gravy Boat .... 7.50 To 18.00
Lid, Medium Teapot 10.00
Mug .... 18.50 To 23.00
Mustard, Covered ...... 50.00 To 55.00
Nappy, 8 1/2 In. 10.00
Pitcher, Ice .... 30.00 To 40.00
Plate, Chop, 12 In. 18.00
Plate, Chop, 13 In. ..... 10.00 To 15.00
Plate, Grill, 10 1/2 In. .. 11.00 To 18.00
Plate, 6 In. .... 1.50 To 3.50
Plate, 7 In. .... 2.00 To 4.50
Plate, 7 1/2 In. 3.25
Plate, 9 In. .... 2.00 To 5.50
Plate, 9 1/2 In. 4.50
Plate, 10 In. .... 4.00 To 12.50
Plate, 15 In. 30.00
Platter .... 15.00 To 17.50
Platter, Oval 10.00
Saltshaker 3.00
Saucer .... 1.00 To 5.00
Soup, Cream .... 12.50 To 17.50
Soup, Dish 7.00
Soup, Onion, Covered
    .... 145.00 To 150.00
Spoon 30.00
Sugar & Creamer, Covered
    .... 14.00 To 18.75
Sugar, Open .... 5.00 To 5.50
Tray, Figure 8 .... 26.00 To 30.00
Tray, Relish, Multicolored Insert .. 60.00
Tray, Utility 10.00

Tumbler, Juice .... 9.00 To 10.00
Tumbler, Water .... 15.00 To 19.00
Vase, Bud .... 20.00 To 35.00

DARK GREEN
Bowl, Straight, 6 In. 10.00
Bowl, 4 3/4 In. .... 6.00 To 10.00
Bowl, 5 1/2 In. 10.00
Creamer .... 6.00 To 9.00
Cup & Saucer .... 6.00 To 17.00
Mug .... 25.00 To 35.00
Nappy 10.00
Plate, 6 In. 2.25
Plate, 7 In. 4.75
Plate, 9 In. .... 5.50 To 7.50
Platter, 12 In. .... 10.00 To 14.00
Salt 6.00
Saucer .... 1.25 To 3.00
Soup, Dish .... 14.00 To 16.00
Sugar, Covered 14.00
Sugar, Open 9.00

GRAY
Bowl, 4 3/4 In. .... 10.00 To 12.00
Bowl, 5 1/2 In. .... 10.00 To 14.00
Bowl, 6 In. 19.00
Creamer 8.00
Cup & Saucer .... 15.00 To 22.00
Gravy Boat 24.00
Jug, Pint 38.00
Mug .... 35.00 To 42.00
Pitcher, Juice 50.00
Pitcher, Water 40.00
Plate, Grill, 10 1/2 In. 18.00
Plate, 6 In. .... 1.25 To 5.00
Plate, 7 In. .... 4.00 To 9.00
Plate, 9 In. .... 4.50 To 5.00
Plate, 10 In. 9.00
Platter, 12 In. 17.50
Salt & Pepper 17.50
Saucer .... .50
Soup, Cream .... 15.00 To 22.00
Soup, Dish .... 12.00 To 15.00
Sugar, Covered 14.00
Teapot, Medium .... 52.00 To 60.00
Teapot, Small 40.00

LIGHT GREEN
Ashtray .... 14.75 To 25.00
Berry Bowl 6.00
Bowl, 4 3/4 In. .... 5.50 To 7.00
Bowl, 5 In. .... 6.50 To 7.50
Bowl, 5 1/2 In. .... 6.50 To 10.00
Bowl, 6 In. 9.00

Bowl, 6 1/4 In. 12.50
Bowl, 7 5/8 In. 45.00
Bowl, 8 1/2 In. 12.50
Bowl, 9 1/2 In. 15.00
Bowl, 11 3/4 In. 50.00
Cake Plate 22.00
Candleholder, Bulb 13.00
Candleholder, Bulb, Pair 29.00
Candleholder, Tripod 50.00
Casserole, Covered .... 38.00 To 45.00
Coffeepot With Lid, After Dinner
.... 60.00
Compote, Sweets 20.00
Creamer, Ring Handle .... 5.00 To 6.00
Creamer, Stick Handle ... 7.00 To 11.50
Cup .... 12.00 To 14.00
Cup & Saucer .... 10.00 To 18.00
Cup & Saucer, After Dinner 22.00
Eggcup .... 17.00 To 19.00
Gravy Boat .... 11.00 To 13.00
Jug, Pint 27.50
Jug, 2 Pint 20.00
Marmalade, Covered 67.00
Mug .... 20.00 To 25.00
Mustard 45.00
Nappy, 8 1/2 In. .... 6.00 To 12.50
Pitcher, Syrup 35.00
Pitcher, 22 Oz. 24.00
Plate, Chop, 13 In. 12.50
Plate, Chop, 15 In. .... 10.00 To 15.00
Plate, Deep, 8 In. 11.00
Plate, Grill, 10 1/2 In. .... 8.00 To 12.50
Plate, 6 In. .... 1.00 To 4.25
Plate, 7 In. .... 2.50 To 4.00
Plate, 7 1/4 In. 3.00
Plate, 9 In. .... .75 To 4.00
Plate, 9 1/2 In. 3.50
Plate, 10 In. .... 5.50 To 10.00
Platter .... 10.00 To 12.00
Platter, Oval, 12 In. ..... 8.00 To 15.00
Salt & Pepper .... 5.00 To 10.00
Saucer .... 1.00 To 1.50
Shaker, Single 4.50
Soup, Cream .... 10.00 To 17.50
Soup, Dish .... 10.00 To 13.00
Soup, Onion, Covered 145.00
Sugar 3.50
Sugar & Creamer, Covered
.... 14.00 To 38.00
Sugar, Open .... 3.50 To 7.00
Syrup 35.00
Syrup, Covered .... 80.00 To 85.00
Teapot, Small 35.00
Tray, Relish 60.00
Tray, Utility 10.00

Tumbler, 5 Oz. .... 5.00 To 18.00
Tumbler, 10 Oz. .... 20.00 To 24.00

MEDIUM GREEN
Ashtray 40.00
Bowl, 4 3/4 In. 45.00
Bowl, 5 1/2 In. .... 15.00 To 17.00
Bowl, 6 In. 40.00
Cup & Saucer .... 11.25 To 20.00
Cup, Ring Handle 8.00
Mug 25.00
Plate, 7 In. .... 2.00 To 10.00
Plate, 9 In. .... 7.00 To 12.00
Plate, 10 In. 18.00
Shaker 11.00
Soup, Dish, 8 In. 22.00
Sugar, Open 10.00

OLD IVORY
Ashtray 16.00
Berry Bowl 6.00
Bowl, Fruit, Flat 85.00
Bowl, Fruit, Footed 32.00
Bowl, No.7 .... 65.00
Bowl, Salad, 11 1/2 In. 100.00
Bowl, 4 3/4 In. .... 5.50 To 10.00
Bowl, 5 1/2 In. .... 6.50 To 10.00
Bowl, 6 In. .... 10.00 To 14.00
Bowl, 9 1/2 In. 15.00
Candleholder, Bulb, Pair 35.00
Coffeepot 48.00
Compote, 12 In. .... 40.00 To 45.00
Creamer 5.00
Cup & Saucer .... 11.00 To 17.50
Cup & Saucer, After Dinner 16.00
Eggcup 17.00
Gravy Boat .... 13.00 To 15.00
Juice .... 10.00 To 12.00
Marmalade 20.00
Mug .... 25.00 To 38.00
Mug, Tom & Jerry 5.00
Mustard, Covered ...... 50.00 To 57.00
Pitcher, 2 Qt. 23.00
Plate, Calendar, 10 In. 15.00
Plate, Calendar, 1954 .... 32.00
Plate, Chop, 15 In. ..... 12.00 To 15.00
Plate, Deep 10.00
Plate, Grill, 10 1/2 In. 12.50
Plate, 6 In. .... 1.25 To 3.00
Plate, 7 1/4 In. .... 2.50 To 4.00
Plate, 9 In. .... 3.00 To 5.00
Plate, 10 In. .... 5.50 To 10.00
Platter 7.00
Platter, Oval, 12 In. ..... 5.00 To 15.00
Salt & Pepper 4.25

Saucer .... 1.00 To 3.00
Soup, Cream .... 10.00 To 14.00
Soup, Dish .... 9.50 To 14.00
Soup, Onion, Covered

.... 150.00 To 155.00
Sugar, Covered 14.00
Syrup 160.00
Tea Cup 5.00
Teapot, Covered 42.00
Teapot, Lid, Medium 13.00
Tray, Relish 50.00
Tray, Utility .... 10.00 To 12.50
Tumbler 22.00
Tumbler, Juice 10.00
Tumbler, 10 Oz. 15.00
Vase, Bud 33.00

RED

Ashtray .... 20.00 To 30.00
Bowl, No.2 .... 25.00
Bowl, No.4 .... 30.00 To 42.50
Bowl, 4 3/4 In. .... 6.00 To 15.00
Bowl, 5 1/2 In. .... 2.00 To 15.00
Bowl, 6 In. .... 17.00 To 26.00
Bowl, 8 1/2 In. .... 16.00 To 18.00
Bowl, 9 1/2 In. 34.00
Cake Plate 35.00
Candleholder, Bulb, Pair

.... 35.00 To 45.00
Candleholder, Tripod, Pair 115.00
Carafe, 3 Pint 78.00
Casserole, Covered 65.00
Coffeepot 55.00
Coffeepot, After Dinner 90.00
Compote, 12 In. .... 40.00 To 45.00
Creamer, Stick Handle, Large

.... 12.00 To 16.00
Cup & Saucer .... 16.00 To 25.00
Cup & Saucer, After Dinner 35.00
Eggcup .... 21.00 To 39.75
Gravy Boat 23.00
Marmalade .... 75.00 To 100.00
Mug 39.00
Mustard, Covered ...... 55.00 To 60.00
Pitcher, Juice 55.00
Pitcher, Syrup .... 125.00 To 155.00
Pitcher, Water 39.00
Plate, Chop, 13 In. ..... 16.00 To 20.00
Plate, Chop, 15 In. 16.00
Plate, Grill, 11 1/8 In. 22.00
Plate, 6 In. .... 1.00 To 18.00
Plate, 7 In. .... 4.00 To 8.00
Plate, 9 In. .... 4.00 To 10.00
Platter, Oval 12.00
Salt & Pepper .... 7.00 To 12.50

Saucer .... 2.00 To 4.00
Soup, Cream .... 14.00 To 19.00
Soup, Dish .... 19.00 To 20.00
Sugar, Open 6.00
Teapot, Large 52.00
Teapot, Medium .... 40.00 To 45.00
Tray, Utility .... 15.00 To 18.00
Tumbler, 5 Oz. .... 10.00 To 22.00
Tumbler, 10 Oz. 9.50
Vase, Bud .... 30.00 To 42.00

ROSE

Bowl, 4 3/4 In. 10.00
Bowl, 6 In. .... 10.00 To 11.00
Bowl, 8 1/2 In. .... 14.00 To 20.00
Creamer 3.50
Cup 10.00
Cup & Saucer .... 10.00 To 16.50
Mug, Tom & Jerry ..... 30.00 To 35.00
Plate, Chop, 13 In. 15.00
Plate, 6 In. .... 2.00 To 4.25
Plate, 7 In. 2.25
Plate, 9 In. .... 5.50 To 7.50
Platter, Oval, 12 In. .... 12.50 To 20.00
Saucer .... .50 To 1.50
Soup, Dish 15.00
Sugar, Covered 18.00
Teapot, Medium 48.00
Tumbler, 5 Oz. 12.50

TURQUOISE

Ashtray .... 14.75 To 20.00
Bowl, No.5 .... 30.00
Bowl, No.6 .... 45.00
Bowl, 4 1/2 In. .... 5.50 To 6.00
Bowl, 5 In. 6.50
Bowl, 5 1/2 In. .... 6.00 To 10.00
Bowl, 6 In. .... 9.00 To 12.50
Bowl, 7 5/8 In. 25.00
Bowl, 8 1/2 In. .... 12.00 To 13.00
Bowl, 9 1/2 In. .... 15.00 To 17.50
Candleholder, Bulb, Pair 28.50
Carafe 48.00
Casserole, Covered 38.00
Coffeepot, Lid 35.00
Compote, Footed ...... 30.00 To 40.00
Creamer .... 6.00 To 7.00
Cup & Saucer .... 10.00 To 17.50
Cup & Saucer, After Dinner 25.00
Cup, After Dinner ...... 14.00 To 16.50
Gravy Boat .... 10.00 To 14.00
Mug .... 22.00 To 25.00
Plate, Chop, 13 In. ..... 10.00 To 12.50
Plate, Deep, 8 In. 11.00

Plate, Grill, 10 1/2 In. . . . 9.00 To 12.50
Plate, 6 In. . . . . 1.00 To 3.00
Plate, 7 In. . . . . 2.00 To 4.00
Plate, 9 In. . . . . 3.00 To 5.00
Plate, 10 In. . . . . 5.00 To 10.00
Platter, Oval, 12 In. . . . . . 8.00 To 15.00
Relish 20.00
Salt & Pepper 8.50
Saucer . . . . .50 To 1.25
Saucer, After Dinner 5.00
Soup, Cream . . . . 7.50 To 14.50
Soup, Flat . . . . 10.00 To 12.00
Sugar, Cover . . . . 8.00 To 15.00
Tidbit, 2 Tier 28.00
Tray, Individual, Sugar, Creamer . . 85.00
Tray, Utility . . . . 12.00 To 12.50
Tumbler, 5 Oz. 12.00
Tumbler, 10 Oz. . . . . 5.00 To 15.00
Vase, Bud 30.00

YELLOW
Ashtray . . . . 18.50 To 20.00
Bowl, Mixing, Set Of 7 . . . . 180.00
Bowl, No.5 . . . . 25.00
Bowl, No.7 . . . . 65.00
Bowl, Salad, 9 1/2 In. 32.00
Bowl, 4 1/2 In. 5.50
Bowl, 4 3/4 In. . . . . 5.50 To 10.00
Bowl, 5 1/2 In. . . . . 6.00 To 10.00
Bowl, 6 In. . . . . 10.00 To 12.50
Bowl, 7 5/8 In. 35.00
Bowl, 8 1/2 In. . . . . 10.00 To 12.00
Candleholder, Bulb, Pair 28.50
Carafe . . . . 48.00 To 57.50
Casserole, Covered 30.00
Casserole, French 77.50

Coffeepot, Lid 50.00
Compote, Sweets 18.00
Creamer, Stick Handle . . . 7.50 To 12.00
Cup 11.00
Cup & Saucer, After Dinner
. . . . 18.00 To 22.50
Cup & Saucer, Tea 12.00
Eggcup . . . . 18.00 To 20.00
Gravy Boat . . . . 13.00 To 15.00
Marmalade . . . . 67.50 To 75.00
Mug . . . . 20.00 To 32.00
Pitcher, Disk, Qt. 22.00
Pitcher, Juice . . . . 9.50 To 10.00
Pitcher, 2 Qt. . . . . 23.00 To 29.00
Plate, Chop, 13 In. . . . . . . 7.00 To 12.50
Plate, Chop, 15 In. 17.50
Plate, Grill, 10 1/2 In. . . 10.00 To 12.50
Plate, Grill, 11 1/2 In. . . 11.00 To 12.00
Plate, 6 In. . . . . 1.00 To 3.00
Plate, 7 In. . . . . 2.00 To 4.00
Plate, 9 In. . . . . 2.50 To 5.00
Plate, 10 In. . . . . 4.00 To 10.00
Platter, Oval, 12 In. . . . . . 9.00 To 15.00
Relish 18.00
Salt & Pepper . . . . 5.00 To 9.00
Saucer . . . . .50 To 2.00
Saucer, After Dinner . . . . . 3.50 To 4.00
Soup, Cream . . . . 12.00 To 17.50
Soup, Dish . . . . 10.00 To 13.00
Sugar, Cover . . . . 8.00 To 12.50
Tidbit, 2 Tier 28.00
Tray, Utility . . . . 10.00 To 14.50
Tumbler, 5 Oz. . . . . 8.00 To 12.00
Tumbler, 10 Oz. . . . . 5.00 To 8.00
Vase, Bud 33.00

Fiesta Casual, see Daisy; Yellow Carnation

Fiesta Ironstone

Fiesta Ironstone by Homer Laughlin Company, Newell, West Virginia, was made from 1970 to 1972. It was made in antique gold, turf green or mango red.

ANTIQUE GOLD
Bowl, Small 3.50
Cup 5.00
Cup & Saucer 7.50
Mug 10.00
Soup, Dish 10.00

MANGO RED
Bowl, 9 In. 15.00
Creamer 5.00

TURF GREEN
Bowl, Salad, 9 1/2 In. . . . . 7.00 To 9.00
Bowl, 8 1/2 In. . . . . 6.00 To 7.00
Creamer . . . . 3.50 To 4.00
Cup & Saucer . . . . 5.00 To 5.50
Plate, 10 In. . . . . 3.00 To 4.00

Fiesta Kitchen Kraft

Fiesta Kitchen Kraft was a bake-and-serve line made in the early 1940s by Homer Laughlin Company, Newell, West Virginia. It was made in red, yellow, green or blue.

DARK BLUE

Bowl, Nesting, No.3	19.50
Bowl, Stack	6.50 To 19.50
Cake Plate	25.00
Cake Server	30.00 To 35.00
Casserole, Covered	33.00
Cookie Jar, Large	75.00
Fork	32.50
Jar, Covered, Small	115.00
Spoon, Pair	9.00

LIGHT GREEN

Bowl, No.2	20.00
Bowl, No.3	27.50
Bowl, No.5	40.00
Bowl, Stack	15.00
Casserole, Bottom, 8 1/2 In.	25.00
Casserole, 7 1/2 In.	20.00
Fork	38.00
Jar, Medium	135.00

Platter, Goes In Metal Holder	35.00
Salt & Pepper	45.00
Spoon	17.50

RED

Cake Server	47.00
Casserole	55.00
Casserole, 8 1/2 In.	58.00
Jar, Covered, Large	175.00
Jar, Covered, Small	165.00
Jug, Covered	129.50
Shaker	50.00
Salt & Pepper	52.00
Spoon	35.00 To 42.50

YELLOW

Bowl, Stack	15.00
Cake Plate	21.00 To 37.00
Casserole, Metal Holder, 7 1/2 In.	55.00
Casserole, 8 1/2 In.	15.00
Fork	25.00
Jar, Covered	95.00
Shaker	23.00

Flower Pot

Hall China Company, East Liverpool, Ohio, made Flower Pot pattern kitchenware. The decal shows a flowerpot with a plant growing up a trellis. The bowls are made from the banded shapes.

Plate, 10 In.	4.00
Syrup, Covered	15.00

Fruit

Stangl Pottery, Trenton, New Jersey, made Fruit pattern from 1942 to 1974. The dishes had center designs that were different fruits. Some pictured apples, some pears, some grapes or other fruit. This pattern, No. 3697, was sometimes called Festive Fruit.

Chop Plate, 14 1/2 In.	12.00
Plate, 9 In.	4.00

Fruit & Flowers

Fruit & Flowers pattern, No. 4030, was made by Stangl Pottery, Trenton, New Jersey, from 1957 to 1974. The design shows a mixed grouping of flowers, leaves, grapes and fanciful shapes. Pieces have a colored border.

Bowl, Cereal	3.50
Plate, 9 In.	5.00

Fuzz Ball

The strange name Fuzz Ball has little to do with the pink and green decoration on the decal-decorated Hall dinnerware made in East Liverpool, Ohio, in the 1930s.

Casserole, Big Lip .... 8.00 To 10.00
Shaker 5.00

Garden Lane

Garden Lane is a hand-painted pattern made by Southern Potteries, Inc., Erwin, Tennessee. Yellow tulips, blue daisy-like flowers and a pink stylized rose are featured on the plate.

Plate, 6 In. 1.50
Plate, 10 In. 3.00

Gingham

Vernon Kilns, Vernon, California, made six different plaid patterns. Each plaid was given a special name, Gingham is the pattern with a dark green border and green and yellow plaid.

Cup .... 5.00 To 6.00
Pitcher, 1 Qt. 10.00
Plate, 10 In. 8.00
Saucer 3.00

Hacienda

Another Mexican-inspired pattern, Hacienda was made by Homer Laughlin China Company, Newell, West Virginia, in 1938. The dinnerware was made on Century shape. A decal showed a bench, cactus and a portion of the side of a Mexican home. Most pieces have red trim at the handles and at the edge of the plate well.

Berry Bowl, 5 In. .... 4.00 To 5.00
Bowl, Oval, 9 In. 10.00
Creamer 4.00
Cup & Saucer 8.00
Plate, 6 1/2 In. 2.00
Plate, 9 In. 3.50
Platter, Square, Well, 11 3/4 In. ... 9.00
Saucer 2.50
Soup, Flat, 8 In. 7.00
Sugar & Creamer 10.00

Hall Teapots

Teapots of all sizes and shapes were made by the Hall China Company of East Liverpool, Ohio, starting in the 1920s. Each pot had a special design name such as Airflow or Boston. Each shape could be made in one of several colors, often with names like Cadet (light blue), Camellia (rose), Dresden (deep blue), Delphinium (purple blue) or Indian Red (orange). Coffeepots were also made.

Airflow, Canary & Gold
.... 14.50 To 24.00
Airflow, Cobalt & Gold
.... 18.00 To 45.00
Airflow, Emerald & Gold 33.00
Aladdin, Canary & Gold
.... 12.50 To 20.00
Aladdin, Cobalt & Gold 35.00
Aladdin, Delphinium Blue & Gold, Infuser
.... 11.50
Aladdin, Marine & Gold 7.50
Aladdin, Marine & Gold, Infuser
.... 24.00 To 33.00
Aladdin, Pink & Gold 14.00
Albany, Brown & Gold
.... 32.00 To 35.00
Albany, Mahogany & Gold 45.00
Automobile, Black & Gold 300.00
Baltimore, Delphinium Blue & Gold
.... 25.00
Baltimore, Lettuce & Gold 26.00
Baltimore, Maroon & Gold
.... 17.00 To 22.00
Birdcage, Cobalt & Gold, 6 Cup .. 20.00
Boston, Cadet & Gold, 2 Cup 20.00
Boston, Cadet & Gold, 8 Cup 35.00
Boston, Camellia & Gold 22.50
Boston, Delphinium Blue & Gold, 6 Cup
.... 22.50
Boston, Ivory & Gold, 1 Cup 15.00
Boston, Ivory & Gold, 2 Cup 15.00
Boston, Maroon & Gold, 4 Cup .. 12.00
Boston, Poppy & Gold, 8 Cup ... 50.00
Boston, Stock Green & Gold, 1 1/2 Cup
.... 17.50
Boston, Stock Green & Gold, 4 Cup
.... 12.00
Boston, Turquoise & White, 4 Cup
.... 18.00
Boston, Warm Yellow & Gold 22.50
Cleveland, Canary & Gold 32.00

Cleveland, Emerald Green & Gold
.... 35.00
Cleveland, Forest Green & Gold .. 45.00
Cleveland, Turquoise & Gold 35.00
Cleveland, Yellow & Gold 18.00
Disraeli, Pink 12.00
Doughnut, Cadet & Gold 24.00
Football, Green & Gold 200.00
French, Cadet & Gold, 4 Cup
.... 15.00 To 45.00
French, Cadet & Gold, 6 Cup 20.00
French, Delphinium Blue & Gold, 6 Cup
.... 20.00
French, Light Russet & Gold 25.00
French, Stock Green & Gold 22.00
French, Turquoise & Gold, 6 Cup
.... 18.00
French, Warm Yellow & Gold, 6 Cup
.... 22.00
Hollywood, Black & Gold 18.00
Hollywood, Camellia & Gold
.... 15.00 To 18.00
Hollywood, Ivory & Gold, 6 Cup
.... 18.00
Hollywood, Lettuce & Gold 20.00
Hollywood, Maroon & Gold
.... 15.00 To 25.00
Hollywood, Seaspray & Gold 20.00
Hook Cover, Cadet & Gold
.... 12.00 To 15.00
Hook Cover, Delphinium Blue & Gold
.... 18.00
Lipton, Black .... 13.00 To 17.00
Lipton, Cadet 15.00
Lipton, Delphinium Blue . 15.00 To 18.00
Lipton, Delphite, 6 Cup 15.00
Lipton, Hi-Black 18.00
Lipton, Maroon 5.00
Lipton, Warm Yellow ... 15.00 To 20.00
Los Angeles, Camellia & Gold 20.00
Los Angeles, Canary & Gold
.... 12.00 To 15.00
Los Angeles, Celadon 16.00
Los Angeles, Celadon & Gold
.... 27.00 To 30.00
Los Angeles, Cobalt & Gold
.... 20.00 To 30.00
McCormick, Green ..... 21.00 To 34.00
McCormick, Maroon ... 12.00 To 22.00
McCormick, Silver 34.00
McCormick, Turquoise .. 18.00 To 22.00
McCormick, Yellow, 1 Cup 7.50

Moderne, Cadet & Gold
.... 12.00 To 18.00
Moderne, Canary & Gold
.... 10.00 To 22.00
Moderne, Cobalt & Gold 40.00
Moderne, Ivory & Gold 12.00
New York, Cadet & Gold, 6 Cup
.... 17.00 To 17.50
New York, Cobalt & Gold 9.00
New York, Cobalt & Gold, 4 Cup
.... 12.00
New York, Daffodil & Gold 12.00
New York, Lettuce & Gold 20.00
New York, Stock Green & Gold, 8 Cup,
Label 30.00
Parade, Cobalt & Gold
.... 18.00 To 24.00
Parade, Daffodil & Gold
.... 12.00 To 20.00
Parade, Rose & Gold 17.50
Philadelphia, Cadet & Gold 10.00
Philadelphia, Daffodil & Gold, 6 Cup
.... 18.00
Philadelphia, Green Lustre & Gold
.... 12.00

Philadelphia, Ivory & Gold 20.00
Philadelphia, Turquoise & Gold
.... 21.00 To 22.50
Sani-Grid, Red & Gold 15.00
Star, Cadet & Gold 45.00
Star, Turquoise & Gold
.... 13.00 To 22.00
Streamline, Canary & Gold 15.00
Streamline, Indian Red & Gold ... 45.00
Sufside, Canary & Gold 49.00
Surfside, Green Lustre & Gold 75.00
Surfside, Lettuce & Gold 72.00
Twinspout, Canary 33.00
Twinspout, Maroon 45.00
Twinspout, Turquoise 65.00
Victoria, Celadon 33.00
Windshield, Camellia & Gold, 6 Cup
.... 14.00 To 22.00
Windshield, Ivory & Gold
.... 22.00 To 24.00
Windshield, Maroon & Gold
.... 5.00 To 15.00
Windshield, Rose & Gold 12.00

Harlequin

Harlequin, a solid color dinnerware made by Homer Laughlin Company, Newell, West Virginia, was less expensive than Fiesta. It was made from 1938 to 1964 and sold unmarked in Woolworth stores. The rings molded into the plate were at the edge of the plate well and the rim was plain. Dishes were made in blue, yellow, turquoise, gray, rose, forest green, dark blue, light green, chartreuse, maroon, mauve blue, spruce green, ivory and tangerine (red).

In 1979 Woolworth stores started to sell a reissue known as Harlequin Ironstone made in turquoise, green, yellow or a new deep coral color. A few of the shapes were redesigned. Plates have the mark Homer Laughlin, although the old Harlequin plates did not.

BLUE

Animal, Deer 37.00
Animal, Duck 45.00
Animal, Fish 20.00
Bowl, Nut .... 4.00 To 5.00
Bowl, Salad 5.00
Bowl, Soup, 8 In. .... 4.50 To 7.00

Bowl, Vegetable, Oval 6.00
Bowl, 5 1/2 In. 3.00
Creamer 7.00
Cup .... 3.50 To 4.00
Cup & Saucer 4.50
Eggcup 6.00
Gravy Boat .... 6.00 To 8.00

Pitcher, 22 Oz. .... 6.00 To 8.00
Plate, 6 In. 2.00
Plate, 7 In. 1.50
Plate, 9 1/4 In. 2.50
Platter, 11 1/2 In. 4.50
Platter, 13 In. 5.50
Salt & Pepper 2.50
Saucer 1.00
Sugar, With Cover 5.00
Tumbler, 10 Oz. .... 10.00 To 18.00

CHARTREUSE
Bowl, 5 1/2 In. 3.00
Bowl, 6 1/2 In. 5.00
Bowl, 9 In. 10.00
Creamer .... 4.00 To 15.00
Cup 4.50
Cup & Saucer .... 5.50 To 10.00
Eggcup 6.00
Gravy Boat .... 8.00 To 9.00
Plate, 6 In. .... 1.25 To 1.75
Plate, 7 1/4 In. 2.50
Plate, 9 In. .... 2.50 To 3.00
Saucer 1.00
Soup, Cream 6.00
Soup, Flat 6.00
Sugar & Creamer, Covered 10.00
Sugar, Open 2.00

CORAL
Cup 3.00
Plate, 10 In. 5.00
Saucer 1.50

DARK GREEN
Bowl, Nut 5.75
Cup .... 2.50 To 3.50
Cup & Saucer .... 5.50 To 10.00
Gravy Boat 6.50
Plate, 6 In. .... 2.00 To 3.00
Plate, 7 In. 3.00
Plate, 9 In. .... 2.50 To 5.00
Plate, 10 In. 6.00
Salad, Individual .... 8.00 To 12.00
Saucer 1.50
Soup, Flat 6.00
Sugar & Creamer, Covered 10.00
Sugar, Covered .... 3.50 To 7.50

FOREST GREEN
Cup 4.50
Cup & Saucer 5.50
Plate, 6 1/4 In. 1.75
Saucer 1.00

GRAY
Bowl, Salad .... 7.00 To 8.00
Bowl, 5 1/2 In. 3.00
Casserole, Covered 25.00
Creamer .... 3.50 To 5.00
Cup .... 2.00 To 4.50
Cup & Saucer .... 5.50 To 10.00
Eggcup, Double 12.00
Gravy Boat 7.00
Pitcher, Water 14.00
Plate, 6 In. .... 1.00 To 1.75
Plate, 7 In. .... 2.00 To 3.00
Plate, 9 In. .... 3.00 To 4.00
Plate, 9 3/8 In. 5.25
Plate, 10 In. 6.00
Saucer 1.00
Shaker .... 6.00 To 8.00
Soup, Cream .... 6.00 To 9.00
Soup, Flat 6.50
Sugar & Creamer, Lid 12.00
Sugar, Covered .... 3.50 To 5.50
Teapot, Covered 29.50

GREEN
Bowl, Nut .... 3.00 To 6.00
Bowl, Soup 5.00
Bowl, 5 1/2 In. .... 2.00 To 3.00
Bowl, 6 1/4 In. 3.00
Casserole, Top 10.00
Creamer .... 3.00 To 4.00
Cup .... 2.00 To 4.50
Cup & Saucer .... 3.00 To 4.50
Eggcup 4.00
Plate, 6 In. .... 1.00 To 1.25
Plate, 7 In. .... 1.25 To 2.00
Plate, 9 In. .... 2.00 To 3.00
Plate, 10 In. 3.00
Salt & Pepper 2.50
Saucer 1.00
Soup, Cream 6.50
Sugar, Covered .... 3.00 To 4.00
Teapot 21.00

LIGHT GREEN
Cup 2.50
Cup & Saucer 3.00
Jug, Water, 22 Oz. 8.00
Plate, 6 In. 1.00
Saucer .... .75

MAROON
Animal, Donkey 45.00
Animal, Fish 48.00
Animal, Lamb 48.00

Bowl, Nut .... 4.00 To 6.00
Bowl, Vegetable, Oval 7.00
Bowl, 5 1/2 In. 4.50
Casserole, Covered .... 25.00 To 39.00
Creamer .... 6.00 To 15.00
Cup & Saucer 10.00
Eggcup 6.00
Gravy Boat .... 6.00 To 10.00
Jug, Water 18.00
Pitcher, 22 Oz. .... 6.00 To 8.00
Plate, 6 In. .... 1.00 To 2.00
Plate, 9 1/4 In. 4.75
Platter, 11 In. .... 6.00 To 7.50
Salt 4.50
Soup, Cream .... 5.00 To 14.00
Sugar & Creamer, Covered 10.00
Sugar & Lid 7.50
Teapot 17.00
Tumbler 22.00

MAUVE BLUE
Animal, Lamb 48.00
Animal, Penguin 60.00
Bowl, Nut .... 3.00 To 6.00
Bowl, Salad, 7 In. .... 6.00 To 10.00
Bowl, Vegetable, Oval .... 6.00 To 7.00
Bowl, 5 1/2 In. .... 2.00 To 3.00
Bowl, 6 1/2 In. 5.00
Casserole, Covered 25.00
Creamer 4.00
Cup .... 2.00 To 4.00
Cup & Saucer .... 3.00 To 5.00
Eggcup .... 5.00 To 8.50
Gravy Boat .... 6.00 To 8.00
Jug, Pint 13.00
Jug, Water 26.00
Plate, 6 In. .... 1.00 To 1.75
Plate, 7 In. .... 1.50 To 2.00
Plate, 9 3/8 In. 5.00
Platter, Oval, 11 In. 5.50
Salt .... 2.00 To 4.00
Saucer .... .75 To 2.00
Saucer, After Dinner 6.00
Soup, Cream .... 5.00 To 8.50
Soup, Flat 6.00
Sugar, Covered 6.00
Tea Set, 5 Piece 70.00
Teapot, Covered .... 22.00 To 25.00
Tumbler 17.00

MEDIUM GREEN
Creamer 3.00
Plate, 10 In. 5.00

RED
Animal, Lamb 145.00
Ashtray 17.50
Bowl, Nut 5.00
Bowl, 5 1/2 In. .... 3.00 To 4.00
Butter, Covered, 1 Pound 15.00
Candleholder 45.00
Creamer .... 3.50 To 9.50
Cup .... 4.00 To 4.50
Cup & Saucer 4.00
Dish, Nut .... 4.00 To 6.75
Eggcup .... 11.00 To 15.00
Gravy Boat .... 6.00 To 8.00
Jug, Water .... 18.00 To 32.00
Marmalade, Covered 50.00
Pitcher, 22 Oz. 18.00
Plate, 6 In. .... 1.50 To 3.00
Plate, 7 1/4 In. .... 2.50 To 2.75
Plate, 9 In. .... 3.00 To 5.00
Platter, Oval, 11 In. 12.00
Platter, Oval, 13 In. ...... 6.00 To 7.00
Salt & Pepper 9.00
Saucer 1.00
Soup, Cream .... 6.00 To 15.00
Soup, Flat 6.00
Sugar & Creamer, Covered
.... 15.00 To 21.00
Sugar, Covered .... 6.50 To 10.00
Teapot, Covered .... 25.00 To 40.00
Tumbler 19.00

ROSE
Ashtray, Basket .... 22.00 To 24.00
Bowl, Salad, Individual .... 6.00 To 8.00
Bowl, Vegetable, Oval 9.00
Bowl, Vegetable, Round 8.00
Bowl, 5 1/2 In. .... 2.00 To 4.00
Bowl, 6 1/2 In. 3.00
Casserole, Covered 25.00
Creamer .... 3.00 To 6.00
Cup .... 2.00 To 4.50
Cup & Saucer .... 3.00 To 6.50
Cup With Saucer, After Dinner ... 15.00
Dish, Nut .... 4.50 To 6.00
Eggcup 5.00
Eggcup, Double 6.50
Gravy Boat .... 6.00 To 9.00
Pitcher, Water .... 6.00 To 15.00
Plate, 6 In. .... 1.00 To 1.50
Plate, 7 In. .... 1.50 To 3.00
Plate, 9 In. .... 2.00 To 3.00
Plate, 9 3/8 In. 5.00
Plate, 10 In. 6.00
Platter, 11 In. .... 4.00 To 6.00

Salt 2.00
Saucer .... .75 To 1.50
Saucer, After Dinner 4.00
Soup, Cream .... 4.00 To 6.00
Soup, Flat .... 4.50 To 8.00
Sugar & Creamer, Covered
.... 8.00 To 10.00
Sugar, Covered .... 5.00 To 6.50
Teapot 30.00

SPRUCE GREEN

Animal, Fish .... 37.00 To 45.00
Animal, Penguin 48.00
Bowl, Salad 10.00
Creamer .... 4.00 To 6.00
Cup 4.50
Cup & Saucer .... 4.50 To 5.50
Dish, Nut .... 3.00 To 6.00
Eggcup .... 6.00 To 12.00
Gravy Boat 7.00
Plate, 6 In. .... 1.00 To 2.00
Plate, 7 1/4 In. 2.50
Plate, 9 In. .... 3.00 To 4.50
Platter, 11 1/4 In. .... 5.00 To 6.00
Salt & Pepper 2.00
Saucer 1.00
Soup, Cream 5.00
Sugar & Creamer, Covered
.... 7.50 To 12.00
Sugar, Covered 4.50
Tumbler, Water 14.00

TURQUOISE

Ashtray, Basket .... 18.00 To 30.00
Bowl, Salad, 7 In. ...... 6.00 To 8.00
Bowl, Vegetable, Oval .... 5.00 To 6.00
Bowl, 5 1/2 In. .... 2.00 To 4.00
Bowl, 6 1/2 In. .... 3.00 To 4.00
Butter, Covered 7.00
Casserole, Covered .... 18.00 To 20.00
Creamer .... 3.00 To 5.00
Cup .... 2.00 To 4.00
Cup & Saucer .... 3.00 To 4.75
Cup, After Dinner ...... 10.50 To 18.00
Dish, Nut .... 4.00 To 5.50
Eggcup, Double .... 4.00 To 6.00
Gravy Boat .... 4.00 To 7.50
Jug, Water 15.00
Marmalade, Covered 40.00
Pitcher, Water 12.00
Plate, 6 In. .... .75 To 1.25

Plate, 7 In. .... 1.25 To 2.25
Plate, 9 In. .... 1.75 To 5.00
Plate, 10 In. 6.00
Platter, Oval, 11 In. ...... 4.00 To 6.00
Platter, Oval, 13 In. 8.00
Salt & Pepper .... 4.00 To 7.50
Saucer .... 1.00 To 1.50
Saucer, After Dinner 4.00
Soup, Cream .... 5.00 To 12.00
Soup, Flat .... 4.75 To 6.00
Sugar & Creamer, Covered 10.00
Sugar, Covered .... 3.00 To 5.00
Teapot, Small Lid 17.50
Tumbler, 10 Oz. 18.00

YELLOW

Animal, Cat 25.00
Animal, Donkey 48.00
Animal, Fish 35.00
Animal, Penguin 48.00
Ashtray, Basket Weave 14.00
Baker, Oval, 9 In. 5.50
Bowl, Vegetable, Oval 6.00
Bowl, 5 3/4 In. .... 2.50 To 4.00
Bowl, 6 1/2 In. .... 3.00 To 4.00
Bowl, 7 1/2 In. .... 5.00 To 10.00
Casserole, Covered .... 18.00 To 20.00
Creamer .... 2.00 To 9.00
Cup .... 2.00 To 4.00
Cup & Saucer .... 3.00 To 5.00
Cup, After Dinner ...... 10.50 To 19.00
Dish, Nut .... 3.50 To 6.00
Eggcup .... 4.00 To 6.50
Jug, Water .... 15.00 To 23.00
Pitcher, Water 23.50
Plate, 6 In. .... 1.00 To 1.75
Plate, 7 In. .... 1.25 To 4.00
Plate, 9 In. .... 2.00 To 4.00
Plate, 10 In. .... 5.00 To 6.00
Platter, Oval, 11 1/2 In. .. 3.00 To 4.50
Salt & Pepper .... 2.50 To 6.00
Saucer 1.00
Saucer, After Dinner 4.50
Soup, Cream 5.00
Soup, Flat .... 5.00 To 6.50
Spoon Rest 85.00
Sugar & Creamer, Covered
.... 8.00 To 10.00
Sugar, Covered .... 3.00 To 4.00
Teapot .... 15.00 To 25.00
Tumbler, 10 Oz. 18.00

Hawaiian Coral

Hawaiian Coral was made by Vernon Kilns, Vernon, California. It has a spattered edge.

Cup & Saucer 6.00
Plate, 10 In. 3.00

Hawaiian Daisy, see Daisy

Hawaiian Flowers

Hawaiian Flowers was a well-known Vernon Kilns, Vernon, California, tableware designed by Don Blanding. It was first made in 1939.

Cup & Saucer 10.00
Plate, 10 In. 10.00

Hilda

A large red flower and an assortment of blue and yellow flowers surround the rim of the Hilda plate. The pattern, made on the Candlewick shape, was made by Southern Potteries, Inc., Erwin, Tennessee.

Bowl, 5 In. 1.50
Bowl, 6 In. 2.00

Bowl, 9 In. 6.00
Plate, 6 In. 1.25
Plate, 6 3/4 In. 2.00
Plate, 9 1/2 In. 2.50
Platter 2.50
Soup, Plate 2.50

Holland, see Crocus

Holly

From 1967 to 1972 the Stangl Pottery, Trenton, New Jersey, made Holly pattern dinnerware.

Bowl, 10 In. 7.25
Plate, 12 1/2 In. 7.50

Homespun

Homespun, a yellow, green and reddish-brown plaid pattern, was made by Vernon Kilns, Vernon, California.

Plate, 10 In. 8.00
Punch Bowl, Shaped Like A Large Cup
.... 65.00

Iroquois

Russel Wright was an important industrial designer. His dinnerwares were made by at least four companies. Iroquois Casual China was a Russel Wright modern design made by Iroquois China Company, Syracuse, New York. The dinnerware was less expensive than American Modern, heavier and less breakable, It was advertised as cook-and-serve. The first pieces were marked "China by Iroquois" with the signature of Russel Wright. In the 1950s the ware was redesigned and the mark was changed to "Iroquois Casual China" by Russel Wright. The dishes were made in a number of colors, designed to be mixed and matched. Sets were often sold with pieces of several colors. The original Iroquois was glazed Ice Blue, Forest Green, Avocado Yellow, Lemon Yellow, Nutmeg Brown or Sugar White. In 1951 more colors were added, including Lettuce Green, Charcoal, Ripe Apricot, Pink Sherbet, Parsley Green, Canteloupe, Oyster Gray, Aqua, Brick Red or Grayed-Blue.

In 1959 some Iroquois pieces were decorated with patterns and sold under other names. Glass tumblers were made in matching colors.

CHARCOAL

Bowl, Flared, 10 In.	8.00
Bowl, Soup, Flat	4.00 To 7.00
Bowl, 5 In.	3.00
Bowl, 8 In.	5.00
Bowl, 11 3/4 In.	10.00
Creamer	15.00
Cup & Saucer	5.00
Plate, 6 1/4 In.	2.00
Plate, 7 1/4 In.	3.00
Plate, 9 3/4 In.	4.00
Platter, Well, Tree, 17 1/2 In.	20.00
Saucer	3.00
Sugar, Open	3.50

LEMON YELLOW

Cup & Saucer	9.00
Dish, Serving, 7 X 10 In.	5.00
Plate, 8 In.	2.00
Plate, 10 In.	3.00
Saltshaker	2.00

PINK SHERBET

Bowl, Handled, 5 In.	3.00
Bowl, Vegetable	10.00
Bowl, 8 In.	5.00 To 7.00
Bowl, 9 3/4 In.	8.00
Casserole, Covered	15.00
Creamer	4.00 To 7.00
Cup	5.00
Cup & Saucer	5.00 To 7.50
Dish, Serving, 7 X 10 In.	5.00
Plate, 6 In.	1.50 To 2.00
Plate, 7 1/4 In.	3.00
Plate, 9 3/4 In.	4.00
Plate, 10 In.	3.00 To 5.00
Saucer	1.00 To 1.50
Sugar & Creamer	8.00
Sugar & Creamer, Covered	8.75
Wine Carafe	65.00

RIPE APRICOT

Bowl, 5 In.	4.00
Casserole, Covered, 1 1/2 Qt.	35.00
Creamer, Stacking	7.00
Cup & Saucer	8.00
Dish, Gumbo, Handled, 21 Oz.	12.00
Plate, 5 In.	2.50
Plate, 10 In.	5.00
Vegetable, Divided, Covered	30.00
Vegetable, Open, 8 In.	18.00

WHITE

Creamer, Restyled	8.50
Creamer, Stacking	9.00
Cup	3.00
Cup & Saucer	10.00
Pitcher, Open, 1 1/2 Qt.	20.00
Plate & Cup, Party Set	20.00
Plate, 6 1/2 In.	2.00
Plate, 10 In.	3.00 To 6.00
Platter, 12 3/4 In.	15.00
Salt & Pepper, Stacking	12.00
Soup, Dish, 8 1/4 In.	8.00

Kitchen Kraft

Kitchen Kraft oven-to-table pieces were made by Homer Laughlin China Company, Newell, West Virginia, from the early 1930s. The pieces were made in plain, solid colors or with decals. If decorated with decals they are listed in this book under the decal's name. If solid colors they are listed here.

BLUE
Casserole, Covered, Individual, Marked
.... 38.00

Saltshaker 18.00

GREEN
Stack Set, Marked 15.00

YELLOW
Bowl, Mixing, 6 In. 15.00
Bowl, Mixing, 13 In. 18.00
Casserole, 8 In. 15.00
Saltshaker 18.00

Kumquat

Kumquat is a Stangl Pottery pattern introduced in 1950.

Cup & Saucer .... 5.00 To 6.00
Plate, 8 In. 4.00

Lipton

Lipton is the name of a line of teapots, sugars and creamers marked with the name Lipton Tea on the bottom. These pieces were made by Hall China Company. The teapot is the French shape, the sugar and creamer are Boston shape.

CADET
Sugar & Creamer, Covered
.... 10.00 To 15.00

HI-BLACK
Creamer 5.00

YELLOW
Creamer 8.50

Lotus

Lotus was made by Red Wing Pottery in the Concord shape.

Bowl, Fruit 3.00
Bowl, Vegetable, 8 1/2 In. 7.00
Cup & Saucer 6.00

Gravy Boat, Tray Attached 6.00
Plate, 6 1/4 In. 3.00
Plate, 10 1/2 In. 5.00
Platter, 11 X 13 In. 5.00
Saucer 2.00

Lu-Ray

The characteristic slightly speckled glass of the solid-colored Lu-Ray makes it easy to identify. Taylor, Smith and Taylor, Chester, West Virginia, made this pattern after 1938. Pastel colors include Windsor Blue, Persian Cream, Sharon Pink, Surf Green and Chatham Gray.

BLUE

Bowl, Handled, 6 In. 2.00
Bowl, Round, 9 In. 6.00
Bowl, Vegetable, Oval 6.50
Bowl, 5 In. . . . . 1.00 To 3.00
Creamer . . . . 2.00 To 4.00
Cup 2.00
Cup & Saucer . . . . .75 To 3.25
Cup & Saucer, After Dinner
. . . . 6.00 To 9.00
Eggcup 4.00
Jug, Water, Tall 17.50
Plate, Grill, 10 In. 6.00
Plate, 6 1/2 In. . . . . 1.00 To 2.00
Plate, 7 1/2 In. . . . . 1.50 To 2.00
Plate, 8 In. . . . . 1.50 To 2.00
Plate, 9 In. . . . . 2.25 To 4.00
Plate, 10 In. . . . . 2.50 To 3.00
Platter, 11 1/2 In. . . . . 7.00 To 9.50
Platter, 13 5/8 In. 5.00
Salt & Pepper . . . . 4.50 To 8.00
Saucer . . . . .50 To 1.25
Soup, Cream 3.50
Soup, Flat . . . . 2.75 To 4.00
Sugar, Covered 2.50
Vegetable, Oval 6.00

GRAY

Cup 2.50
Plate, 7 In. 10.00
Saucer 1.50

GREEN

Berry Bowl . . . . 1.00 To 3.00
Bowl, Vegetable, Oval 3.50
Bowl, 5 1/2 In. 1.75
Butter, Covered 5.00
Creamer . . . . 2.00 To 2.50
Cup & Saucer . . . . 3.25 To 4.50
Cup & Saucer, After Dinner
. . . . 6.00 To 9.00
Jug, Water, Tall 17.50
Plate, Grill, 10 In. 6.00
Plate, 6 1/2 In. . . . . 1.25 To 2.00

Plate, 7 1/2 In. . . . . .75 To 1.50
Plate, 8 In. 1.50
Plate, 9 In. . . . . 2.25 To 4.00
Plate, 10 In. . . . . 2.50 To 3.00
Platter, Oval, 11 5/8 In. 4.00
Platter, Oval, 13 1/2 In. 5.00
Salt & Pepper . . . . 4.50 To 6.00
Saucer . . . . .50 To .75
Saucer, After Dinner 3.00
Shaker 4.00
Soup, Flat, 8 In. . . . . 2.75 To 3.50
Sugar, Covered . . . . 3.75 To 4.50

PINK

Berry Bowl . . . . 1.00 To 1.50
Bowl, Handled, 6 In. 2.00
Bowl, Vegetable, 9 In. 4.00
Bowl, 5 In. . . . . 1.50 To 5.00
Creamer . . . . 2.00 To 4.00
Cup . . . . 2.00 To 3.00
Cup & Saucer . . . . 3.25 To 3.50
Cup & Saucer, After Dinner 6.00
Eggcup 4.00
Gravy Boat . . . . 8.00 To 10.00
Pitcher, Ice Lip 22.50
Plate, 6 1/2 In. . . . . 1.00 To 1.50
Plate, 7 In. . . . . .75 To 2.00
Plate, 9 In. . . . . 2.25 To 5.00
Plate, 10 In. . . . . 2.75 To 4.00
Plate, 13 In. 8.00
Platter, 11 3/4 In. 3.75
Platter, 13 1/2 In. . . . . 5.00 To 6.50
Salt & Pepper . . . . 6.00 To 8.00
Saucer . . . . .75 To 1.25
Saucer, After Dinner 3.00
Soup, Cream . . . . 3.00 To 3.50
Soup, Flat . . . . 2.75 To 4.00
Sugar, Covered . . . . 3.00 To 6.00

YELLOW

Bowl, Vegetable 5.50
Bowl, 5 In. . . . . 1.00 To 3.00
Butter, Covered, 1/4 Pound
. . . . 15.00 To 18.00
Creamer . . . . 2.00 To 4.00
Cup . . . . 3.00 To 4.50
Cup & Saucer . . . . 3.25 To 3.50
Eggcup 4.00
Gravy Boat, Underplate 7.50
Jug, Ball 15.00
Jug, Water, Short 17.50
Plate, 6 1/2 In. . . . . 1.00 To 1.50

Plate, 7 In. .... .75 To 2.00	Salt .... 2.50 To 4.00
Plate, 8 In. 1.50	Saucer .... .50 To .75
Plate, 9 In. .... 2.25 To 4.00	Saucer, After Dinner 3.00
Plate, 10 In. .... 2.50 To 4.00	Soup, Cream 2.50
Platter, 11 3/4 In. 3.75	Soup, Flat 4.00
Platter, 13 In. 8.00	

Magnolia

A wide bright cranberry red band borders Magnolia pattern by Stangl Pottery, Trenton, New Jersey. The pattern, No. 3870, was made from 1952 to 1962. Another version of Magnolia is known that does not have the banded edge.

Bowl, Fruit 4.00

Bowl, 7 In. 4.00	
Creamer 6.00	
Cup & Saucer 7.00	
Plate, Dinner, 10 1/2 In. 5.00	
Platter, 13 In. 5.00	
Sugar 2.00	

Mardi Gras

Southern Potteries, Inc., Erwin, Tennessee, made Mardi Gras, a hand-painted dinnerware. The flowers pictured are only half seen on the plate. A large blue daisy and a large pink-petaled flower are surrounded by leaves and buds.

Cup & Saucer 4.00
Plate, 10 In. 5.00

Max-i-cana

The Mexican-inspired dinnerwares can be confusing. Max-i-cana is a Homer Laughlin China Company pattern. The decal design shows a Mexican napping amid pottery jars and cactus. It was made on a Yellowstone shape with octagonal plates. Do not confuse it with Mexicana.

Bowl, 6 In. .... 4.50 To 6.50	
Eggcup, Rolled Top .... 10.00 To 15.00	
Gravy Boat 15.00	
Plate, 9 In. .... 3.50 To 4.50	
Platter, Oval, 11 1/2 In. 10.00	
Platter, 11 1/2 In. 5.00	
Platter, 13 1/2 In. 10.00	

Mayflower

Mayflower is a pattern by Vernon Kilns, Vernon, California.

Bowl, Sauce, 5 1/4 In. 2.00
Plate, 9 1/2 In. 3.50

Mexicana

The first of the Mexican-inspired patterns that became popular as a dinnerware in the 1930s was Mexicana. This decal-decorated set was first offered in 1938. The design shows a collection of orange and yellow pots with a few cactus. The edge of the dishwell is rimmed with red or occasionally yellow, green or blue. Almost all of the pieces are Century line, a popular Homer Laughlin dinnerware shape.

Bowl, Fruit, Handled, 5 In.
.... 3.00 To 4.00
Bowl, Soup, Handles 2.25
Bowl, 5 In. 4.50

Bowl, 6 In. 6.00
Bowl, 8 In. 6.50
Creamer .... 4.00 To 6.00
Cup 6.50
Eggcup, Double 7.50
Plate, Deep, 7 3/4 In. 6.00
Plate, 6 In. .... 2.00 To 4.00
Plate, 7 In. .... 1.00 To 5.00
Plate, 9 In. .... 2.00 To 4.00
Plate, 9 1/2 In. 5.00
Platter, 11 1/2 In. .... 7.00 To 8.00
Platter, 13 1/4 In. .... 6.50 To 9.00
Saucer .... 1.00 To 1.50
Sugar, Covered 12.00
Tray, 7 X 13 In. 20.00

Mexicana Kitchen Kraft

The kitchenwares that matched the dinnerware Mexicana were made with the same decorations. Mixing bowls, casseroles, pie plates, pie servers, cake plates and other pieces were made by the Homer Laughlin Company.

Casserole, 8 1/2 In. .... 25.00 To 30.00
Pie Plate, 10 In. 18.00
Salt & Pepper 25.00
Server 22.00

Modern California

Modern California was made in the 1930s by Vernon Kilns, Vernon, California. Colors include azure blue, orchid, pistachio, straw, sand or gray.

AZURE
Cup & Saucer .... 7.00 To 8.50
Plate, 10 In. .... 3.50 To 6.00

PISTACHIO
Creamer 7.00
Plate, 9 In. .... 3.00 To 5.00

Morning Glory

From 1942 to 1949 the Hall China Company, East Liverpool, Ohio, made a dinnerware called Morning Glory. The outside of the pieces was Cadet blue, the inside had a Morning Glory decal decoration.

Bowl, No.3 .... 6.50
Coffee, Drip 35.00
Teapot 25.00

Moss Rose

Moss Rose was made by Southern Potteries, Inc., Erwin, Tennessee, under the trade name Blue Ridge, from 1920 to 1957. It was a hand-painted pattern. Another pattern called Moss Rose was made by the Universal Potteries, Cambridge, Ohio, from 1953 to 1955. It had decal decorations.

Cup & Saucer	5.00 To 6.00
Plate, 6 In.	2.00

Mountain Nosegay

A blue tulip, yellow, dark purple, pink and rose colored flowers are hand-painted on the Mountain Nosegay plate. It is a dinnerware made by Southern Potteries, Inc., Erwin, Tennessee.

Bowl, Saucer, 5 1/4 In. 3.00

Cup	3.00
Plate, 6 In.	2.00
Plate, 7 In.	3.50
Plate, 9 1/2 In.	4.50
Plate, 10 In.	5.50
Saucer	2.50
Sugar, Large	5.00

Nautilus

Nautilus is a Homer Laughlin pattern. The decorations were put on Century-shaped dishes.

Creamer	5.00
Plate, 8 In.	1.50

Orange Poppy, see Poppy

Orchard Song

Orchard Song was made by Stangl Pottery, Trenton, New Jersey, from 1962 to 1974.

Creamer	4.00
Tray, Relish	6.00

Organdie

Organdie is one of six different plaid patterns made by Vernon Kilns, Vernon, California. It is an overall brown pattern with a yellow and brown plaid border.

Butter	13.00
Carafe	12.00
Casserole, Open-Handled	3.00

Plate, 6 1/2 In.	1.00
Plate, 7 1/2 In.	2.00
Plate, 9 1/2 In.	3.00
Plate, 12 1/4 In.	4.00
Saucer	.50
Shaker, Pair	5.00
Sugar, Covered	5.00
Vegetable, Round, 8 In.	5.00

Patio

Patio is a Paden City Mexican-decal-decorated dinnerware. It was made on the Shell-Crest Shape. The Paden City, West Virginia, pottery made dinnerwares from 1907 to the 1950s. The Patio decal shows a doorway and a group of pots in blue, purple and yellow. One orange blossom on a long stem is pictured in a pot. The handled pieces often have red trim on the edge.

Cup & Saucer	6.00
Plate, 6 In.	3.00
Plate, 10 In.	4.00

Petit Point Leaf

Petit Point Leaf is yet another design that looks like stitches. It was made by the Crooksville China Company, Crooksville, Ohio. The company made a similar pattern called Petit Point House.

Plate, 10 In.	2.50

Petit Point Rose

Notice the spelling of the name Petit Point. The pattern shows a border of roses that seem to have been stitched together. It was made by Harker Pottery Company of Chester, West Virginia.

Coffeepot, Cover	10.00
Cup	5.00

Petitpoint

Petitpoint is a confusing pattern and even the spelling can be odd. Petitpoint, a decal showing patterns that seem to have been made of small stitches, was used by Homer Laughlin China Company, Newell, West Virginia, in a variety of shapes in the 1960s.

Petit Point Rose is a similar pattern by Harker Pottery.

Cake Plate, Kitchen Kraft	15.00
Pie Plate, Kitchen Kraft	10.00
Pitcher	25.00

Pink Cosmos

Pink Cosmos is a 1966 design made by Stangl Pottery, Trenton, New Jersey.

Creamer	6.50
Cup & Saucer	5.50 To 8.00
Plate, 8 In.	4.00 To 6.00
Plate, 10 In.	6.00 To 8.00
Platter, Oval, 15 In.	15.00

Pink Mums

Pink Mums is a decal-decorated design made by the Hall China Company, East Liverpool, Ohio, possibly in the 1930s.

Creamer 4.00
Shaker 4.00

Pinkie

Pinkie is a Blue Ridge, hand-painted dinnerware made by Southern Potteries, Inc., Erwin, Tennessee. The main flower has five pink flowers and a sponged center. Dark leaves complete the spray design.

Cup, Regular 3.50
Plate, 9 1/2 In. 3.50
Saucer 2.00

Poinsettia

Poinsettia pattern shows large red flowers and green leaves. The hand-painted pattern was made by Southern Potteries, Inc., Erwin, Tennessee.

Plate, 6 In. 4.00
Plate, 10 In. 4.00

Poppy

Poppy, sometimes called Orange Poppy by collectors, was made by the Hall China Company, East Liverpool, Ohio, from 1933 through the 1950s. The decals picture realistic groups of orange poppies with a few leaves. Another Hall pattern called Red Poppy has bright red stylized flowers with black leaves and trim.

Baker, Fluted, 7 3/4 In. . . 9.00 To 10.00
Baker, Fluted, French, 3 Part 15.00
Bean Pot, New England
. . . . 22.50 To 35.00
Bowl, Cereal . . . . 5.00 To 8.50
Bowl, Drip, Covered 15.00
Bowl, Mayonnaise, Plate 15.00
Bowl, Mixing, Set Of 4 . . . . 25.00
Bowl, Salad . . . . 9.00 To 13.00
Bowl, Soup, Flat 10.50
Bowl, Sunshine, No.1 . . . . 3.00
Bowl, Sunshine, No.3 . . . . 7.00
Bowl, Sunshine, No.4 . . . . 8.00
Bowl, Sunshine, No.5 . . . . 10.00
Bowl, Vegetable, Round, 9 1/2 In.
. . . . 12.50
Bowl, 5 1/4 In. 2.00
Bowl, 6 In. . . . . 5.00 To 8.50
Bowl, 6 1/4 In. 6.50
Bowl, 8 3/4 In. 9.00
Cake Plate . . . . 12.00 To 18.00
Casserole, Oval, Covered
. . . . 28.00 To 35.00

Coffee & Drip, Lid 45.00
Coffeepot, Dripolator, Covered
. . . . 32.00 To 45.00
Coffeepot, Golden Key
. . . . 25.00 To 28.00
Cookie Jar, Covered 40.00
Creamer . . . . 7.50 To 9.00
Cup 6.00
Dish, Leftover, Loop Handle
. . . . 37.00 To 40.00
Drippings Jar, Covered . . 15.00 To 20.00
Jug, Ball, No.3 . . . . 19.00
Jug, Milk 17.50
Jug, Sunshine, No.5 . . . . 15.00 To 19.00
Mustard, Covered . . . . . . 20.00 To 25.00
Pepper 8.50
Pepper, Range 8.00
Pitcher, Milk . . . . 12.50 To 15.00
Plate, 6 In. 3.50
Plate, 9 In. 25.00
Plate, 9 1/2 In. 15.00
Platter, 13 In. 13.75
Shaker, Handle Range 12.00
Soup, Dish 10.50
Soup, Flat . . . . 9.75 To 10.50
Sugar & Creamer, Golden Key
. . . . 10.00 To 20.00
Sugar, Covered . . . . 12.00 To 14.00
Teapot, Covered, Melody
. . . . 52.00 To 55.00
Teapot, Doughnut . . . . . 50.00 To 90.00
Teapot, Melody 55.00

Poppy & Wheat

Poppy & Wheat is a design that seems to have been made in the 1930s. It was made by Hall China Company, East Liverpool, Ohio. The design shows a realistic spray of orange flowers and wheat heads. It is sometimes called Wheat.

Shaker, Flour 12.00
Shaker, Pepper 12.00
Teapot, 6 Cup 16.00

Poppy Trail

Metlox Poppy Trail Manufacturing Company of California made many dinnerwares marked with the words Metlox or Poppy Trail. Solid colored wares and hand-decorated pieces were made. Listed here are solid pieces marked Metlox Poppy Trail.

BLUE
Carafe 15.00
Tumbler, Ribbed 5.00

ORANGE
Plate, 10 In. 3.50

Tumbler, Ribbed 5.00
Tumbler, Straight Sided 5.00

ROSE
Plate, 10 In. 3.50
Tumbler, Ribbed 5.00

RUST
Tumbler, Straight Sided 5.00

TURQUOISE
Plate, 10 In. 3.50
Tumbler, Ribbed 5.00

WHITE
Plate, 10 In. 3.50

YELLOW
Bowl, Fruit, 5 1/2 In. 3.00
Bread & Butter 1.00
Cup & Saucer 4.00
Plate, Chop, 12 In. 5.50
Plate, 8 In. 2.00
Plate, 10 In. .... 3.00 To 3.50
Platter, 13 In. 5.00
Soup, Set, 7 In. 3.50
Tumbler, Ribbed 5.00
Vegetable, Open, 9 In. 4.50

Prelude

Prelude is a pattern with a stylized flower design. It was made by Stangl Pottery, Trenton, New Jersey, from 1949 to 1957.

Plate, 10 In. 5.00
Sugar & Creamer, Covered 7.50

Priscilla

Priscilla was made by Homer Laughlin China Company, Newell, West Virginia. It is a decal-decorated ware with pale pink roses and sprigs of flowers.

Cake Plate 4.00
Pitcher 12.50
Plate, 10 In. 4.00

Provincial

Provincial is a bordered plate with a floral center made by Stangl Pottery, Trenton, New Jersey, from 1957 to 1967.

Eggcup, Bake-Ware 2.50
Plate, 12 1/2 In. 12.00
Saucer 2.00

Quilted Fruit

Southern Potteries of Erwin, Tennessee, made Quilted Fruit from 1920 to 1957. The hand-painted decorations resembled pieces of fruit made from printed calicoes. Stitching outlined the leaves and the fruit.

Cup & Saucer	5.50
Plate, 6 In.	1.50
Plate, 10 In.	5.00
Sugar & Creamer, Covered	17.50

Red Poppy

Bright red flowers and black leaves were used on this popular Hall pattern called Red Poppy. The pattern, made in East Liverpool, Ohio, from 1930 through 1950, was a premium item for Grand Union Tea Company. Matching metal pieces were made, such as wastebaskets and bread boxes, and glass tumblers are known.

Berry Bowl	5.00
Bowl, No.3	7.00 To 13.00
Bowl, No.4	10.00
Bowl, No.5	9.00 To 13.00
Bowl, Salad	6.00 To 12.00
Bowl, Soup, 9 In.	6.00
Bowl, Vegetable, Round, 9 1/2 In.	10.00
Bowl, 5 1/2 In.	5.00
Bowl, 6 1/4 In.	5.00
Cake Plate	8.00 To 10.00
Casserole	7.00
Clock, Electric	90.00 To 95.00
Coffeepot, Electric	40.00
Coffeepot, Rickson	18.00 To 20.00
Creamer, Mary Lou	5.00 To 8.50
Cup & Saucer	5.00 To 6.00
Cup, Poppy Inside	3.00
Cup, Poppy Outside	3.00
Custard Bowl	3.00
Jug, No.286	15.00
Jug, Water, Sunshine No.5	17.00 To 20.00
Matchsafe, 2 Pocket	15.00
Pitcher	7.50
Plate, 7 1/2 In.	3.00
Plate, 9 In.	3.00 To 5.50
Platter, Oval, 11 In.	7.00 To 11.00
Salt & Pepper, Egg Drop	9.00 To 14.50
Salt & Pepper, Handled	10.00 To 17.50
Saucer	2.50
Soup, Flat	6.00 To 10.50
Sugar & Creamer, Covered	18.00
Sugar, Rickson	3.00 To 6.00
Teapot, New York	34.50

Red Riding Hood

One of the easiest patterns of American dinnerware to recognize is Red Riding Hood.
Three-dimensional figures of the little girl
with the red hood have been adapted into
saltshakers, teapots and other pieces. The
pattern was made by the Hull Pottery Company, Crooksville, Ohio.

Bank 195.00
Butter, Covered, Rectangular
.... 85.00 To 98.00
Cookie Jar, Blue Skirt ... 30.00 To 55.00
Creamer .... 32.00 To 35.00
Dish, Mustard, Covered, Spoon
.... 125.00
Pitcher, Milk, Tall, 8 In. 90.00
Pitcher, 6 1/2 In. 55.00
Pitcher, 7 1/2 In. 65.00
Salt & Pepper, 3 1/4 In. 23.00
Salt & Pepper, 5 1/4 In.
.... 34.00 To 35.00
Sugar & Creamer 50.00

Teapot, Covered .... 85.00 To 95.00
Wall Pocket 150.00

Red Rose

A single red rose on one side of the plate and
perhaps a rosebud on the other is the design
for the Paden City Red Rose pattern. The
dinnerware was made in Paden City, West
Virginia.

Bowl, Soup, Handled 3.00
Bowl, 5 1/4 In. 2.00
Plate, 6 In. 1.50
Plate, 8 1/2 In. 3.00
Plate, 10 1/4 In. 4.00

Refrigerator Ware

Refrigerator sets were made by the Hall
China Company, East Liverpool, Ohio, from
the late 1930s. For Westinghouse the company made Patrician in 1938, Emperor in
1939, Aristocrat in 1940-1941 and Prince in
1952. They also made King and Queen
ovenware to match the Refrigerator Ware.
Sears, Roebuck, Montgomery Ward, Hotpoint and General Electric also used Hall Refrigerator Ware. The company also made
some pieces sold with the Hall name. They
were Bingo in the late 1930s, Plaza in the
1930s to the 1960s and Norris.

Hotpoint, Leftover, Round, 9 In., Yellow
.... 17.00

Montgomery Ward, Bowl, Covered, 8 In.
.... 10.00
Montgomery Ward, Pitcher, Blue
.... 18.00
Sears, Roebuck, Leftover, 3 Piece
.... 16.00
Westinghouse, Leftover, Patrician Blue
.... 6.00 To 7.50
Westinghouse, Pitcher, Water,
Emperor, Blue ...... 12.00 To 16.00
Westinghouse, Roaster, Covered, King,
Canary 8.00
Westinghouse, Roaster, Open, King, Canary
.... 4.00

Rhythm Rose

Rhythm Rose was made by Homer Laughlin China Company, Newell, West Virginia, from the mid-1940s to the mid-1950s. The pattern featured a center rose decal.

Plate, Cake	5.00
Teapot	19.50

Ring

Ring, sometimes called Beehive, was made by J. A. Bauer Company, Los Angeles, California, from 1932 to 1962. It was made in many colors. Bright shades include black, burnt orange, green, ivory, maroon, orange and yellow. Pastel shades were chartreuse, gray, green, light yellow, olive, pale blue, pink, turquoise or white.

HEMLOCK GREEN

Cup	.75
Plate, 6 1/4 In.	2.25
Tumbler, Flat, Platinum Trim, 5 In.	4.50
Tumbler, 5 Oz., Set Of 6	3.50
Tumbler, 9 Oz.	1.25
Tumbler, 12 Oz., Set Of 9	5.00

Riviera

Riviera was solid color ware made by Homer Laughlin China Company, Newell, West Virginia, from 1938 to 1950. It was unmarked and sold exclusively by the Murphy Company. Plates and cup handles were squared. Colors were ivory, light green, mauve blue, red, yellow and, rarely, dark blue.

GREEN

Baker, 9 In.	8.00 To 12.00
Bowl, Oval, 9 1/4 In.	8.50 To 10.00
Bowl, 5 1/4 In.	2.00 To 4.00
Bowl, 8 1/2 In.	7.50 To 8.00
Butter, 1/4 Pound	25.00 To 32.00
Casserole, Covered	38.50
Creamer	4.00
Cup	2.50 To 5.00
Cup & Saucer	5.00 To 10.00
Jug, Covered, 8 In.	60.00
Plate, 6 1/2 In.	1.00 To 2.75
Plate, 7 In.	2.00 To 3.50
Plate, 9 In.	3.00 To 4.50
Plate, 10 In.	5.00
Platter, Oval, Well, 11 1/2 In.	10.00 To 12.00
Platter, Square, Well, Handle, 12 In.	8.00
Salt & Pepper	8.00 To 8.50
Saucer	1.00 To 1.50
Soup, Flat	5.00 To 6.00
Sugar & Creamer, Covered	5.50 To 15.00
Tumbler, Handle	12.50

IVORY

Bowl, 5 In.	3.00 To 3.50
Butter, 1/4 Pound	35.00
Creamer	5.00
Platter, Square, 12 In.	8.00 To 10.00
Shaker, Pair	4.00
Soup, Dish	3.00
Sugar, Covered	7.50 To 11.50
Tumbler, 5 Oz.	6.00 To 11.50

LIGHT GREEN
Jug, Covered, 8 In. 50.00
Salt & Pepper 5.00
Sugar, Covered 6.00
Tumbler, Handle 16.00
Tumbler, Juice 27.50

MAUVE BLUE
Bowl, Serving, Square, 8 In. 4.00
Bowl, 5 In. .... 3.50 To 4.50
Bowl, 6 In. 6.00
Bowl, 8 In. .... 7.00 To 8.00
Bowl, 8 1/4 In. 7.00
Butter, 1/4 Pound ..... 34.00 To 45.00
Casserole, Covered 23.00
Creamer .... 3.00 To 4.00
Cup 5.50
Cup & Saucer .... 4.00 To 8.50
Plate, Deep 6.50
Plate, 6 In. 1.50
Plate, 6 1/2 In. .... 1.00 To 2.75
Plate, 7 In. 4.00
Plate, 9 In. .... 2.50 To 5.00
Platter, 11 1/2 In. 6.00
Salt & Pepper .... 8.00 To 8.50
Shaker, Pair 8.50
Sugar .... 1.00 To 4.00
Sugar & Creamer, Covered 15.00
Tea Set, 5 Piece ...... 80.00 To 100.00
Teapot, Lid 30.00
Tumbler, Juice 27.50

OLD IVORY
Cup & Saucer .... 6.00 To 7.50
Gravy Boat 9.00
Plate, Deep .... 4.50 To 6.50
Plate, 6 1/2 In. .... 1.50 To 2.75
Plate, 9 In. 3.50
Saucer 2.00

RED
Bowl, 5 1/4 In. .... 4.00 To 6.00
Bowl, 8 In. 9.00
Butter, 1/2 Pound 45.00

Creamer .... 4.50 To 8.00
Cup .... 4.50 To 6.50
Cup & Saucer .... 5.00 To 10.00
Dish, 8 1/4 In. 9.00
Gravy .... 6.00 To 8.75
Plate, 6 1/4 In. .... 1.50 To 3.25
Plate, 9 In. .... 3.50 To 7.50
Platter, Square, Well, Handle, 12 In.
.... 10.00 To 12.00
Salt & Pepper, Pair ...... 8.00 To 12.00
Saucer .... 1.00 To 3.00
Sugar & Creamer, Covered 18.00
Syrup, Covered 45.00
Tumbler, Juice 27.50

YELLOW
Berry Bowl .... 2.00 To 4.00
Bowl, Square, 8 1/4 In. 7.50
Bowl, Vegetable, Oblong, 9 In. 5.00
Bowl, Vegetable, Oval 6.00
Bowl, 6 In. .... 4.00 To 7.00
Bowl, 8 1/4 In. 4.00
Butter, 1/4 Pound 45.00
Casserole, Covered 30.00
Creamer .... 2.50 To 4.00
Cup 3.00
Cup & Saucer .... 4.00 To 8.50
Dish, 8 1/4 In. 8.00
Gravy Boat 6.00
Pitcher, Juice 55.00
Plate, Deep 6.50
Plate, 6 1/2 In. .... 1.00 To 2.25
Plate, 7 In. .... 3.50 To 4.00
Plate, 9 In. .... 3.50 To 5.00
Platter, Oval, Well, Handle, 11 1/4 In.
.... 6.00 To 7.00
Platter, Square, Well, 13 In.
.... 12.00 To 14.00
Salt & Pepper .... 3.50 To 8.50
Saucer .... 1.50 To 2.00
Soup, Flat .... 5.00 To 6.50
Sugar & Creamer, Covered 12.00
Teapot, Covered 22.00
Tumbler, Juice .... 25.00 To 27.50

Rock Rose

Rock Rose is a pink and green floral-decorated pattern made by Southern Potteries, Erwin, Tennessee. It is hand-painted on Colonial-shape dishes.

Bowl, 9 1/2 In. 8.00
Plate, 10 In. 4.00

Rooster

Roosters of many sorts were used as decorations on Southern Potteries pieces. The plain rooster in front of a fence is called Rooster pattern. The Rooster crowing from the fence top with a sun and a barn in the distance is a pattern called Cock O' the Morn. There is also another pattern called Rooster made by Stangl Pottery.

Box, Cover 10.00
Plate, 10 In. .... 3.00 To 6.50

Rose Parade

The Hall China Company, East Liverpool, Ohio, sometimes made surprising color and decal-decorated wares. Rose Parade had a solid Cadet Blue body with contrasting Hi-white knobs and handles. A rose decal was added to the white spaces. Sometimes the flower is pink, sometimes blue. The pattern was made from 1941 through the 1950s. Serving pieces, not dishes, were made.

Bean Pot .... 20.00 To 30.00
Casserole, Tab-Handled
.... 20.00 To 25.00

Coffeepot, Covered, Drip
.... 10.00 To 15.00
Creamer 5.00
Cup 22.00
Dish, Custard 6.00
Grease Jar, Covered .... 10.00 To 15.00
Jug, Ball, Small 15.00
Pitcher, Medium 12.00
Salt & Pepper, Sani-Grid
.... 10.00 To 17.00
Sugar & Creamer, Sani-Grid
.... 10.00 To 17.00
Teapot, Sani-Grid, 6 Cup 24.00

Rose White

Rose White, first made in 1941 by Hall China Company, is similar to Rose Parade. The same shapes were used but the pieces were all white with a slightly different rose-decal decoration. There is silver trim on many pieces.

Bean Pot, Covered ..... 20.00 To 25.00
Bowl, Mixing, Straight Side, 9 In.
.... 18.00

Casserole, Covered, Tab-Handled
.... 17.50 To 20.00
Jug, Medium 9.00
Salt & Pepper, Handled
.... 11.00 To 15.00
Sugar & Creamer, Covered
.... 20.00 To 25.00
Teapot, Sani-Grid, 6 Cup 24.00

Rosebud

Rosebud was made by Coors Pottery, Golden, Colorado, in the 1940s. It is a solid color ware with a stylized flower and leaves on the edge of plates or sides of cups. It was made in blue, green, ivory, maroon, turquoise or yellow.

BLUE
Plate, 6 In. 4.00
Plate, 10 In. 6.00

GREEN
Honeypot 35.00

IVORY
Plate, 6 In. 4.00
Plate, 10 In. 6.00

MAROON
Jug, Water 50.00
Platter, 8 In. 14.00

YELLOW
Plate, 10 In. 6.00

Royal Rose

Royal Rose is a Hall China Company pattern that can confuse you. It is Cadet Blue with Hi-white handles and knobs. The floral decal is the one used on Rose White. Pieces have silver trim. The shapes are different from those used for Rose Parade.

Bowl, Big Lip, 6 1/2 In. 6.00
Bowl, Big Lip, 7 1/2 In. 8.00
Bowl, Big Lip, 8 3/4 In. 9.00
Salt & Pepper, Handled 10.00

Russel Wright, see American Modern; Iroquois

Saf-Handle

Saf-Handle is a kitchenware line that had, as would be expected from the name, an unusual handle on some pieces. Most pieces are found in Chinese Red, but other colors were also used. The line was made from 1938 until the 1960s. Some pieces were made in several variations and there are three different style creamers.

CHINESE RED
Casserole No.4, 8 1/8 In. 18.00
Syrup 45.00

Sani-Grid

Sani-Grid is a colorful kitchenware line usually found in Cadet Blue or Chinese Red. It has white knobs and handles. The pattern was made by the Hall China Company, East Liverpool, Ohio, after 1941.

CHINESE RED
Creamer 6.00
Jug, Large 12.00
Jug, 6 1/2 In. 18.00
Salt & Pepper 15.00
Saltshaker 7.00
Teapot 18.00

Shellware, see Cameo Shellware

Silhouette

Silhouette looks just like its name. The pattern is a black silhouette of two people eating at a table. A dog is begging for food in front of the table. The plates are trimmed in platinum. It is a 1930s pattern. The pattern, made by Crooksville China Company, Crooksville, Ohio, is similar to the pattern Taverne, but Taverne has no dog. Matching metal pieces and glasswares were made.

Bowl	8.00
Coffeepot	45.00 To 50.00
Creamer	5.00
Cup & Saucer	6.00 To 8.00
Plate, 6 In.	1.00 To 2.00
Plate, 9 In.	4.50 To 5.00
Platter, 13 In.	9.00
Shaker, Ball	10.00

Silhouette Blue Ridge

Another pattern named Silhouette was made under the trade name Blue Ridge by Southern Potteries, Inc., Erwin, Tennessee. It is a very plain pattern with light-colored lines crossing the plate, giving the appearance of a heavy textured cloth.

Plate, 9 In.	3.25
Saucer	2.00

Spring Glory

A bright blue flower and bud with green leaves is hand-painted on the center of the Spring Glory pattern dishes by Southern Potteries, Inc., Erwin, Tennessee.

Plate, 8 In.	2.50
Plate, 10 In.	4.00

Springtime

Springtime is a dinnerware made by Hall China Company, East Liverpool, Ohio. It has a pink floral arrangement.

Cake Plate	15.00
Creamer	5.00
Plate, 9 In.	3.00

Spun Gold

Spun Gold was a pattern made by Stangl Pottery, Trenton, New Jersey, from 1965 to 1967.

Plate, 6 In.	4.00
Server	8.00

Star Flower

Star Flower is a pattern of dinnerware made by Stangl Pottery from 1952 to 1957.

Plate, 10 In.	4.00
Sugar & Creamer, Covered	6.00

Sunflower

A bright yellow flower with an orange center is partially seen in the hand - painted design on Sunflower, a dinnerware by Southern Potteries, Inc., Erwin, Tennessee, about 1947.

Ashtray	8.00
Creamer	9.00

Cup	6.50
Cup & Saucer	9.50
Plate, 9 In.	8.50
Sugar & Creamer	18.00
Tumbler, Footed	12.50

Sunshine

Sunshine is a dinnerware pattern by Stangl Pottery, Trenton, New Jersey.

Jug, No.5	5.00
Salt & Pepper	8.00
Sugar, Covered	9.00

Tam O'Shanter

Tam O'Shanter is one of the many plaid patterns made by Vernon Kilns, Vernon, California. It was colored forest green, lime and reddish-brown plaid with a forest green border.

Bowl, Salad	2.00
Plate, 6 In.	1.50 To 2.00
Soup, Bowl	4.00

Tampico

Tampico, a brown, green and watermelon colored pattern on a Futura shape, was made by Red Wing Pottery, Red Wing, Minnesota. This modern design was introduced in 1955. Many other patterns were also made on the Futura bodies.

Plate, 6 1/2 In.	3.00
Plate, 8 1/2 In.	4.00
Saucer	2.00

Taverne

Taverne serving pieces were made by the Hall China Company, East Liverpool, Ohio, in the 1930s. Matching dinnerware was made by Taylor, Smith and Taylor, Chester, West Virginia. A rolling pin was made by Harker Potteries. The silhouetted figures eating at a table are very similar to those seen on the pattern Silhouette, but there is no dog in this decal. In some of the literature, Taverne is called Silhouette.

Baker, Swirl	7.00
Bowl, Mixing, No.3	6.00
Bowl, Mixing, No.4	3.00
Bowl, Mixing, No.5	10.00
Bowl, 5 In.	3.00
Bowl, 6 1/4 In.	7.00
Bowl, 7 3/4 In. .... 16.00 To 17.50
Casserole, Covered, 8 1/4 In.	30.00
Coffeepot, Banded ..... 29.00 To 40.00
Coffeepot, Colonial	25.00
Coffeepot, Covered, Drip	8.00
Creamer	5.00
Cup & Saucer	5.00
Drip Jar, Covered, Colonial	18.00
Jug, Ball, No.3	15.00
Jug, Classic .... 20.00 To 45.00
Jug, Milk, 5 In.	12.00
Pitcher, Milk, 24 Oz.	14.00
Plate, 9 1/4 In.	8.50
Platter, Oval	12.00
Salt & Pepper, Banded	24.00
Sugar & Creamer, Covered	18.00
Tile, Tea	12.00

Thistle

Thistle, or No. 3847, is a pattern made by Stangl Pottery, Trenton, New Jersey. The hand-painted decoration is purple thistle and green spiked thistle leaves. The dishes were made from 1951 to 1967.

Bowl, Vegetable, 11 In.	12.50
Bowl, 5 In. .... 2.00 To 4.50
Creamer, 4 In.	9.50
Cup & Saucer	7.50
Plate, 6 In.	3.00
Plate, 8 In. .... 4.00 To 7.50
Plate, 10 In.	8.50
Sugar & Creamer, Covered	12.50
Vegetable, 11 In.	12.50

Tiger Lily

Stangl pottery made Tiger Lily pattern from 1957 to 1962.

Cup	4.00
Plate, 8 In.	4.00

Tom & Jerry

Tom & Jerry sets were made to serve the famous Christmas punch. A set was usually a punch bowl and six matching cups.

Bowl, Black Footed, Hall	40.00
Bowl, Ivory Handle, Covered, Hall	50.00
Mug, Black Footed, Hall	10.00

Trojan

Trojan is a solid color dinnerware made by Catalina Pottery of Catalina Island. The company was bought in 1937 by Gladding, McBean & Company. The solid color dinnerware was made until the 1940s.

YELLOW

Plate, 6 In.	4.50
Plate, 7 1/4 In.	7.50
Sherbet, Tall	14.50

Tulip

Tulip is a 1930s pattern made by Hall China Company, East Liverpool, Ohio. It remained popular until the 1950s. Most of the pieces were distributed by Cook Coffee of Cleveland, Ohio. Pale yellow and purple tulips are applied by decal. The ware is trimmed with silver. The same design is found on a Harker Pottery pattern called Pastel Tulip. Other patterns called Tulip were made by Stangl Pottery; Edwin H. Knowles; Paden City Pottery; Universal Pottery; Leigh and Leigh Crescent Pottery; and Royal Pottery. Other patterns called Tulips were made by Homer Laughlin Company; Pottery Guild; Taylor, Smith and Taylor; and Blue Ridge.

Baker, French	10.00
Bowl, Big Lip, 7 1/2 In.	12.00
Bowl, Mixing, 6 In.	8.50
Bowl, Mixing, 8 3/4 In.	15.00
Bowl, 9 In.	8.00
Console, Oval	10.00
Creamer	4.50
Cup	2.50 To 4.50
Cup & Saucer	9.00
Plate, 8 In.	4.00
Plate, 10 In.	13.00
Platter	10.00
Sugar & Creamer	10.00
Vegetable, Oval	10.00

Virginia Rose

Virginia Rose is the name of a shape of dishes made by Homer Laughlin Company, Newell, West Virginia. The shapes were decorated with a variety of decal decorations. The dishes with a design of a spray of roses and green flowers is the most often called Virginia Rose pattern by collectors.

Bowl, Deep, 5 In.	6.00
Bowl, Mixing, Set Of 3, Kitchen Kraft	30.00
Bowl, Round, 9 In.	7.00
Bowl, Vegetable, Oval	7.00
Bowl, 6 In.	3.00
Butter, Covered	25.00
Casserole, Covered, Kitchen Kraft, 8 In.	14.00
Cup & Saucer	3.50
Plate, 6 In.	1.50
Plate, 9 3/4 In.	10.00
Plate, 10 In.	4.00
Platter, 11 1/2 In.	7.00
Salt & Pepper, Short	6.00
Soup, Flat	6.00
Sugar & Creamer, Covered	9.00

Vistosa

Taylor, Smith and Taylor, Chester, West Virginia, made a solid color dinnerware about 1938 called Vistosa. The plates had piecrust edges and the other pieces had some bands or ridges. The glaze colors were cobalt blue, deep yellow, light green or mango red. Pieces were marked with the name Vistosa and the initials T. S. & T. Co. U.S.A.

BLUE
Bowl, 5 1/2 In.	2.50
Cup & Saucer	3.50
Plate, 6 In.	1.00
Plate, 10 In.	6.00

Saucer	.75
Sugar	4.00

GREEN
Eggcup	15.00
Plate, 10 In.	6.00

RED
Plate, Chop	20.00
Plate, 10 In.	3.00
Sugar, Covered	6.00 To 8.00

YELLOW
Cup & Saucer	3.50
Plate, 10 In.	6.50

White Dogwood

White Dogwood was made by Stangl Pottery, Trenton, New Jersey, from 1965 to 1974. Stangl also made patterns called Dogwood and Colonial Dogwood.

Plate, 6 In.	2.00
Plate, 10 In.	6.00 to 8.00
Teapot	20.00

White Rose

White Rose is a cameo ware made by Harker China Company, Chester, West Virginia, in the 1940s. The rose pattern is cut into the glaze. It has white leaves and an outline of a single rose. The background is blue, pink or yellow. The pieces are marked White Rose, Carv-Kraft by Harker. Both dinnerware and kitchenware were made in this pattern. It was made for Montgomery Ward.

BLUE
Cake Plate	5.00
Cup	5.00
Salt & Pepper	6.00
Sugar, Covered	3.00

YELLOW
Pitcher	10.00

Wild Rose

Wild Rose was a decal-decorated set made by the Homer Laughlin China Company, Newell, West Virginia. Other dinnerware sets by the same name were made by Knowles, Taylor, Knowles about 1933, Stangl Pottery about 1955 to 1973, Blue Ridge about 1941, Hall China Company and Paden City Pottery.

Creamer	5.00
Cup & Saucer	10.00 To 12.00
Plate, 6 In.	2.00 To 3.00
Plate, 9 In.	3.00 To 4.00

Wild Strawberry

Wild Strawberry pattern was made by Southern Potteries, Inc., under the trade name of Blue Ridge.

Bowl, Sauce, 5 1/2 In.	2.00
Bowl, 6 In.	3.00
Creamer, Large	4.00
Plate, 9 1/2 In.	3.50
Platter, Oval, 11 In.	5.00
Saucer	2.00
Sugar, Large, Covered	5.00

Wildfire

Great American Tea Company gave Wildfire pattern as a premium. This Hall pottery pattern of the 1950s has a Hi-body and a flower garland decal decoration.

Bowl, Covered, 5 1/4 In.	12.00
Bowl, Mixing, Set Of 3	25.00
Bowl, No. 3, 6 In.	7.00
Bowl, Salad	12.00
Bowl, Vegetable, Oval	10.00
Bowl, 9 In.	6.00 To 7.50
Casserole, Covered, Tab-Handled	14.00 To 25.00
Coffeepot, S Lid	22.00 To 23.50
Creamer	3.50
Cup	3.00
Cup & Saucer	5.50 To 7.00
Custard	4.00
Drip Jar & Lid	10.00 To 12.00
Gravy Boat	7.00
Jug, Sunshine, 6 1/2 In.	11.00 To 14.00
Plate, 6 In.	1.50 To 2.00
Plate, 7 In.	2.00 To 2.50
Plate, 10 In.	4.00 To 7.50
Platter, 10 In.	11.00
Platter, 11 In.	8.00 To 10.00
Platter, 13 In.	11.00 To 12.00
Saltshaker, Egg Drop	4.00 To 10.00
Saltshaker, Sani-Grid	7.00
Soup, Flat	6.50 To 7.50
Sugar & Creamer	9.00
Sugar, Covered	6.50
Tidbit, 3 Tier	20.00

Wildflower

Wildflower was made by Edwin M. Knowles, Newell, West Virginia.

Bowl, Mixing, Set Of 3 .... 28.00
Bowl, 9 In. .... 5.00 To 6.00
Butter Tub, 6 In. 37.50
Cup & Saucer .... 4.00 To 5.00
Drip Jar, Covered 10.00

Goblet, Gold Trim 23.75
Lamp, 11 In. 175.00
Plate, 6 In. 1.50
Plate, 7 In. .... 1.75 To 2.00
Plate, 8 In. 9.00
Plate, 10 In. .... 4.00 To 5.00
Platter, 13 In. 11.00
Soup, Dish 6.00

Woodfield

Woodfield was a dinnerware made by the Steubenville pottery, Steuben, Ohio. The dishes were shaped like leaves and were colored in many of the colors used for American Modern dishes also made by the same pottery. Full dinner sets were made.

BLUE
Cup 5.00
Plate, Snack 3.50
Plate, 8 3/4 In. 4.50
Tray, Plate, 9 In. 4.50

GRAY
Cup 5.00

Cup & Saucer .... 5.00 To 6.00
Plate, Snack 3.50

LIGHT GREEN
Cup & Saucer 5.00
Plate, 9 In. 4.50

PINK
Cup 5.00
Cup & Saucer 5.00
Plate, Server, 13 1/2 In. 15.00
Plate, Snack 3.50
Plate, 9 In. 4.50
Sugar, Covered 6.00

Yellow Carnation

Yellow Carnation is a Fiesta casual design with yellow and brown flowers on a white background. The rim is edged with yellow. It was made from 1962 to 1968 by Homer Laughlin Company.

Cup & Saucer .... 10.00 To 12.00
Plate, 7 In. .... 4.00 to 6.00
Plate, 10 In. .... 6.00 To 8.00
Platter, 12 1/2 In. 20.00

American Dinnerware Pattern List

(* = listed in book)

Pattern	Shape	Maker	Date	Description
ABC	Kiddieware	Stangl	Mid-1940s–1974	Solid colors
Abingdon	Square	Abingdon	1935	
Acacia Flowers	Shellcrest	Paden City		
Acorn		Harmony House		Blue, pink; Cameo ware
Adam	Antique	Steubenville		Rich ivory glaze; heavily embossed
Adobestone	Ceramastone	Red Wing	1967	
Adrian		Stangl	1972–1974	
Al Fresco	Al Fresco	Franciscan	1952	Hemlock green, coffee brown, lime olive green, misty gray
Alia Jane	Round	Taylor-Smith, and Taylor	1933–1934	Decal
All Apple		Purinton		Hand-painted; large apple
Aloha		French-Saxon		
Amapila	Amapila	Franciscan		Hand-painted
Amber Glo		Stangl	1954–1962	
* Amberstone	Fiesta	Homer Laughlin	1967–	Solids; brown designs
American Beauty	Minion	Paden City		Large pink rose
American Beauty		Stetson		
* American Modern	American	Steubenville (Russel Wright)	1938	Chartreuse, seafoam blue, coral, granite gray, bean brown, black chutney, canteloupe, glacier blue or clear green
American Provincial		Homer Laughlin		Pennsylvania Dutch designs
Americana pattern	A2000	Stangl		
Amy		Harker		Gold trim; multicolored flowers

Pattern	Shape	Maker	Date	Description
Anemone	Piecrust	Blue Ridge		
Anniversary		Salem China	1943	
Antiqua		Stangl	1972–1974	
Antique Leaf	Lace Edge	Blue Ridge		
Anytime		Vernon Kilns		
Appalachian Spring	Candlewick	Blue Ridge		
Apple	Apple	Franciscan	1940	
Apple	Watt Ware	Watt Pottery	1922–1960	
Apple & Pear	Woodcrest	Blue Ridge		
Apple Blossom		Crooksville		Pink flowers
Apple Blossom	Nautilus Eggshell	Homer Laughlin	1935–1955	Flowered border; gold trim
Apple Crunch	Piecrust	Blue Ridge		
Apple Delight		Stangl	1965–1974	
Apple Jack	Skyline	Blue Ridge		
Apples		Pottery Guild		Apple tree branch
April		Homer Laughlin		Flowered border
Arabescue	Arabesque	Catalina	1935	Solids
Arabian Night		Paden City		
Arcadia		Vernon Kilns	C. 1947	
Ardennes	Provincial	Red Wing	1941	Laurel leaf band
Argosy		W. S. George	1930	Ivory body
Aristocrat		Homer Laughlin		Flowered border
Aristocrat	Century	Salem		Delphinium blue; black & platinum band
Arlene	Trellis	Blue Ridge		
Art Deco	Art Deco	Catalina	Early 1930s	Solids
Asbury	Pegasus	Sebring	1940s	
Atlanta	Skyline	Blue Ridge		
Autumn Apple (No. 3735)	Colonial	Blue Ridge	1941	
Autumn Breeze	Skyline	Blue Ridge		

Pattern	Shape	Maker	Date	Description
Autumn Fancy		Universal		Decals
Autumn Harvest	Versatile	Taylor, Smith, and Taylor		
* Autumn Leaf				
Autumn Leaf		Blair		Floral decals
Autumn Leaf		Crooksville China		Floral decals
Autumn Leaf		Crown		Floral decals
Autumn Leaf		Hall China for Jewel T.	1933–present	Floral decals
Autumn Leaf		Harker Potteries		Floral decals
Autumn Leaf		Paden City		Floral decals
Avenue	Coupe, La-Grande	Crooksville		Reddish-brown plant sprigs
Aztec		Stangl	1967–1968	
Aztec	Citation	Steubenville		
Aztec on Desert Sand	Citation	Steubenville		
Bachelor's Button		Stangl	1965	
* Ballerina	Ballerina	Universal Potteries	1947–1956	Solids: forest green, burgundy, chartreuse, dove gray, jade green, jonquil yellow, periwinkle blue, charcoal, pink; abstract designs
Bamboo		Blair		Stylistic bamboo design
Bamboo	Woodcrest	Blue Ridge		
* Banded	Banded	Hall	1937	Kitchenware; floral decals; solid colors: Chinese red, marine maroon, cadet, canary, Indian red
Barkwood		Vernon Kilns		Beige and brown; like tree bark
Basket		Hall	1932–1960	Small flower basket & diamond shaped designs
Basket	Harker			Flower basket border
Basket		Leigh & Leigh Crescent		Flower basket & individual small flowers

Pattern	Shape	Maker	Date	Description
Basket		Salem		Center flower basket; border of leaves and individual flowers
Basket of Tulips	Bonjour	Salem		Various colored tulips; platinum rim
Basket Petit-point	Victory	Salem		Decals
Basketweave	Skyline	Blue Ridge		

J. A. Bauer is a mark found on pottery by a firm later using the mark "J. A. Brushe."

Pattern	Shape	Maker	Date	Description
Bauer, see Ring				
Beaded Apple	Colonial	Blue Ridge		
Beatrice	Skyline	Blue Ridge		Black-haired girl
Becky		Harker		Blue & red flowers
Becky	Colonial	Blue Ridge		Large red flowers
Beehive, see Ring				
Bel Air		Vernon Kilns		Three lines crossing three lines
Bella Rosa		Stangl	1960–1962	Spray of roses & lily of the valley; pale gray background
Bench	Deanna	Knowles		Mexican styled jugs & cactus
Bermuda		Homer Laughlin	1977–1978	
Berry		Blue Ridge	1920–1957	Hand-painted
* Betty	Candlewick	Blue Ridge		
Big Apple	Colonial	Blue Ridge		
Bimini		Homer Laughlin	1977–1978	
Bird	Derwood	W. S. George		Red & brown bird on border
Bird		Blair		Sgraffito bird
Bird in the Heart		Universal Cambridge		
Bird Pottery		Vernon Kilns	Early 1930s	
Birds and Flowers		Harker		Multicolored flowers, small birds
Bit Series	Kiddieware	Stangl	Mid-1940s–1974	
Bittersweet		Hall		Flowers
* Bittersweet	Skyline	Blue Ridge		
Bittersweet		Stangl		Sgraffito decoration

Pattern	Shape	Maker	Date	Description
Bittersweet		Universal Pottery	1949	Decals; orange
Black Tulip		Crooksville	1950s	Hand-painted; black on pink
Bleeding Heart	Candlewick	Blue Ridge		
Blossom Ring		Stangl	1967/68–1970	
Blossom Time	Concord	Red Wing	1947	
Blossom Time	Coupe	Crooksville		Off-center decoration; branch of pink flowers
Blossoms	Shellcrest	Paden City		Large flower spray
Blossoms	Fruits	Crooksville		Red & pink flowers
Blossoms	Lido	W. S. George		Pink blossoms border
Blue Bell		Stangl	19??–1942	
Blue Bird		Crown	1941	Blue birds perched on pink apple blossoms; turquoise blue rim
Blue Blossom		Hall	C. 1939	Blue background, floral decals
Blue Blossoms		Crooksville		Flowers in shades of blue
* Blue Bouquet	D-Line	Hall (Premium for Standard coffee)	1950–1960s	Thin blue border with roses
Blue Carousel	Kiddieware	Stangl	Mid-1940s–1974	
Blue Daisy		Stangl	1963–1974	
Blue Dresden	Virginia Rose	Homer Laughlin	1949	
Blue Elf	Kiddieware	Stangl	Mid-1940s–1974	
* Blue Garden		Hall	1939	Blue background, floral decals
Blue Heaven	Colonial	Blue Ridge		
Blue Medallion		Homer Laughlin	1920	Decals
Blue Moon	Candlewick	Blue Ridge		
Blue Parade, see Rose Parade				

Pattern	Shape	Maker	Date	Description
Blue Rhythm (Cameo)		Harker	1959	
Blue Shadows	True China	Red Wing	1964	
Blue Symphony		Homer Laughlin		
Blue Willow	Cavalier	Royal	Late 1940s–early 1950s	Overall Oriental design; also pink or green
Blue Willow		Homer Laughlin	1942	Blue & pink
Blue Willow		Sebring-Limoges		
Bluebell		Paden City		Floral sprig
Bluebell Bouquet	Candlewick	Blue Ridge		
* Blueberry		Montgomery Ward	1921	Decals
* Blueberry		Stangl	C. 1940	Red with yellow border; blueberries in center
Bluebird		Salem		Small bluebirds on border
Bluebird	Derwood	W. S. George		Bluebird on border; thin blue trim
Blushing Rose, see Lido Dalyrymple				
Bo Peep	Kiddieware	Stangl	Mid-1940s–1974	
* Bob White		Red Wing	1956	Hand-painted; stylized bird; figurals
Bolero		Homer Laughlin	1977–1978	
Bonita		Caribe-Sterling	1950s–c. 1963	Modernistic flowers
Bonita		Stangl		Della-Ware mark
Boquet	Astor	Blue Ridge		
Bouquet		Crown		Multicolored flowers & bow
Bouquet		Hall		Random flower sprays
Bouquet		Harker		
Border Boquet	LaGrande	Crooksville		Border of small flowers
Border Rim		Knowles		Border design of flowers
Border Rose		Crooksville		Continuous border design

Pattern	Shape	Maker	Date	Description
Bountiful	Colonial	Blue Ridge		
Boyce		Harker		Flowers in shades of pink
Breakfast Nook		W. S. George		Open windows with flower trellis
Breeze	Bountiful	Salem China; French-Saxon	1948	
Brentwood	Cavalier	Royal		Ironstone; bold flower center design
Briar Rose	Century	Homer Laughlin	1933	Sprays of wild rose; platinum edge
Bridal Boquet	Colonial	Blue Ridge		
Bridal Flower		Taylor, Smith, and Taylor		
Bridge	Tricorne	Salem		Decals
Bridle Rose		W. S. George		
Brilliance	Coupe	Crooksville		Multisized pink flowers
Brim		Harker		Bold-colored flower border
Brittany	Provincial	Red Wing	1941	Yellow rose
Brocade	True China	Red Wing	1964	
Brown Satin		Stangl		
* Brown-eyed Susan		Vernon Kilns	1940s	Flower
Brushes	Al Fresco	Bauer		
Bryn-Mawr	Symphony	Salem		Floral sprays in brown, lavender & gray
Bud	Concord	Red Wing	1947	
Buddah	Corinthian	Sebring		
Bunny Lunch	Kiddieware	Stangl	Mid-1940s–1974	
Buttercup	Colonial	Blue Ridge		
Cabaret	Cabaret	Franciscan		
Cactus or Cactus Banded	Banded	Hall	1937–1940s	Decal; cactus in flowerpots
Cactus & Cowboy, see Ranger				
Cadenza	Piecrust	Blue Ridge		Red & green flowers

Pattern	Shape	Maker	Date	Description
Cadet Series		Salem		Fluted edge; thin bands of color
Cal-Art		Bauer		
Calico	Colonial	Blue Ridge		
Calico		Vernon Kilns		Blue border; pink & blue plaid
Calico Chick	Coupe	Crooksville		Calico-print chickens
Calico Farm	Skyline	Blue Ridge		
Calico Flower		Pottery Guild		Red band; calico print flowers
Calico Flowers	Dartmouth	Crooksville		Calico-print tulips
Calico Fruit		Pottery Guild		Red band; calico-print fruits
* Calico Fruit		Universal Potteries	1940s	White background; bright red & blue fruits
Calico Tulip		Harker		
* Caliente		Paden City	1940s	Solids: blue, green, tangerine or yellow
California James Poppy	LaGrande	Crooksville		Large sprays of pastel flowers
California Pottery		Bauer		Solid colors
California Provincial	Poppytrail	Metlox	1965	
California Series		Vernon Kilns	1930s	Red, brown, green, blue
California Shadows		Vernon Kilns		Colored edge
California Strawberry	Poppytrail	Metlox		
Call Rose	Century	Homer Laughlin		Floral decal
* Cameo Rose	E-Shape	Hall	1970s	Gray & white leaf decorations
* Cameo Rose		Harker	1940s	Solid white roses; blue, pink, gray or yellow background
* Cameo Shellware	Shell	Harker	1940s	White, blue, pink, gray, yellow background; same cameo flower design as Cameo Rose; fluted plate edge

Pattern	Shape	Maker	Date	Description
Cantata	Piecrust	Blue Ridge		
Canton	Encanto	Franciscan	1953	
Capistrano	Anniversary	Red Wing	1953–1967	Swallow design
Capri		Paden City	1933	
Capri	Rhythm Coupe	Homer Laughlin		
Caribe Casual		Caribe-Sterling	1950s–c.1963	
Carnation Beauty		Homer Laughlin	1920	Decal
Carnival	Candlewick	Blue Ridge		
Carnival	Fruits	Crooksville		Abstract
* Carnival		Stangl	1954–1957	Pink, green & black abstract starlike pattern
Caroline		Blue Ridge	1920–1957	
Carriage		Crown		Coach & horses, manor
Casa California		Vernon Kilns	1938	Blue; green leaves; pink flowers; yellow border
Casa del Sol	Cavalier	Royal		Indian-style design
Casablanca	Cavalier	Royal		Ironstone; large center sunflower design
Cascade		Montgomery Ward	1936	White with red lines; solids
Cashmere		Homer Laughlin		Border of small sprays of flowers
Cassandra	Waffle Edge	Blue Ridge		Wide blue or pink border; center flowers
Casual California	Casual California	Vernon Kilns		
* Casualstone	Fiesta	Homer Laughlin	1970	Solids; marked Coventry
Cat & the Fiddle	Kiddieware	Stangl	Mid-1940s–1974	
* Cat-Tail	Camwood; Old Holland; Laurelle	Universal for Sears, Roebuck, & Co.	1934–1956	Red & black decals
Cattail		Hall	1927	
Cattails	Trailway	Blue Ridge		

Pattern	Shape	Maker	Date	Description
Century		Homer Laughlin		Floral decals; ivory
Champagne Pinks	Colonial	Blue Ridge		Overall large floral
Chanticleer		Blue Ridge	1920–1957	
Charstone Bleu	Ceramastone	Red Wing	1967	
Chartreuse		Montgomery Ward	1936	Decals; green; green border
Chateau		Homer Laughlin		
Chateau-France		Sebring-Limoges		
Cheerio	Skyline	Blue Ridge		
Cherry		Harker		Brightly colored fruits
Cherry		Salem China	1951	
Cherry	Stangl	1940		Brown band with tan glaze & blue lines; blue band with tan glaze & yellow lines or blue band with blue glaze & green lines; cherry stems in center
Cherry Blossom		Harker		Sprig of cherries & flowers
Cherry Cobbler	Colonial	Blue Ridge		
Cherry Coke	Colonial	Blue Ridge		
Cherry Trim		Harker		Border of groups of cherries
Chesterton	Royal Gadroon	Harker	1945–1965	Gray, green, blue, pink, yellow
Chevron	Gypsy Trail	Red Wing	1935	Blue, ivory, turquoise, orange, yellow
Chicken Pickins	Skyline	Blue Ridge		
Chickory	Colonial	Blue Ridge		
Chicory		Stangl	1961	
Children's Plates		Harker		Blue & pink Cameo ware; duck, teddy bear, dog

* Chinese Red (color used by Hall)

Pattern	Shape	Maker	Date	Description
Chintz	Colonial	Blue Ridge		
Chintz		Vernon Kilns	1940s	Floral design
Christmas Tree	Colonial	Blue Ridge		
Chrysanthe-mum	Colonial	Blue Ridge		
Chrysanthe-mum	Concord	Red Wing	1947	
Circus Clown	Kiddieware	Stangl	Mid-1940s–1974	
Clear Day	Cavalier	Royal		Ironstone
Clio	Corinthian	Leigh Potters		Floral
Clive	Brittany	Homer Laughlin		Border of maroon panels & floral sprays
Clover		Blue Ridge	1947–1954	
Clover		Hall	1940–1960	Bright colors; Impressionistic design
* Cock o' the Morn	Skyline	Blue Ridge		Crowing rooster
Cock-o-the-Morn (Harker), see Engraved Rooster				
Cock O' Walk		Blue Ridge	1948	
Cocolo	Cocolo	Franciscan		
* Colonial		Hall	1932	Kitchenware; lettuce green, daffodil, hi-white, delphinium, ivory, Chinese red, golden glo; decals
Colonial		Salem		Red & green stencil-like decorations
Colonial		Stangl	1926	Silver-green, Persian yellow, Colonial blue, tangerine, aqua blue, rust, brown, surf white
Colonial Dogwood		Stangl		Marked Prestige
Colonial Lady		Harker		
Colonial Rose		Stangl	1970–1974	
Colonial Silver		Stangl	19??–1970	
Colonnes	Futura	Red Wing	1960	Pillars

Pattern	Shape	Maker	Date	Description
Colorado				Brown
Columbine	Century	Homer Laughlin		Floral decal; off-center
Columbine	Skyline	Blue Ridge		
Commodore		Salem		Gold medallions & trim
* Conchita	Century	Homer Laughlin	1938	Mexican-inspired decal
* Conchita Kitchen Kraft		Homer Laughlin	1930s	Ovenwares; Mexican-inspired decal
Concord		Stangl	1957	
Concord		Continental Kilns	1944–1957	
Contempo	Al Fresco	Bauer	1950s	
Contemps		Brusche	1952	Slate, champagne white, desert beige, indigo brown, pumpkin, spicy green
Cookie Twins	Kiddieware	Stangl	Mid-1940s–1971	
Coors, see Rosebud				
Coral Reef		Vernon Kilns	1939	
Coreopsis	Colonial	Blue Ridge		
Corn		American Pottery		
Corn		Brush McCoy		
Corn		Brush Pottery		
Corn		J. W. McCoy		
Corn		Paden City		
Corn		Standard Pottery		
Corn		Stanford Pottery	1945–61	
Corn Gold		Montgomery Ward	1921	Decals
Corn Is Green		Paden City		Cornstalk center design
* Corn King	Corn King	Shawnee	C. 1950	Yellow & green; three-dimensional

Pattern	Shape	Maker	Date	Description
* Corn Queen	Corn Queen	Shawnee	1954–1961	Three-dimensional; lighter kernel than Corn King; dark foliage
Cornflower Blue		Knowles	1930s	Decals
Coronado	Coronado	Franciscan	1940s	Turquoise
Coronado	Coronado	Vernon Kilns (grocery promotion)	1939	Orange, turquoise, yellow, dark blue
Coronation Organdy		Vernon Kilns		Gray & rose plaid
Corsage	Astor	Blue Ridge		
Cosmos	Skyline	Blue Ridge		Large brown flowers
Cosmos		Stangl		Marked Prestige, Cosmos flower border
Cosmos		Vernon Kilns		Allover floral
Cosomi	Skyline	Blue Ridge		Large red & blue flowers
Cottage		Harker		Flowered path leading to red-roofed cottage
Country Classics		Haeger		
Country Garden	Anniversary	Red Wing	1953	Floral
Country Garden	Candlewick	Blue Ridge		
* Country Garden		Stangl	1956–1974	Stylized flowers
Country Gardens		Red Wing	1953	
Country Home	Fruits	Crooksville		Cottage with mountains in background
Country Life		Stangl	1956–1967	
Country Road		Homer Laughlin	1977–1978	
Countryside		Harker		Cottage with smoking chimney
County Fair	Colonial	Blue Ridge		

Cowboys & Cactus, see Ranger

Pattern	Shape	Maker	Date	Description
Cowslip	Colonial	Blue Ridge		
* Crab Apple		Blue Ridge	C· 1930–1957	Hand-painted decorations; red spatter border
Cranberry		Stangl		
Crazy Quilt		Homer Laughlin	1977–1978	
Crazy Rhythm	Futura	Red Wing	1960	Abstract; hand-painted
Crestone		Hull		Turquoise
Crocus	Colonial	Blue Ridge		
Crocus		Hall	1950	Floral decal; platinum trim
* Crocus	D-Line	Hall	1930s	Floral decals; black, lavender, red, green & pink
Crocus	True China	Red Wing	1960	Floral
Crocus		Stangl		
Croydon	Sovereign	Crown	1941	Black trellis border with multicolored flowers
* Cumberland		Blue Ridge	1948	Hand-painted blue & white flowers
Currier & Ives	Cavalier	Royal		Ironstone; scenic center design
Currier & Ives	Coupe	Scio		
Currier & Ives		Homer Laughlin	Present	Blue decal on white
Cut-A-Way		Hall	1930	Multicolored flowers
Cynthia		Blue Ridge	1949	
Cynthia	Lido	W. S. George		Sprigs of small pink flowers (Peach Blossom has same decal on Bolero shape)
* Daffodil	Piecrust	Blue Ridge		Single flower
Dahlia	Candlewick	Blue Ridge	1948	
Dahlia		Stangl	1970–1974	Marked Prestige
Dainty		Vernon Kilns		
Daisies	Deanna	Knowles		Field of flowers
* Daisy	Fiesta	Homer Laughlin	1962–1968	Turquoise band; daisies

Pattern	Shape	Maker	Date	Description
Daisy		Stangl	1936–1942	
Daisy	Versatile	Taylor, Smith, and Taylor		
Daisy Chain	True China	Red Wing	1960	Floral
Daisy Wreath	Daisy Wreath	Franciscan		
Damask	True China	Red Wing	1964	
Daydream	Colonial	Blue Ridge		
Deanna		Knowles		
Deco-Dahlia		Harker		Stylized red flowers
Deco-Delight		Stangl		Deco shaped; colonial blue or silver green
Del Mar	Del Mar	Franciscan		
Delft Rose	Colonial	Blue Ridge		
* Delicious	Candlewick	Blue Ridge		Painted fruit
Della Robbia	Piecrust	Blue Ridge		
Della Robbia	Vernonware	Metlox	1965	
Delmar		Stangl	1972–1974	
Delores		Vernon Kilns		
Delta Blue	Village Green	Red Wing	1954	Light blue with floral decor
Desert Flower	Skyline	Blue Ridge		
Desert Rose	Desert Rose	Franciscan		
Desert Sun	New Shape	Red Wing	1962	Geometric
Design 69		Taylor, Smith, and Taylor		Pale blue & brown
Dewberry	Colonial	Blue Ridge		
Diana		Stangl	1972–1974	
Dick Tracy	Century	Homer Laughlin	1950	Decal; child's set
Dinner Rose, see Queen Rose				
Disney		Vernon Kilns	1940s	
Dixie Harvest (No. 3913)	Piecrust	Blue Ridge	1949	
D-Line		Hall	1936	Plain; round; floral decals

Pattern	Shape	Maker	Date	Description
Dogwood	Dogwood	Franciscan		
* Dogwood	Century	Homer Laughlin	1960s	Pink & white floral decals
Dogwood		Stangl	1965	Della-Ware mark; raised border of pink flowers & pale green leaves
Dogwood	Skyline	Blue Ridge		Large yellow flowers
Dogwood		Taylor, Smith, and Taylor	1942	Underglaze pattern; overall flowers
Dolores		Vernon Kilns	1940s	Floral border
Dominion	Victory	Salem		Poppies, wheat, blue flowers; decal
Dorset		Scio		
Dragon Flower		California Pottery		Stylized brown plant
Dream Flower	Colonial	Blue Ridge		
Dresden		Crown	1941	Sprays of assorted flowers; gold trim
Dresden Doll	Colonial	Blue Ridge		
Driftwood	Anniversary	Red Wing	1953	Tree branch design
Duchess		Paden City	1942	Small flowers & scrolls
Ducky Dinners	Kiddieware	Stangl	Mid-1940s–1974	
* Dutch Boquet	Candlewick	Blue Ridge		Red tulip decoration
Dutch Iris	Candlewick	Blue Ridge		
Dutch Petit Point	Tricorne; Bonjour	Salem		Decals; Dutch boy & girl
Dutch Tulip	Candlewick	Blue Ridge		
Dynasty	Cavalier	Royal		Ironstone
Early American		Homer Laughlin	1960s	Floral
* Early California	Early California	Vernon Kilns	1930s	Solid: orange, turquoise, green, brown, blue, pink, yellow
Early Days		Vernon Kilns		
Ecstasy		Vernon Kilns		
Edmonton		Syracuse		

Pattern	Shape	Maker	Date	Description
Eggshell Nautilus		Homer Laughlin	1935–1955	Floral decals
Eggshell Polka Dot		Hall	1934	Matte white, ivory glaze, red, green or blue dots; floral decals
Eggshell Theme		Homer Laughlin	1940s	English look; decals; floral border
El-Chico		Bauer		
El Rosa				Della-Ware mark; pink rose & lavender flowers; border of dark green, white & yellow
El Vuelo		Caribe-Sterling	1950s–c.1963	Modernistic swirls
Emerald		Montgomery Ward	1921	Decals
Emma Susan	Washington Square	Taylor, Smith, and Taylor	1933–1934	Decals
Enchantment		Harker		
English Countryside		Hall		
English Garden	Century	Homer Laughlin	1933	Landscape design
Engraved Rooster		Harker		Cameo Ware
Epicure		Homer Laughlin	1955	Solid: dawn pink, snow white, charcoal gray, turquoise blue
Eureka Homewood		Hall (made for Eureka Co.)		Decal
Eureka Serenade	D-Line	Hall		
Evening Flower	Skyline	Blue Ridge	1950	
Eventide		Blue Ridge	1920–1957	
Fairlawn		Stangl	1959–1962	
Fairy Bells	Colonial	Blue Ridge		
Falling Leaves	Colonial	Blue Ridge		
Fantasia	Skyline	Blue Ridge		

Pattern	Shape	Maker	Date	Description
Fantasy	Ball	Hall	1930s–1940s	Decal; bright flowers
Fantasy	Concord	Red Wing	1947	Abstract
Fantasy Apple	Skyline	Blue Ridge		
Far East	Shellcrest	Paden City		Oriental design
Farmer Takes a Wife	Colonial	Blue Ridge		
Farmhouse	Woodcrest	Blue Ridge		Large scenic design
Fashion White		Montgomery Ward	1936	Decals
Federal		Sebring-Limoges	1942	
Festival		Stangl	1961–1967	Della-Ware mark
Festive	Skyline	Blue Ridge		
Festive Fruit, see Fruit (Stangl)				
Field Daisy	Colonial	Blue Ridge		
Field Daisy		Stangl	1941–1942	White daisies on blue or yellow background
* Fiesta	Fiesta	Homer Laughlin	1936–1972	Bright green, red, yellow, dark blue, old ivory, turquoise, gray, rose, forest green, light green, chartreuse, turf green, mango red, antique gold
* Fiesta Ironstone	Fiesta	Homer Laughlin	1970–1972	Antique gold, turf green, mango red
* Fiesta Kitchen Kraft		Homer Laughlin	1939–early 1940s	Bake & serve line; red, yellow, green, blue
Fiesta Wood	Fiesta	Homer Laughlin		Colored border stripes; sleeping Mexican
First Love		Stangl	1968–1973	
Five Little Pigs	Kiddieware	Stangl	Mid-1940s–1974	
Flaming Rose		Paden City		Brightly colored floral design
Flamingo	Gray Lure	Crooksville		Sprig of delicate flowers

Pattern	Shape	Maker	Date	Description
Flamingo		Hall		
Flare Ware Gold Lace		Hall	1960s	Overall stars & scalloped border
Fleur de Lis	Kitchen Kraft	Homer Laughlin		
Fleur de Lis		Vernon Kilns		Large pastel center design
Fleur de Lis Iris, see Iris (Universal)				
Flight	New Shape	Red Wing	1962	Birds
Flight of the Swallows	New Art	Homer Laughlin	1930s	Foliage spray & group of flying birds
Flora		Stangl	1947–1957	
Floral	Floral	Franciscan		
Floral	Lido	W. S. George		Decal of multicolored small flowers
Floral		Paden City		
Floral		Stangl	1941–1942	
Floral Bird-song	Sabina II	Sabin	C. 1946	
Floral Border		Montgomery Ward	1936	Decals
Floral Bouquet	Fairway	Taylor, Smith, and Taylor	Early 1930s	
Floral Plaid		Stangl	1940–1942	
Florence	Squared-Off Edges	Knowles	1933–1934	Decals
Florence		Pope Gosser	1940s	Border of small flowers
Florentine		Stangl	1958	
Florette		Stangl	1961–1962	
Flower Basket	Yorktown	E. M. Knowles		
Flower Fair	Coupe	Crooksville		Muted flowers
Flower Fantasy		Blue Ridge	1954	
* Flower Pot	Banded	Hall		Early decal
Flower Power		Homer Laughlin	1977–1978	
Flower Rim	Lido	W. S. George		Bands of small flowers

Pattern	Shape	Maker	Date	Description
Flower Ring	Colonial	Blue Ridge		
Flower Wreath	Candlewick	Blue Ridge		
Flowering Berry	Candlewick	Blue Ridge		
Flowers of the Dell	New Art	Homer Laughlin	1930s	Two floral sprays
Flute		Hall	1935	Kitchenware; russet, Chinese red, hi-white marine
Flying Blue-bird	Empress	Homer Laughlin	1920	Decal
Fondoso	Gypsy Trail	Red Wing	1938	Blue, yellow, turquoise, pastels
Forest Flower	Shellridge	Harker		Light brown & yellow
Forest Fruits	Skyline	Blue Ridge	1950	
Forever Yours	Shellridge	Harker		Rosebud garland
Formal		Salem		Rust & gold rim; gold border design
Forman		Hall		
Fountain	Ballerina	Universal	1950	Abstract
French Peasant	Colonial	Blue Ridge		
French Provincial				Silhouette decal
Frontenac	Futura	Red Wing	1960	Abstract flowers
Frosted Fruit		Stangl	1957	
Fruit	Concord	Red Wing	1947	
* Fruit		Stangl	1942–1974	Center designs of fruit
* Fruit & Flowers		Stangl	1957–1974	Center design; colored border
Fruit & Flowers		Universal		Subdued colors; large center design
Fruit Basket		Homer Laughlin	1977–1978	
Fruit Basket		Salem		Narrow checkerboard band; border of fruit baskets
Fruit Fantasy	Colonial	Blue Ridge		Painted fruits
Fruit Punch	Colonial	Blue Ridge		
Fruit Sherbet	Colonial	Blue Ridge		

Pattern	Shape	Maker	Date	Description
Fruitdale		Vernon Kilns	C. 1945	Flower & fruit center
Fruitful	Colonial	Blue Ridge		Painted fruits
Fruits		Harker		Large stem of fruit
Fruits		Knowles		Brightly colored individual fruits
Fuchsia		Leigh & Leigh Crescent		Predominately orange & green floral spray
Fuji		Hall		Oriental-styled flower
Futura		Red Wing	1961	Hand-painted
* Fuzz Ball		Hall	1930s	Pink & green
Galaxy		Stangl	1963–1970	
Garden Design		Salem China	1940s	
Garden Flower		Stangl	1947–1957	
* Garden Lane	Colonial	Blue Ridge		Hand-painted tulips, daisies & roses
Garden Party	Garden Party	Franciscan		
Garden Pinks	Skyline	Blue Ridge		
Garden Trail	Shellridge	Harker		Center bouquet; floral border
Garland	Colonial	Blue Ridge		
Garland	Monarch	Crown	1941	Garland of small roses
Garland		Pickard		
Garland		Stangl	1957–1967	
Gascon		W. S. George		Bright blue flowers, gray leaves; sold by Sears, Roebuck & Co.
Gay Plaid		Blair		Yellow, green & brown; large plaid
Ginger Boy	Kiddieware	Stangl	Mid-1940s–1974	
Ginger Cat	Kiddieware	Stangl	Mid-1940s–1974	
Ginger Girl	Kiddieware	Stangl	Mid-1940s–1974	
Gingersnap	Gingersnap	Franciscan		

Pattern	Shape	Maker	Date	Description
* Gingham		Vernon Kilns		Green & yellow plaid; dark green border
Gingham Fruit	Trailway	Blue Ridge		
Glamour		Vernon Kilns		
Glenedon		Leigh Potteries		
Glenwood	Cavalier	Homer Laughlin	1961–1968	
Gloria		Blue Ridge	1949	
Gloucester Fisherman	Ballerina	Universal Pottery	1950	
Godey Prints	Victory	Salem		Decals; service plates
Gold & Cobalt	Empress	Homer Laughlin	1920	Decal
Gold Band		Montgomery Ward	1920	Decals
Gold Band		Montgomery Ward	1936	Decals
Gold Drape		Crooksville		Floral design; gold border, draped effect
Gold Floral Band		Homer Laughlin	1920	Decal
Gold Garland		Homer Laughlin	1920	Decal
Gold Initial		Montgomery Ward	1921	Decal
Gold Label		Hall	1950s	Gold stamped decorations
Gold Lace over Cobalt Blue		Homer Laughlin	1920	Decal
Gold Stripe		Montgomery Ward	1936	Decals
Golden Blossom		Stangl	1964–1974	Golden blossoms, green leaves
Golden Crown	Queen Anne	Sabin		
Golden Grape		Stangl	1963–1972	
Golden Harvest	Coupe	Stangl	1953–1973	Yellow flowers, gray background
Golden Laurel		Knowles	1930	Decals
Golden Viking	Futura	Red Wing	1960	Geometric; gold
Golden Wheat	Rhythm Coupe	Homer Laughlin	1953–1958	

Pattern	Shape	Maker	Date	Description
Golden Wheat	Yorktown	E. M. Knowles	1936	Decals
Goldtrim	Briar Rose	Salem	1952	Gold rim; gold border design
Good Luck		Lee Mfg. Co.	1926	
Gooseberry	Candlewick	Blue Ridge		
Granada		French-Saxon	1939–1940	Solid: yellow, blue, green or tangerine
Granada	True China	Red Wing	1960	Floral
Grandiose	Coupe	Paden City	1952	Muted large flowers
Grand-mother's Garden	Colonial	Blue Ridge		
Grape		Stangl	1973–1974	
Green Briar	Piecrust	Blue Ridge		
Green Dots	Avona	Taylor, Smith, and Taylor	Early 1930s	Wide border of dots
Green Eyes	Skyline	Blue Ridge		
Green Grapes		Stangl		
Green Valley		Homer Laughlin	1977–1978	
Green Wheat	Yorktown	E. M. Knowles		Decals
Green Wheat		Leigh & Leigh Crescent		Separate wheat stalks
Greenwich-stone	Ceramastone	Red Wing	1967	
Gumdrop Tree	Candlewick	Blue Ridge		
Gypsy	Colonial	Blue Ridge		
Gypsy Trail		Red Wing	1930s	
Hacienda	Hacienda	Franciscan		Hacienda green
* Hacienda	Century	Homer Laughlin	1938	Decal; cactus, bench, side of Mexican house; red trim
Hallcraft	Classic	Hall		Eva Zeisel design; solid white or patterned

Pattern	Shape	Maker	Date	Description
* Harlequin	Harlequin	Homer Laughlin	1938–1964, 1979	Ironstone; light green, chartreuse, forest green, dark blue, ivory, cobalt blue, yellow, tangerine, gray, turquoise, rose, maroon, mauve blue, spruce green; 1979— green, yellow, turquoise, deep coral
Harvest	Concord	Red Wing	1947	
Harvest		Stangl		
Harvest	Ultra California	Vernon Kilns	1930s	Fruits in center; pears, green apples, plum, cherries & a peach
Harvestime	Skyline	Blue Ridge		
Hawaii		Vernon Kilns		
* Hawaiian Coral		Vernon Kilns		Spatter edge
* Hawaiian Flowers		Vernon Kilns	1939	
Hawaiian Fruit	Cinchfield; Piecrust	Blue Ridge		
Hawaiian 12 Point Daisy, see Daisy				
Hawthorne	Qena	Crown		Pastel pink & blue flowers; gold rim
Hawthorne	Hawthorne	Franciscan		
Hazel	Ranson	Scio		
Hazelnut		Universal		Decals
Hearthstone	Casual	Red Wing	1961	Solids: beige, orange
Hearthstone	Ceramastone	Red Wing	1967	Beige or orange
Heather Rose		Hall		Rose branch
Heavenly Days		Vernon Kilns		Blue
Heirloom	Corinthian	Sebring		Wide gold floral border; garland & bouquet in center
Heritage		Stangl		
Heritance		Harker		

Pattern	Shape	Maker	Date	Description
Heyday		Vernon Kilns		
Hibiscus, Crooksville, see Flamingo				
Hidden Valley	Cavalier	Royal		Ironstone; colored band and large center stencil-like flowers
Hi-Fire		Bauer	1930s	
Highland Ivy	Piecrust	Blue Ridge	1949	
Highlight		Paden City	1948	Heavy quality oven & craze proof colors; white, citron, blueberry, nutmeg & pepper
* Hilda	Candlewick	Blue Ridge		Red, blue & yellow flowers
Hilo		Vernon Kilns		
Holland, see Crocus (Hall)				
* Holly		Stangl	1967–1972	
Hollyberry	Colonial			Traditional Christmas plant
Hollyhock	Colonial	Blue Ridge		
Hollyhock	New Art	Homer Laughlin		Decal; pink flowers on stem
Hollyhocks		Universal		Multicolored flowers
*Homespun		Vernon Kilns		Brown, yellow, green plaid
Homestead in Winter	Iva-Lure	Crooksville		Winter scene
Honeycomb		Bennington		Oats, blueberry, brown sugar
Hostess Pantry Ware		Pottery Guild	1954	Hand-painted
Housetops		Leigh & Leigh Crescent		Variety of buildings
Humpty Dumpty	Kiddieware	Stangl	Mid-1940s–1974	
Hunting	Iva-Lure	Crooksville		Scenic

Pattern	Shape	Maker	Date	Description
Indian Camp-fire	Kiddieware	Stangl	Mid-1940s–1974	
Indian Tree		Leigh & Leigh Crescent		Large floral spray; pink & blue
Indian Tree	Victory	Salem		Decals; Minton-style floral
Inspiration		Stangl	1967–1968	Marked Prestige
Iris	Concord	Red Wing	1947	
Iris		Universal		Pastel pinks
Iris Bouquet		Leigh & Leigh Crescent		Brightly colored flowers
Isle of Palms	Commonwealth	James River Pottery		
Iroquois		Iroquois China (Russel Wright)		Brick red, grayed-blue canteloupe, oyster gray, aqua, ripe apricot, pink sherbet, parsley green, ice blue, forest green, avocado yellow, lemon yellow, nutmeg brown, sugar white, lettuce green, charcoal
Iroquois Red	Ranchero	W. S. George		Red banded design
Ivy	Ivy	Franciscan	1948	Hand-painted
Ivy	Regal	Harker		Fall colors
Ivy Vine	Coupe	Crooksville		Pastel greens
Ivy Vine		Harker		Border of ivy
Jack in the Box	Kiddieware	Stangl	Mid-1940s–1974	
Jacobean	Queen Anne	Sabin	C. 1946	
Jade Ware		Sebring	1940s	
Jamoca	Jamoca	Franciscan		
Jane Adams	Victory	Salem	1950s	Yellow & green floral sprays
Jean	Nancy	Steubenville		
Jeanette	New Yorker	Salem		Flowerpot center design
Jessica		Harker		Brightly colored flowers

Pattern	Shape	Maker	Date	Description
Jessie		Crooksville		Pastel pink; floral sprays on border & center
Joan of Arc	Diana	Sebring-Limoges		
Jonquil		Paden City		Pastel flowers or border of yellow sprays
Jonquil	Tricorne	Salem		Decals
Jonquil		Stangl		
J-Sunshine		Hall		Floral decals
Jubilee		Homer Laughlin	1948–?; 1977–1978	Pastel; celadon green, shell pink, mist gray, cream beige; solids
June Apple	Woodcrest	Blue Ridge		
June Boquet	Colonial	Blue Ridge		
June Bride	Colonial	Blue Ridge		
June Rose	Colonial	Blue Ridge		
Kaleidoscope	Birds	Crooksville		Floral pattern with green divider
Karen		Sebring-Limoges	1940	
Kashmir	True China	Red Wing	1964	
Kitchen Bouquet	Century-Kitchen Kraft	Homer Laughlin		Floral decals
* Kitchen Kraft	Kitchen Kraft	Homer Laughlin	1930s	Red, blue; also decals under pattern name
Kitten Capers	Kiddieware	Stangl	Mid-1940s–1974	
Kitty	Harker			Blue & pink Cameo ware
* Kumquat		Stangl		
La Gonda		Gonder	1950s	Modern shapes; aqua, yellow, pink
Lady Alice	Brittany	Homer Laughlin		Maroon border; bluebells & roses
Lady Greenbriar	Liberty	Homer Laughlin		Green border
Lady Stafford	Liberty	Homer Laughlin		Maroon border
La-Linda		Bauer		Solid colors; smooth (no ridges)

Pattern	Shape	Maker	Date	Description
Landscape		Salem China	1940s	
Lanterns	Concord	Red Wing	1947	Abstract
Largo		Universal		Border of fall leaves; small center decal
Laurel	Monarch	Crown	1941	Black & gold wreath border
Laurel		Stangl	19??–1942	
Laurelton		Harker		Green or beige
Laurie	Colonial	Blue Ridge		
Laurita		Stangl		Della-Ware mark
Lazybone		Frankoma		Solids
Leaf		Taylor, Smith, and Taylor		Coral
Leaf & Flower		Harker		Cameo-type design
Leaf Spray		Knowles		Muted colors
Leaf Swirl	Shellridge	Harker		Fall colors
Leilani		Vernon Kilns	1939	
Lenore	Monticello; Olivia	Steubenville		
Lexington	Concord	Red Wing	1947	Rose
Lexington		Homer Laughlin		Wide solid-colored border
Lexington Rose		Red Wing		Large flowers
Lido		Homer Laughlin	1977–1978	
Lido Dalrymple		W. S. George		Tiny buds
Lime		Stangl	1950	
Linda		Vernon Kilns	Late 1930s	Burgundy border; pink & blue flowers
* Lipton	French; Boston	Hall		Teapots, sugars & creamers; marked Lipton
Little Bo Peep, see Bo Peep				
Little Bouquet	LaGrande	Crooksville		Small flower groupings
Little Boy Blue	Kiddieware	Stangl	Mid-1940s–1974	

Pattern	Shape	Maker	Date	Description
Little Quackers	Kiddieware	Stangl	Mid-1940s–1974	
Los Angeles		Bauer		
* Lotus	Concord	Red Wing	1947	
Louise	Virginia Rose	Homer Laughlin		
Louisiana Lace	Candlewick	Blue Ridge		
Luna		Blue Ridge	1920–1957	
Lupine	Futura	Red Wing	1960	Floral
* Lu-Ray	Laurel, (1932); Empire (1936)	Taylor, Smith, and Taylor	1930s–1950s	Pastel; Windsor blue, surf green, Persian cream, sharon pink, Chatham gray solids
Lute Song	True China	Red Wing	1960	Musical instruments
Lyric		Stangl	1954–1957	Black & brown free-form shapes; white background
Madison		Leigh Potteries		
Madrid		Homer Laughlin	1977–1978	
Magic Flower	Candlewick	Blue Ridge		
Magnolia	Piecrust	Blue Ridge		
Magnolia	Liberty	Homer Laughlin		Decal
Magnolia	Concord	Red Wing	1947	
* Magnolia		Stangl	1952–1962	Red border
Majestic	True China	Red Wing	1960	White
Mandarin Red		Salem		Solid colored: bright red & white
Mandarin Tri-corne	Tricorne	Salem		Red borders, white interiors
Mallow		Harker		Pastel flower arrangements
Mango	Mango	Franciscan		
Manhattan		Leigh & Leigh Crescent		Bordered with rings of gold
Maple Leaf		Salem		Fall leaf design
Maple Whirl		Stangl	1965–1967	
Mar-Crest				
* Mardi Gras		Blue Ridge	1943	Blue daisy & pink flower

Pattern	Shape	Maker	Date	Description
Margaret Rose		Homer Laughlin		Thick colored border; floral center
Mary	Astor	Blue Ridge		
Mary Quite Contrary	Kiddieware	Stangl	Mid-1940s–1974	
Marylou		Hall		Floral decals; creamer & sugar
* Max-i-cana	Yellowstone	Homer Laughlin	1930s	Mexican decal: man, cactus, pots; octagonal plates
May and Vieve Hamilton		Vernon Kilns		
Mayan Aztec		Frankoma		Solids
Mayfair		Leigh & Leigh Crescent		Bold flower decal
Mayflower	Skyline	Blue Ridge		
* Mayflower		Vernon Kilns	1940s–late 1950s	Fully covered center; floral
Maypole	Maypole	Franciscan		
Meadow Beauty	Colonial	Blue Ridge		
Meadow Flowers	Coupe	Crooksville		Brightly colored floral border
Meadow Flowers	Ball	Hall		Decal; teapot
Meadow Rose	Meadow Rose	Franciscan	1977	
Mealtime Special	Kiddieware	Stangl	Mid-1940s–1974	
Medallion		Crooksville		Small floral border
Medici	Cavalier	Royal		Ironstone; wide, elaborate scroll border
Mediterranean	True China	Red Wing	1960	Floral
Mediterranean		Stangl	1965–1974	
Mello-Tone		Coors		
Mermaid	Ballerina	Universal	1950	Abstract
Merrileaf	True China	Red Wing	1960	Floral
Mesa	Encanto	Franciscan		
Metlox Poppy Trail, see Poppy Trail				
* Mexicana	Century	Homer Laughlin	1930s	Decal; orange & yellow pots

Pattern	Shape	Maker	Date	Description
* Mexicana Kitchen Kraft		Homer Laughlin	1938	Mexican decals, scenes with different-colored bands
Mexi-Gren		W. S. George		Mexican-style archway, pots, blanket
Mexi-Lido		W. S. George		Mexican-style pots
Mickey	Colonial	Blue Ridge		
Middlebury	Cavalier	Royal		Ironstone; large flower burst center design
Midnight Rose	Anniversary	Red Wing	1953	Rose
Midsummer	Victory	Salem		Decals
Midsummer		Sebring-Li-moges	1940	
Ming Tree (No. 4387)	Woodcrest	Blue Ridge	1920–1957	
Mini Flowers	Deanna	Knowles		Small red flowers
Mirador		Homer Laughlin	1977–1978	
Mirasol	Mirasol	Franciscan		
Moby Dick		Vernon Kilns	1939	
Mod Tulip	Colonial	Blue Ridge		
Modern		J. A. Bauer	1935	Solids
* Modern California	Modern California	Vernon Kilns	1930s	Azure, orchid, pistachio, straw, sand, gray
Modern Orchid	Round; Trend	Paden City		Large center orchid; gold border
Modern Tulip	Plymouth	Harker	1930s	Stencil-type tulip design; muted colors
Monogram		Salem		Gold-initialed
Monterey		Stangl	1967–1968–1970	
Monterey		Vernon Kilns		
Monterey Moderne		J. A. Bauer	1948	Olive green, gray, black, yellow, pink, chartreuse, brown, burgundy solids
Monticello	E-Shape	Hall	1941	Border; small, individual, pale flowers
Monticello		Steubenville		

Pattern	Shape	Maker	Date	Description
Montmartre	Futura	Red Wing	1960	French street scene
Moon Flower		Salem		
Moon Song		J. A. Bauer		
Morning Blue		Stangl	1970	
Morning Glory	Concord	Red Wing	1947	
* Morning Glory		Hall	1942–1949	Cadet blue with decal
Morning Glory	Shenandoah	Paden City		Floral sprays
Morningside	Delphian	Taylor, Smith, & Taylor	Late 1920s	Flower garden scene
* Moss Rose (No. 4486)	Trailway	Blue Ridge	1920–1957	Hand-painted
Moss Rose		Universal Pottery	1953–1955	Decals
Mother Hubbard	Kiddieware	Stangl	Mid-1940s–1974	
Mount Vernon		Hall	1941	Wreath with center floral decal, Granitetone
Mountain Aster	Colonial	Blue Ridge		
Mountain Bells	Colonial	Blue Ridge		
Mountain Cherry		Blue Ridge	1920–1957	
Mountain Cherry		Blue Ridge	1951	
Mountain Ivy	Candlewick	Blue Ridge	1951	
Mountain Laurel		Stangl	1947–1957	
* Mountain Nosegay	Candlewick	Blue Ridge		Blue tulip and multi-colored flowers
Mountain Sweetbriar	Skyline	Blue Ridge		
Nassau		Homer Laughlin		Border of large roses
Nasseau	Concord	Red Wing	1947	
Nasturtium	Shell-Crest; Shenandoah	Paden City	1940s	Bright orange flower
Native American		Vernon Kilns	1930s	Mexican scenes; soft pastel colors

Pattern	Shape	Maker	Date	Description
Native California	Native California	Vernon Kilns	Late 1930s	Pastels
Nautical	Candlewick	Blue Ridge		
* Nautilus	Century	Homer Laughlin		Floral decals
Navajo		Crown		Mexican design; red banded rim
Neville		W. S. George		Small rosebuds interspersed on colored border; sold by Sears, Roebuck
New Art	New Art	Homer Laughlin	1930s	Solid colors
New Princess		Sebring-Limoges		
* Newport		Stangl	1940–1942	Blue shading from dark to pale; matte finish; sailboat
Night Flower	Skyline	Blue Ridge	1952	
Night Song	Cavalier	Royal		Ironstone; bold patterned border
Nocturne	Colonial			Rose-red flower; red brushed edge
Nordic		Homer Laughlin	1977–1978	
Norma	Colonial	Blue Ridge		
Norma		Stangl		Della-Ware mark; pear branch in center; rings of color on rim
Normandy	1941 Provincial	Red Wing	1941	Blue & maroon bands, later apple blossoms added
Norway Rose		Homer Laughlin		Floral decal
Northern Lights	Futura	Red Wing	1960	Geometric blue
Nove Rose	Colonial	Blue Ridge		
Nut Tree	Nut Tree	Franciscan		
Octagon	Octagon	Catalina	1930s	Solids
October	October	Franciscan	1977	
Old Dutch		Sebring-Limoges		
Old English		Homer Laughlin		Decal scene with castle

Pattern	Shape	Maker	Date	Description
Old Mexico	Alara	Limoges		
Old Orchard		Stangl	1941–1942	
Old Provincial		Red Wing	1943	Aqua, brown bottom
Olivia		Stangl		Della-Ware mark
Orange Blossom	Regina	Paden City		Orange floral
Orange Poppy, see Poppy (Hall)				
Orange Tree	Orange Tree	Homer Laughlin		Raised design on outside of nested bowls
Orchard Glory	Colonial	Blue Ridge		Yellow pear & pink flower
* Orchard Song		Stangl	1962–1974	
* Organdie		Vernon Kilns	1930s	Yellow & brown plaid border
Organdy		Homer Laughlin		Pastel borders on eggshell
Oriental Poppy	Colonial	Blue Ridge		
Orleans	1941 Provincial	Red Wing	1941	Red Rose
Our America		Vernon Kilns	1939	Walnut brown, dark blue & maroon on cream ground
Our Barnyard Friends	Kiddieware	Stangl		
Overture	Cavalier	Royal		Ironstone; bold center design
Paden Rose		Paden City		Large, pale rose & bud
Painted Daisy	Colonial	Blue Ridge		
Painted Desert	Ballerina	Universal	1950	Abstract
Paisley		Stangl	1963–1967	
Palm Tree	New Art	Edwin Knowles		
Palo Alto	Encanto	Franciscan		
Pansy		Harker		Pastel flowers
Pantry Shelf	Yorktown	E. M. Knowles		
Paper Roses	Colonial	Blue Ridge		
Paradise	Coupe	Homer Laughlin		
Parsley	Salem	Salem		

Pattern	Shape	Maker	Date	Description
Partridge Berry	Skyline	Blue Ridge		
Passy	Ballerina	Universal	1950	Abstract
Pastel Garden	Sabina	Sabin		
Pastel Poppy	Astor	Blue Ridge		
Pastel Tulip		Harker		Floral decals
Patchwork		Homer Laughlin	1977–1978	
Patchwork Posy	Colonial	Blue Ridge		
Pate Sur Pate		Harker		Scalloped border; solid colors
Pate-Sur-Pate	Shalimar	Steubenville		
* Patio	Shell-Crest	Paden City	1907–1950s	Mexican decal decorated
Pauda (Freesia)	Pauda	Franciscan		Hand-painted
Pauline	Astor	Blue Ridge		
Peach		Pottery Guild		Peaches & lavender flowers
Peach Blossom	Bolero	W. S. George		Sprigs of small pink flowers (Cynthia has same decal on Lido shape)
Pear		Pottery Guild		Fruit grouping
Pear Turnpike		Vernon Kilns		Brown
Pebble Beach	Pebble Beach	Franciscan		
Penny Serenade	Colonial	Blue Ridge		
Penthouse	Yorktown	E. M. Knowles		Flowerpots
Peony	Colonial	Blue Ridge		
Peony Bouquet	Candlewick	Blue Ridge		
Pepe	New Shape	Red Wing	1962	Geometric
Periwinkle	Astor	Blue Ridge		
Petalware		W. S. George	Late 1930s	Solid colors
Peter Rabbit	Kiddieware	Stangl		
Petit Point		Crown	1941	Flower bouquet; cross-stitch effect
Petit Point		Leigh & Leigh Crescent		Floral border

Pattern	Shape	Maker	Date	Description
Petit Point		Montgomery Ward	1936	Decals
Petit Point Basket		Salem		Flower basket; sampler effect
Petit Point Bouquet	Delphian	Taylor, Smith, and Taylor	Late 1920s	
Petit Point House		Crooksville		Decal of houses, trees; sometimes called "House"
* Petit Point Leaf		Crooksville		Decals
* Petit Point Rose		Harker		Rose border
Petit Point Rose	Fleurette	W. S. George		Cross-stitch, floral
Petite Flowers		Stangl	1970–1974	
* Petitpoint		Homer Laughlin	1960s	Floral decal like stitched petit point
Petunia	Colonial	Blue Ridge		
Petunia		Hall	1932–1969	Pink floral decal
Pheasant	LaGrande	Crooksville		Flying birds; scenic
Picardy	Village Green	Red Wing	1960	Yellow rose
Picket Fence	Yorktown	Knowles		Brightly colored floral & fence
Picnic	Picnic	Franciscan		
Pie Crust		Stangl	1969	
Pine Cone		Harker		Wispy, brown design
Pinecone Spray	Fiesta	Homer Laughlin		Decal
Pink Border	LaGrande	Crooksville		Tiny pink flora border
Pink Carousel	Kiddieware	Stangl	Mid-1940s–1974	
* Pink Cosmos		Stangl	1966	Marked Prestige
Pink Dog-wood		Stangl		
Pink Dog-wood	Skyline	Blue Ridge		
Pink Fairy	Kiddieware	Stangl	Mid-1940s–1974	

Pattern	Shape	Maker	Date	Description
Pink Lady	Vernon Ware	Metlox	1965	
Pink Lily		Stangl	1953–1957	
Pink Morning Glory		Hall		Early decal
Pink Moss Rose		Homer Laughlin	1920	Decal
* Pink Mums		Hall	1930s	Floral decals
Pink Pastel		Knowles		Pale pink & white with pink flowers
Pink Print		Montgomery Ward	1936	Decals
Pink Rose		Homer Laughlin	1920	Decals
Pink Rose & Daisy	Plain Edge	Homer Laughlin	1920	Decals
Pink Spice	Anniversary	Red Wing	1953	Butterfly design
* Pinkie	Skyline	Blue Ridge		Pink flowers; sponged center
Pintoria		Metlox	c. 1939	
Pippin	Skyline	Blue Ridge		
Plaid, see Gay Plaid				
Plain	Gypsy Trail	Red Wing	1935	Blue, yellow, ivory, orange, turquoise solids
Plain-Jane	Lido	W. S. George		
Plainsman		Frankoma		
Plantation Ivy	Sky line	Blue Ridge	1920–1959	
Playful Pups	Kiddieware	Stangl	Mid-1940s–1974	
Plaza				Water jugs
Plum	Candlewick	Blue Ridge		
Plum		Stangl	1940	Green, blue or tan
Plum Blossom	Dynasty	Red Wing	1947	Yellow, green, pink, Oriental motif, six-sided
Plum Duff	Candlewick	Blue Ridge		
Plume	Astor	Blue Ridge		
Pocahontas	Common-wealth	James River Pottery		

Pattern	Shape	Maker	Date	Description
Poinsettia	Colonial	Blue Ridge	1950	Hand-painted red flowers
Polka Dot		Hall	1942	
Polo	Tricorne	Salem		Decals
Pom Pom	Candlewick	Blue Ridge		
Pompadour	Sabina	Sabin	C. 1946	
Pompeii	New Shape	Red Wing	1962	Geometric
Pony Trail	Kiddieware	Stangl		
Poppy		Crown		Floral center; pastel vinelike border
Poppy	Rainbow	W. S. George		Center design of three flowers
* Poppy	C-Line	Hall	1933–1950s	Floral decals; orange poppies
Poppy	Deanna	Knowles		Orange floral spray
Poppy	Shenandoah	Paden City		Flora border
* Poppy & Wheat		Hall	1933–c.1939	Decals: orange flowers & wheat
* Poppy Trail		Metlox (California)	C. 1939	Solid: delphinium blue, old rose, canary yellow, turquoise blue, poppy orange, rust
Posey Shop	Triumph	Sebring-Limoges	1944–1945	
Posies	LaGrande	Crooksville		Pastel flowers
Posies	Coupe	Paden City		Abstract flowers
Posies		Stangl	1973–	
* Prelude		Stangl	1949–1957	Stylized design
Pricilla	Clinchfield	Blue Ridge		
Pricilla Bakeware	Century; Kitchen Kraft	Homer Laughlin		Floral decals
Primitive Bird, see Bird				
* Primrose				
Prince		Hall	C. 1952	Refrigerator sets
* Priscilla		Homer Laughlin	1940s–1950s	Pale pink rose decals
* Provincial		Stangl	1957–1967	Floral center

Pattern	Shape	Maker	Date	Description
Provincial Blue	Poppytrail	Metlox	1951	
Provincial Fruit	Poppytrail	Metlox	1965	
Provincial Tulip		Harker	1959	Cameo-ware
Provincial Wreath		Harker		Stoneware; Pennsylvania Dutch design
Puppy-Flower	Floral edge	Knowles	1933–1934	Decals
Puritan	Royal Gadroon	Harker		Plain white
Quaker Maid		Harker		
Quartette	Concord	Red Wing	1947	Four solid colors
Queen Rose	Coupe	Crooksville		Pastel rose stem
* Quilted Fruit		Blue Ridge	1920–1957	Fruit design, printed calicos
Quilted Ivy	Woodcrest	Blue Ridge		
Raffia		Vernon Kilns		Green and brown; like tree bark
Rainbow		Hall		Hall's radiant ware
Rainbow		Stangl	1935	Solids: silver green, Persian yellow, colonial blue, tangerine, aqua blue, rust, brown, surf white
Rainbow	Rainbow	W. S. George	Late 1930s	Solid colors
Raisin	Ring	Vernon Kilns		Drip glaze; solids
Rambler Rose	Aristocrat	Knowles	1930s	Decals
Rambler Rose		Universal		Rose medallions
Rancho		French Saxon		Solid colors
Random Harvest	Futura	Red Wing	1955	Harvest colors
Random Harvest		Red Wing	1961	
Ranger		Stangl		Cowboy & cactus
Ranger Boy	Kiddieware	Stangl	Mid-1940s–1974	
Rawhide		Harker	1960s	Stoneware; dark brown
Raymond	Yellowstone	Homer Laughlin	1926	Floral decal

Pattern	Shape	Maker	Date	Description
Raymor		Roseville (Ben Siebel)	1952	White, brown, mottled green, dark green, blue, rust, brown; modern
Raymore	Contempora	Steubenville (Ben Siebel)		Three-dimensional rippling; faun, mist gray, sand white, charcoal
Red & Gold		Montgomery Ward	1936	Decals
Red Apple 1		Harker		Small, continuous apple decal
Red Apple 2		Harker		Large, individual apple decal
Red Barn	Skyline	Blue Ridge		
Red Berry	Victory	Salem		Decals
Red Cone Flower	Clinchfield	Blue Ridge		
Red Ivy		Stangl	1957	
Red Pony	D-Line	Hall	1930s–1950s	Floral decals
* Red Poppy		Hall	1930–1950	Red flowers, black leaves
* Red Riding Hood	Figural	Hull		Three-dimensional figures
Red Rooster Provincial	Poppytrail	Metlox	1965	
* Red Rose		Paden City		Red rose decal, rosebud decal
Red Tulip	Candlewick	Blue Ridge		
Red Tulip	Kitchen Kraft	Homer Laughlin		Decals
Red Wing Rose	Futura	Red Wing	1960	Rose
Reed	Gypsytrail	Red Wing	1935	Blue, yellow, turquoise, ivory, orange
Regal Rings	Queen Anne	Sabin	C. 1946	
Remembrance	Citation	Steubenville		
Rend Leaf		Blue Ridge	1942–1943	
Rhapsody	Colonial	Blue Ridge		
Rhea	Trend	Steubenville		

Pattern	Shape	Maker	Date	Description
Rhythm		Homer Laughlin	C. 1938–1950s	Solids: yellow, chartreuse, gray, green, burgundy
Rhythm		Paden City	1936	
* Rhythm Rose	Century	Homer Laughlin	Mid-1940s–mid-1950s	Floral decal, large center rose
Rialto		Stangl		Della-Ware mark; yellow flowers on blue background
Ribbon Plaid	Skyline	Blue Ridge		
Richmond		Hall	1941	Granitetone
Rick-Rack		Blair		Yellow & brown
Ridge Rose	Colonial	Blue Ridge		
Ring-O-Roses	Piecrust	Blue Ridge		
* Ring (beehive)		J. A. Bauer	1932–1962	Solids: black, orange, burnt orange, dark blue, yellow, green, ivory, maroon. Pastel: turquoise, olive, green, gray, white, pale blue, light yellow, pink, chartreuse
Ringles		Stangl	1973–1974	
Rio		Salem China	1943	
Rite of Spring		Paden City		
* Riviera	Century	Homer Laughlin	1938–1950	Solids: mauve blue, red, yellow, light green, ivory, dark blue
Rock Garden	Skyline	Blue Ridge		
* Rock Rose	Colonial	Blue Ridge		Hand-painted; pink & green flowers
Rococo	Princess	Paden City	1933	
Romance	Cavalier	Homer Laughlin		
* Rooster		Blue Ridge	1920–1957	Rooster in front of fence
Rooster		Harker		Blue, pink; Cameo ware
Rooster	Poppy Trail	Metlox		Rust yellow; black rooster in center; zigzag border
Rooster		Stangl	1970–1974	

Pattern	Shape	Maker	Date	Description
Rope Edge	Rope Edge	Catalina	1936	Solids
Rosalinde	Colonial	Blue Ridge		
Rose	Deanna	Knowles		Pale rose & buds
Rose & Lattice	Plain edge	Homer Laughlin	1920	Decals
Rose Bouquet	Floral edge	Knowles	1933–1934	
Rose Bud	Horizon	Steubenville		
Rose Garden	Gray Lure	Crooksville		Rose spray
Rose Garland		Crooksville	1920s	Border of tiny roses
Rose Garland Border		Homer Laughlin	1920	Decals
Rose Leaf		Syracuse		
Rose-Marie		Salem		Large cluster of rose-buds; platinum edge
Rose Marie		Sebring-Li-moges		
Rose O'Day		Vernon Kilns		
* Rose Parade		Hall	1941–1950s	Cadet blue body; rose decals; hi-white handles & knobs
Rose Point	Stafford Rose	Pope-Gosser		Embossed roses
Rose Red	Candlewick	Blue Ridge		
Rose Spray		Harker		Allover pattern; tiny pink & yellow flowers
* Rose White		Hall	1941	Hi-white body; floral decals
Rose I		Harker		
Rose II		Harker		
* Rosebud	Horizon	Steubenville		
* Rosebud		Coors, Golden Co.	1930s	Green, turquoise, ivory, yellow, maroon, blue solids; stylized flower border
Roses	Birds; Bolero	Crooksville		Multicolored flowers
Rosetta		Homer Laughlin		Bird hovering over flowers
Rosettes		Harker		Thin sprays of flowers on border & center
Rosita	Ranchero	W. S. George		Rose blossoms

Pattern	Shape	Maker	Date	Description
Roundelay (No. 4499)	Trailway	Blue Ridge		
Round-up	Casual	Red Wing	1958	
Roxanna		Universal		Decals
Roxanne		Stangl	1972–1974	
Royal Harvest	Coupe	Homer Laughlin		
Royal Marina	Sebring	Sebring-Limoges	1944–1945	
* Royal Rose		Hall		Cadet blue exterior; white handles & knobs; silver trim; floral decals
Royal Rose		Harker		Bright single rose decal
Royal Windsor		Salem	1950s	
Ruby	Clinchfield	Blue Ridge		Blue; large red flowered border
Ruffled Tulip		Harker		Bright flowers
Rugosa	Colonial	Blue Ridge		
Russel Wright	Woodfield	Steubenville		Golden fawn, salmon pink, tropic, rust, dove gray
Russel Wright		Edwin Knowles	Mid-1950s	Seeds, grass, Queen Anne's lace; botanica & solar
Russel Wright	Highlight	Paden City	1948–c. 1953	Blueberry, citron, pepper, nutmeg, white
Russel Wright	Iroquois	Garrison Prod.	1946	Ice blue, forest green, avocado yellow, lemon yellow, nutmeg brown, sugar white
Russel Wright (Iroquois), see Iroquois				
Russel Wright (Harker), see White Clover				
Russel Wright		Justin Therod & Sons		
Russel Wright	Vitreous restaurant ware	Sterling	1948	Ivy green, straw yellow, suede gray, cedar brown
Russel Wright, American Modern, see American Modern				
Rust Bouquet	LaGrande	Crooksville		Fall shades

Pattern	Shape	Maker	Date	Description
Rust Floral	Lido	W. S. George		Predominately orange flowers
Rust Tulip	Shell-Crest	Paden City		Assorted flowers
Rust Tulip	Victory	Salem		Assorted pastel flowers
Rustic		Stangl	1965–1974	
Rustic Garden		Stangl	1972–1974	
Rustic Plaid	Skyline	Blue Ridge		
* Saf-Handle		Hall	1938–1960s	Kitchenware; Chinese red most common color
Sailing	Georgette	W. S. George		Variety of boats on borders
Sailing	Tricorne	Salem		Decals, coral & black sailboats
Salamina		Vernon Kilns	1939	
Sampler	Victory	Salem		Decals
Sandra		Salem	1950s	
* Sani-Grid		Hall	1941–	Decal; Chinese red or cadet; white handle & knobs
Santa Barbara		Vernon Kilns		
Saratoga	Skyline	Blue Ridge	1952	
Scotch Plaid	Coupe	Crooksville		Plaid center design
Sculptured Daisy	Poppytail	Metlox	1965	
Sculptured Fruit		Stangl	1966–1974	Marked Prestige
Sculptured Grape	Poppytail	Metlox	1975	
Sculptured Zinnia	Poppytail	Metlox	1965	
Sea Shell		Paden City		
Sears R.		Hall		Cadet, hi-white
Sequoia		Knowles	Late 1930s	Bright floral bouquet
Serenade		Homer Laughlin	1940s	Solids: yellow, green, pink, blue, pastel
Serenade	D-Shape	Hall		Sprigs of orange flowers

Pattern	Shape	Maker	Date	Description
Sesame		Stangl	1972–1974	
Seven Seas		Vernon Kilns		
Sevilla				Solids, similar to Harlequin
Shadow Fruit	Skyline	Blue Ridge		
Shadow Leaf				
Shalimar	Shalimar	Steubenville		
Shawnee				
Sheffield		Salem China	1943	
Shellridge		Harker		Gold decal design
Shellware, see Cameo Shellware				
Sherry	Colonial	Blue Ridge		
Sherwood		Vernon Kilns		
Shoo Fly	Colonial	Blue Ridge		
Shortcake	Lido	W. S. George		Strawberry decal
Showgirl	Candlewick	Blue Ridge		
Sierra		Stangl	1967/1968–1970	Marked Prestige
* Silhouette		Crooksville	1930s	Silhouette decal; dog included
* Silhouette	Skyline	Blue Ridge		Clothlike appearance
	Skytone	Homer Laughlin		Kraft blue
Silver Rose		Homer Laughlin	1960s	Floral decals
Skiffs	Yorktown	E. M. Knowles		
Skyblue		Homer Laughlin	1977–1978	
Skyline		Blue Ridge	1954	
Skytone		Homer Laughlin		Light blue
Sleeping Mexican	Deanna	Knowles		Mexican style; man sleeping under palm tree
Slender Leaf		Harker		Gray border; graceful leaf design
Smart Set	Casual	Red Wing	1955	
Smoky Mountain Laurel	Candlewick	Blue Ridge		

Pattern	Shape	Maker	Date	Description
Smooth		J. A. Bauer	1936–1937	Solids
Snowflake		Homer Laughlin	1920	Decals
Snowflower		Montgomery Ward	1936	Decals
Sombrero		Pottery Guild		Brightly colored fruit in straw basket
Sonata	Skyline	Blue Ridge		
Sonesta		Homer Laughlin	1977–1978	
Sorrento		Homer Laughlin	1977–1978	
Southern Belle	Coupe; Iva-Lure	Crooksville		Large single rosebud
Southern Ca-melia	Piecrust	Blue Ridge	1948	
Southern Dogwood		Blue Ridge	1920–1957	Hand-painted
Speck Ware		J. A. Bauer	1946	Tan, pink, gray, white
Spider, see Spring Blossom				
Spiderweb	Skyline	Blue Ridge		
Spray	Piecrust	Blue Ridge		
Spray	Coupe	Crooksville		Pink ground; gray & black decal
Sprig Crocus		Hall		Several sprigs on border
Spring	Trend	Steubenville		
Spring Blos-som	LaGrande	Crooksville	1940s	Delicate floral sprays
Spring Bou-quet		Montgomery Ward	1936	Decals
* Spring Glory	Candlewick	Blue Ridge		Hand-painted blue flowers
Spring Song	Cavalier	Homer Laughlin		
Spring Song	Concord	Red Wing	1947	Birds
Springblossom	Regina	Paden City		Large multicolored pastel flowers
Springtime		Harker		Large single budding flower
Springtime		W. S. George	1940s	Open window with flower trellis
* Springtime		Hall		Pink flowers

Pattern	Shape	Maker	Date	Description
* Spun Gold		Stangl	1965–1967	
Square Dance	Colonial	Blue Ridge		Party set
Standard		Salem		Narrow floral sprays; blue edge
Stanhome Ivy	Skyline	Blue Ridge		Stylized green ivy leaves
* Star Flower		Stangl	1952–1957	Large center flower
Stardust		Stangl	1967	
Stardust	Skytone	Homer Laughlin	1940s–1950s	Light blue background; stylized flowers
Still Life	Colonial	Blue Ridge		
Strawberry	Shenandoah	Paden City		Strawberry plant border
Strawberry Patch	Colonial	Blue Ridge		
Streamers	Skyline	Blue Ridge		Ribbons
Summer Day		Salem		Blue & white flowerpot with floral sprays
Sun Drops	Astor	Blue Ridge		
Sun-Glo	Olympic	Harker	C. 1955	Harmony House mark
Sun Porch	Fiesta	Homer Laughlin		Decal; striped umbrella, table scene
* Sunflower		Blue Ridge	C. 1947	Large flowers
Sungold	Candlewick	Blue Ridge		
Sunny	Colonial	Blue Ridge		
Sunny Day	Cavalier	Royal		Ironstone; large flower branch
	Sunshine	Hall	1933	Kitchenware; decals, lettering or solid; ivory, Chinese red, Indian red, blue, yellow cadet, canary, delphinium, Dresden emerald, lettuce, marine, maroon, pink, rose, turquoise
* Sunshine		Stangl		
Susan		Blue Ridge		
Susan		Stangl	1972–1974	

Pattern	Shape	Maker	Date	Description
Susan	Trend	Steubenville		
Susannah	Colonial	Blue Ridge		
Swedish		Crown		Modern flowers
Sweet Clover	Candlewick	Blue Ridge		
Sweet Pea	Colonial	Blue Ridge		
Sweet Pea	Empire	Taylor, Smith, & Taylor		Pink decal
Swirl	Coupe	Crooksville		Flower sprigs on border, pointing to center
Symphony	Colonial	Blue Ridge		
Tahiti	Triumph	Sebring-Limoges	1938	
Tahitian Gold	New Shape	Red Wing	1962	Gold
* Tam O'Shanter		Vernon Kilns		Green, lime & reddish-brown plaid; green border
* Tampico	Futura	Red Wing	1955	Modernistic design
Tango		Homer Laughlin	1930s	Blue, green, yellow & red solids
* Taverne		Hall	1930s	Silhouette decal; serving pieces
* Taverne	Laurel	Taylor, Smith, & Taylor		Silhouette decal; no dog; dinnerware
Teal Rose	Aladdin	Harker	1952	Wide border, large rose
Terra Rose		Stangl	1941–1942	
Terrace Ceramics	Corn Shape	Terrace Ceramics		
Thanksgiving Turkey	Skyline	Blue Ridge		Turkey in center
Thistle		Hall		Muted floral
Thistle		Blue Ridge	1954	
Thistle		Universal		Decals
Thistle		French-Saxon		
* Thistle		Stangl	1951–1967	Hand-painted; purple & green decoration
Thorley		Hall		Small starbursts
Tia Juana	Deanna	Knowles		Ivory or white background

Pattern	Shape	Maker	Date	Description
Tickled Pink		Vernon Kilns		Pink
Tiger Flower	Tiger Flower	Franciscan		Pink
Tiger Lily	Colonial	Blue Ridge		
* Tiger Lily		Stangl	1957–1962	Decal
Tiny Roses		W. S. George		Rose medallion
Tip Toe	Casual	Red Wing	1958	
Toledo Delight	Trojan	Sebring	1941–1942	
* Tom & Jerry				Tom & Jerry printed on bowl, mug
Tom Thumb & the Butterfly		Homer Laughlin		Child's set; decal
Touch of Black	Regina	Paden City		Pastel flower sprays with occasional black leaves
Touch of Brown		Taylor, Smith, & Taylor		Brown & white flowered decal
Tower		Leigh		
Town & Country		Red Wing	1946	Metallic brown, forest green, rust, sandy peach, blue, chartreuse
Town & Country		Stangl		Blue, black, green, yellow or honey; graniteware look
Trade Winds		Vernon Kilns		
Trailway		Blue Ridge	1954	
Traveler		Syracuse		Railroad china
Treasured		Stangl	1968	
Trellis	Duckbill	Crooksville	1929	Bright flowers on black trellis
Tricorne		Salem	1934	Red-orange; stripes; modern
Trinidad		Stangl	1972–1974	
Triple Treat	Cavalier	Royal		Ironstone; three modernistic flowers
* Trojan	Trojan	Catalina Gladding, McBean & Co.	1930–1940s	Solids
Tropical		Blue Ridge	1920–1957	
Trotter	Coupe	Crooksville		Racing horse

Pattern	Shape	Maker	Date	Description
True Blue	Vernonware	Metlox	1965	
Tudor Rose	Sabina	Sabin		
* Tulip	D-Line	Hall	1930s–1950s	Decals; yellow & purple tulips
Tulip		Universal		Decals
Tulip		Stangl	1942–1973	Blue & yellow
Tulip		Salem		Tulip & bud
Tulip		Knowles		Bright orange tulip
Tulip		Paden City		Floral bouquet
Tulip		Leigh & Leigh Crescent		Vivid tulips
Tulip Tree		Homer Laughlin	1977–1978	
Tulip Wreath	Coupe	Homer Laughlin		
Tulips		Blue Ridge	1942–	
Tulips		Blue Ridge	1920–1957	
Tulips	Kitchen Kraft	Homer Laughlin	1930s	Decals on ovenware
Tulips		Pottery Guild		
Tulips		Taylor, Smith, & Taylor		
Tuliptime		Knowles		Ruffled tulips
Tuliptime	Candlewick	Blue Ridge		
Tuna Salad	Skyline	Blue Ridge		
Turtle Dove	New Shape	Red Wing	1962	Two Doves
Tweed		Vernon Kilns		Gray, blue plaid
Tweed Tex	Anniversary	Red Wing	1953	White
Twilight		Flintridge China Co.		
Two Step	Village Green	Red Wing	1960	Geometric design
Tyrol	Olivia	Steubenville		Carnation, aster, gardenia, buttercup
Ugly Couple		Blue Ridge	1920–1957	
Ultra California		Vernon Kilns	1930s	Carnation, aster, gardenia, buttercup
Valley Violet	Astor	Blue Ridge		Small flowers
Veggies		Crooksville		

Pattern	Shape	Maker	Date	Description
Vermillion Rose	Triumph	Sebring-Limoges		
Vernon 1860	Village Green	Vernon Kilns	1955	Brown
Vernon Rose	Vernonware	Metlox	1965	
Vestal Rose		Knowles	1930s	Decals
Victory		Salem		Fluted border
Vienna	Victory	Salem China	1940s	
Village Brown	Village Green	Red Wing	1955	Brown
Village Green	Village Green	Red Wing	1953	Green
Vine		Harker		Cameo ware
Vine Yard	Vernonware	Metlox	1965	
Vine Wreath	Laurel	Taylor, Smith, & Taylor	1933–1934	Decals
Vintage	Royal Gadroon	Harker	1947–1949	Red & green ivy
Vintage		Vernon Kilns		
Vintage	True China	Red Wing	1960	Floral
Vintage Pink	Poppytail	Metlox	1965	
Violet	Trend	Steubenville		
Violet		Blue Ridge		
Violet Spray		Homer Laughlin	1920	Decals
* Virginia Rose	Virginia Rose	Homer Laughlin	1935–1960	Decal: spray of roses, leaves
* Vistosa		Taylor, Smith, & Taylor	1938	Solids: cobalt blue, deep yellow, light green, mango red
Vistosa		E. M. Knowles	1936	Solids: cadet blue, yellow, russet, burgundy, red
Vogue		Syracuse		
Wagon Wheels		Frankoma	1933–	Desert gold, prairie green solids
Waldorf		Sebring-Limoges	1939	
Waltz Time	Colonial	Blue Ridge		
Wampum	Ranchero	W. S. George		Floral

Pattern	Shape	Maker	Date	Description
Ward's Garland		Montgomery Ward	1936	Decals
Water Lily	Yorktown	E. M. Knowles		
Water Lily		Stangl	1949–1957	
Waterlily	Astor	Blue Ridge		
Waverly		Homer Laughlin	1977–1978	
Weather Bloom	Squared-Off Edges	Knowles	1933–1934	Decals
Weathervane (No. 4277)	Skyline	Blue Ridge	1920–1957	House & tree
Westwind		Frankoma		Solids
Wheat		Harker	1961	Cameo ware
Wheat	Deanna	Knowles		Wheat stalks
Wheat		W. S. George		Brightly colored wheat stalks
Wheat (Hall), see Poppy & Wheat				
Wheatfield		Sebring-Limoges		
White & Embossed		Montgomery Ward	1920	Decals
White & Gold		Homer Laughlin	1920	Decals
White & Gold Carnation		Homer Laughlin	1920	Decals
White & Green Persian		Homer Laughlin	1920	Decals
White Clover		Harker (Russel Wright)		Cameo ware; green, coral sand, golden spice, charcoal, meadow green
* White Dogwood		Stangl	1965–1974	Marked Prestige
White Gold Ware		Sebring	1940s	
White Grape		Stangl	1967	
White Rose		Corncraft		
* White Rose		Harker Potteries	1940s	Blue or pink Cameo ware; yellow, gray; outlined flower in center

Pattern	Shape	Maker	Date	Description
Wild Bouquet		Homer Laughlin	1977–1978	Corn-Kraft; made for Montgomery Ward
Wild Cherry #1	Skyline	Blue Ridge		
Wild Cherry #2	Skyline	Blue Ridge		
Wild Cherry #3	Piecrust	Blue Ridge		
Wild Irish Rose	Colonial	Blue Ridge		
Wild Rose		Crown	1941	Wild flowers & wheat sheaths
Wild Rose		Hall		
Wild Rose	Princess	Paden City		
Wild Rose	Colonial	Blue Ridge		
Wild Rose	Floral Edge	Knowles	1933–1934	Decals
* Wild Rose		Homer Laughlin		Floral decals
Wild Rose		Stangl	1955–1973	
Wild Rose & Flower	Empress	Homer Laughlin	1920	Decals
* Wild Strawberry	Colonial	Blue Ridge		
* Wildfire	D-Line	Hall	1950s	Hi-white floral decals
* Wildflower	Floral Edge	Knowles	1933–1934	Decals
Wildwood		Stangl		
Willow	Coupe	Crooksville		Pussy willow stalks
Willow	Willow	Franciscan		
Willow Wind	Concord	Red Wing	1947	Abstract
Windfall		Stangl	1955–1957	
Windflower	Colonial	Blue Ridge		
Windmill		Crown		
Windmill		Universal		
Windmill	Victory	Salem		Decals
Winesap	Skyline	Blue Ridge		
Winged Streamliner		Homer Laughlin		Railroad china
Wizard of Oz	Kiddieware	Stangl	Mid-1940s–1974	
Woman in the Shoe	Kiddieware	Stangl	Mid-1940s–1974	

Pattern	Shape	Maker	Date	Description
Wood Rose		Stangl	1973–1974	
Wood Song		Harker		
Woodcrest		Blue Ridge	1954	
* Woodfield		Steubenville		Modern shapes
Woodhue	Flair	Salem		
Woodland	Round Coupe	Salem		
Woodland Gold		Metlox		Marked Poppy Trail
Woodvine		Universal		Small red flowers, large leaves
Wrightwood	Rainbow	Knowles	1930s	Decals
Wrinkled Rose	Colonial	Blue Ridge		
* Yellow Carnation	Fiesta Casuals	Homer Laughlin	1962–1968	Yellow & brown flowers on white background
Yellow Flower		Stangl	1970	
Yellow Matte Gold		Homer Laughlin	1920	Decals
Yellow Matte Gold Band	Plain Edge	Homer Laughlin	1920	Decals
Yellow Plaid		Blair		
Yellow Poppy	Candlewick	Blue Ridge		
Yellow Rose	Minion	Paden City	1952	
Yellow Trim Poppy	Deanna	Knowles		
Yellowridge		Salem		Multicolored flowers
Yorkshire	Swirled Edge	Metlox	C. 1939	Solids: pastel yellow, satin turquoise, peach, satin ivory, opal green, delphinium blue, old rose, canary yellow, turquoise blue, poppy orange
Yorktown	Yorktown	E. M. Knowles	1936	Concentric Deco shape: maroon, terra cotta, periwinkle blue, light yellow
Zeisel		Hall	1950s	

Pattern	Shape	Maker	Date	Description
Zinia	Concord	Red Wing	1947	
Zinnia	Colonial	Blue Ridge		
Zinnia		Homer Laughlin	1977–1978	

We welcome any additions or corrections to this chart. Please write to us c/o Crown Publishers, Inc., One Park Avenue, New York, N.Y. 10016.

Hall Teapots

(Colors listed are most commonly found for that pattern.)

Airflow, canary, 1940
Aladdin, camellia, 1939
Albany, emerald, 1930s
Automobile, Chinese red, 1938
Baltimore, emerald, 1930s
Basket, canary with silver, 1938
Basketball, Chinese red, 1938
Birdcage, maroon, 1939
Boston, warm yellow, early
Cleveland, emerald, 1930s
Doughnut, Chinese red, 1938
Football, delphinium, 1938
French, decorated, early
Globe, 1940s
Hollywood, maroon, late 1920s
Hook Cover, cadet, 1940

Illinois, cobalt, late 1920s early 1930s
Los Angeles, stock brown, 1926
Manhattan, stock brown
Melody, canary, 1939
Moderne, ivory, 1930s
Nautilus, canary, 1939
New York, blue turquoise
Parade, canary, 1942
Philadelphia, cadet, 1923
Rhythm, Chinese red, 1939
Saf-Handle, canary, 1938
Sani-Grid, cadet, 1941
Star, turquoise, 1940
Streamline, canary, 1940
Surfside, emerald, 1939
Windshield, camellia, 1941

Special Teapot Lines by Hall

Cube (made by other companies), red, green, cobalt
Disraeli, pink
Gladstone, pink/gold
Lipton, same shape as French, label on bottom, black lustre, warm yellow, daffodil cozy
McCormick, 1907, maroon, turquoise, green & silver
Miss Terry
T-Ball, designed for Bacharach, Inc., in 1948, maroon, daffodil, delphinium, round & square
Tea for Two, angled top, undecorated, 1930s, sand dust, old rose
Teataster (oval), made for the Teamaster Co. late 1940s, still in production, cobalt, lettuce, daffodil
Twinspout (round), made for the Teamaster Co. late 1940s, maroon
Twin-Tee, flat top, decorated in gold or decal, 1926, stock brown, cobalt, light russet
Victoria & Albert, 1940s, celadon/gold

Hall Coffeepots

Armory, warm yellow
Big Boy, maroon/silver
Blaine, cadet
Carraway, Chinese red
Coffee Queen, Chinese red

Deca-Flip, red & hi-white
Step-Down, red, black & green
(some decals)
Step-Round, ivory

Drip-O-Lator

(This is a line of pots made for the Enterprise Aluminum Company from 1930s through the present. They ordered the pots from Hall, added an aluminum drip section, and marketed them under the name Drip-o-lator.)

Arch
Basketweave
Bell
Bricks 'n' ivy
Bullseye
Crest
Monarch

Panel
Petal
Sash
Step-Round (only one that had been
previously designed)
Sweep
Trellis

Pottery Marks

American Modern mark, Steubenville, Steubenville, Ohio, 1939-1959

Autumn Leaf mark, Hall China Company, East Liverpool, Ohio, 1936-present

Universal Potteries, Inc., Cambridge, Ohio, 1935-1956

Stangl Pottery, Trenton, New Jersey, 1805-1978

Calico Fruit mark, Universal Potteries, Inc., Cambridge, Ohio, 1940s

Cameo Rose mark, Harker Pottery Company, Chester, West Virginia, 1940s

Hall China Company, East Liverpool, Ohio, 1903-present

Fiesta mark, Homer Laughlin China Company, East Liverpool, Ohio, and Newell, West Virginia, 1936-1973

Blue Ridge (Southern Potteries, Inc.), Ervin, Tennessee, 1917-1957

Taylor-Smith-Taylor, Chester, West Virginia, 1899-present

White Rose mark, Harker Pottery Company, West Virginia, 1940s

Coors, Golden, Colorado, c. 1900-1930s

Iroquois Russel Wright mark, Iroquois, Syracuse, New York, 1946-1959

Paden City Pottery, Paden City, West Virginia, 1930-1956

Tricorne mark, Salem China Company, Salem, Ohio, 1940s

Priscilla mark, Homer Laughlin China Company, East Liverpool, Ohio, and Newell, West Virginia, 1940s

Cat Tail mark, Universal Potteries, Inc., Cambridge, Ohio. Pattern made for Sears, Roebuck and Company, 1934–1956

Vistosa mark, Taylor, Smith and Taylor Co., Chester, West Virginia, c. 1938. The outline of the mark is shaped like the edge of the plate.

Early California dinnerware mark, Vernon Kilns, Vernon, California, late 1930s

Prestige mark, Stangl Pottery, Trenton, New Jersey, after 1965

Amberstone mark, Homer Laughlin China Company, East Liverpool, Ohio, and Newell, West Virginia, 1936–1973. Sold through supermarkets as "Genuine Sheffield" dinnerware.

Ballerina mark, Universal Potteries, Inc., Cambridge, Ohio, 1947–1956

Fiesta Kitchen Kraft mark, Homer Laughlin China Company, East Liverpool, Ohio, and Newell, West Virginia, early 1940s

Glossary: China and Glass

Akro Agate: glass made in Clarksburg, West Virginia, from 1932 to 1951. The firm has been known for making marbles but started making children's dishes. The marbleized glassware is sometimes incorrectly referred to as Akro Agate, meaning a color.

Ball jug: round pitcher, Hall China Company shape introduced in 1938.

Berry bowl: a berry set consisted of a master berry bowl about six inches in diameter and six small berry bowls used for individual servings. The small bowl is about three inches in diameter.

Bottom's-Up: drinking glass made so it cannot be put down because the bottom is rounded. Often made with the figure of a girl molded across the sides and bottom.

Butter dish: a covered dish used to hold butter on the table; or a covered storage dish used for butter in the refrigerator.

Chinese red: Hall China Company color.

Chinex: a pattern made by the MacBeth-Evans Division of the Corning Glass Works from the late 1930s to the 1940s. This ivory-colored glass with scrolled edges was made with either a plain or a colored decal decoration. Sometimes confused with Cremax.

Cider set: a metal tray, cookie jar with special metal lid and ladle, and eight round, handleless cups.

Console bowl: a console set usually included an oval low bowl about twelve inches long and a pair of candlesticks or matching small vases. It was made to be displayed on the buffet or a long table.

Coupe soup: flat, shallow round bowl about seven or eight inches in diameter, no handles. Used to serve soup.

Cream soup: two-handled low bowl used for service of cream soup or bisque.

Cremax: an ivory colored glassware made by the MacBeth-Evans Division of the Corning Glass Works in the late 1930s and early 1940s. It is sometimes confused with Chinex but has a ridged edge. Cremax is also used as a color name for a creamy opaque glass used in some other patterns such as American Sweetheart.

Delphite: opaque light-blue colored glass, sometimes incorrectly called "blue milk glass."

Drip-o-lator or dripper: additional piece put between cover and coffeepot. Coffee is put in the top or spreader, hot water is poured in and drips through to the pot to make coffee.

Fired-on colors: colors applied to glass, then baked under high heat at the factory.

Flashed or flashed-on: color added over clear glass.

Flat soup or rimmed soup: similar to coupe shape but with a rim that makes it seem larger.

Fluted baker: sometimes called French flute. Dish with ridges and straight sides, of a type now called a souffle dish. Comes in various sizes.

French flute: see fluted baker.

Goblet sizes: capacity in ounces is determined by the shape.
5¾ in.–9 ounce
7¼ in.–9 ounce

Grill plate: round three-section plate used to serve meat and vegetables in the separate sections. Similar to a modern TV dinner tray.

Ice lip: specially shaped lip of a pitcher curved to keep the ice cubes from falling out when the liquid is poured.

Iridescent: rainbowlike colors that appear on glassware when the light reflects.

Ivy ball: round glass vase, with or without a pedestal stem.

Jade-ite: opaque light-green colored glass.

Jadite: opaque light-green colored kitchenware made by Jeannette Glass Co.

Leftover: covered dish used to hold leftover food in a refrigerator—part of refrigerator sets.

Monax: white colored glass made by the MacBeth-Evans Division of the Corning Glass Works. Has a slightly iridescent coloring and the word "fire" on the edge.

Nappy: a round or oval dish with a flat bottom and sloping sides, about six inches in diameter.

Opalescent: opaque white glass that appears to have colors at the edges.

Plate sizes: 6 in.–dessert or sherbet
        7 in.–bread & butter
    7-7½ in.–salad
      8-9 in.–luncheon
        9 in.–breakfast
     10 in.–dinner
     13 in.–chop

Platonite: heat-resistant white glass made by the Hazel Atlas Glass Company.

Reamer: dish and pointed-top cone used to extract juice from citrus fruits.

Salver: a small footed tray.

Sani-Grid: Hall China Company shape introduced in 1941.

Tidbit: a two- or three-layer serving piece with a metal upright and handle.

Tilt jug: pitcher.

Tumble-Up: glass bottle with small tumbler turned upside down over the neck to serve as a top and a drinking glass.

Tumbler sizes: capacity in ounces is determined by the shape.
   2½ in.–whiskey glass
   3-3½ in.–4 to 5 ounce
   4-4½ in.–7 ounce
   4-6 in.–9 to 10 ounce

Water server: covered pitcher kept filled with water in the refrigerator—part of refrigerator sets.

Particular patterns can be found by using either the Depression Glass or American Dinnerware main listings, both of which are arranged alphabetically. Depression Glass begins on page 1 and American Dinnerware on page 138. There is no index of pattern names in this book as it would only duplicate the main listings.